RENAISSANCE, REFORMATION, AND ABSOLUTISM 1400-1600

A Documentary History of Modern Europe, Volume I

Edited by

Thomas G. Barnes
Gerald D. Feldman

University of California, Berkeley

Originally published by Little, Brown and Company

UNIVERSITY
PRESS OF
AMERICA

LANHAM • NEW YORK • LONDON

PREFACE

"For I do not see the whole of anything; neither do those who promise to show it to us." Michel de Montaigne's frank disclaimer of his own capacity and scathing rejection of the vaunted capacities of others to see all was written almost exactly four centuries ago, in an age of fanaticisms and all-embracing visions. It is relevant for our own age of fanaticisms and all-embracing visions. Fanaticism aside, it is a particularly apt motto for authors and editors of books for introductory courses in history. Where not downright messianic, or even prophetical, such books tend to be pontifical — if not by the authors' intentions, then at least in the student's reading of them. Some notions guided us in this compilation, and it is good to make those notions and their manifestations clear at the outset, not only that we might not be thought messianic, prophetical, or pontifical, but also that those who choose and those who use this book will know what we think it does and does not do. At the outset, we make no claim that it will enable the student to "see the whole" of modern European history, or even as much of it as is treated here.

We believe that even the most general study of history requires awareness of historians' dependence upon the sources for history. It is as well that the novice understands from the start that all historiography is based on a broad but still selected body of sources. The very selectiveness of this collection reflects the nature of the historian's job in writing history. We believe that the student cannot begin to understand either history or the historian's task without himself exercising his intellect on the sources of history. This compilation, highly selective though it is, demands that the student use his critical faculties in weighing what he reads as historical evidence; indeed, it demands that he determine from the variety of sources presented what constitutes historical evidence and how evidence can be analyzed and understood in different ways. For example, a student with the psychological interests of Erik H. Erikson, another with the politico-social bent of Roland H. Bainton, and another given to the avowedly theological focus of James Atkinson would all approach Martin Luther differently, but they would all have to meet and begin with Luther's own writings.

v

For that reason, if for no other, this series includes a major segment of Luther, which, though it comprises only a fraction of his considerable output, provides a common ground for all who would understand Luther and Lutheranism and a common origin for each interpretation of the man and his movement. So have we in every volume of this series aimed at providing a large enough selection from major historical figures (both thinkers and doers), commentaries by lesser men, descriptions of events, laws and government directives, manifestoes and platforms, some correspondence and belles lettres, to suggest the variety of sources for Europe's past, to allow each student to bring into play his own critical acumen, and to provide illustration of men, events, and ideas which might otherwise prove elusive.

This series is intended to be a *documentary history* of Europe. By this we mean that a student using — not merely reading — these volumes can come to some understanding of modern Europe's past by the documents alone aided by the explanation of the headnotes to the selections and the longer introductory essay to each chapter, which provides context and continuity both to the documents in that chapter and with the chapters preceding and succeeding. The series is not meant to serve as a substitute for a text, but it is intended to be as self-sufficient as is necessary to fit with any textbook or narrative history, sometimes in agreement with and sometimes in contrast to the interpretations that will be found elsewhere in what a student can be expected to read in an introductory course in modern European history at any college level. We have sought to make the selections long enough to give real substance for reflection and analysis. Perforce, this has limited the number of selections and therefore has caused us to exclude some men, events, and ideas that others would think of prime importance. We have felt no call to mirror the broad consensus as to which documents are and are not important. Although our colleagues will find a number of selections that all agree are "major," they will also find many that are rarely if ever found in books of readings and a few that have not previously appeared in English. We have sought significance, freshness, insightfulness, and incisiveness in our selections, and these concerns rather than idiosyncrasy, a penchant for novelty, or a commitment to a specific historical interpretation have determined that much of the material in this series will be new and different.

ACKNOWLEDGMENTS

The permission of authors and publishers in whom copyright is vested has been acknowledged where the selection appears. We would, however, tender special thanks to those holders of copyright who allowed us to use material either gratis or for a nominal fee, a practice that is no longer universal. A number of our colleagues assisted us with sage advice and tips for finding materials, and we are in yet greater debt to Lawrence Levine, Martin Malia, Robert Middlekauff, William Slottman, and Engel Sluiter than that already incurred by many years' close service together at Berkeley. Two students, Murray Bilby and Jeffrey Diefendorf, served us as bibliographical assistants and rendered aid beyond what we paid them. Malgorzata I. Winkler of the University of California, Berkeley, Library translated the Union of Lublin from Polish, a difficult task well done. The College Department of Little, Brown and Co. was always helpful, and we perhaps tumble into invidiousness in singling out the history editor, Charles Christensen, and the three copyeditors who wrestled with the series and its authors, Jane Aaron, Lynne Marcus Gould, and Patricia Herbst. To all, our most sincere thanks.

T. G. B.
G. D. F.

CONTENTS

RENAISSANCE, REFORMATION, AND ABSOLUTISM
1400–1660

THE HERITAGE
OF THE EUROPEAN WORLD

Chapter 1

"In the beginning was the Word, and the Word was with God, and the Word was God." The first verse of the Gospel According to St. John, and the first sentence of the first document in this collection, is almost the epitome of the cultural heritage of the European world. The One-God of the Jews, the unalterably monotheistic orthodoxy of both the Judaic and the Christian traditions, is boldly pronounced: God is the Creator, omnipotent and omnicompetent. Yet this God is called *Logos*, the Greek word meaning both "word" and "reason." The doctrine of *Logos* was enunciated by Philo Judaeus, a Jewish philosopher in the city of Alexandria during the Hellenistic period, the twilight of Greek philosophy — a man whose life began before the Christian era and ended during the Christian era. Philo sought to use the allegorical method to reconcile Plato, Aristotle, and the other major Greek philosophers with the Hebrew Scriptures, the Old Testament. *Logos*, meaning both "word" and "reason," was Philo's key concept in his attempt to define the God of the Jews in terms of Greek philosophy, because "word" appears in the Old Testament as one of the personalized mediators of God with man and "reason" was the crux of the Greek philosophical systems. The New Testament and early Christian theology conveyed the Greek emphasis on reason, as well as some of the substance of Greek philosophy, to the European world.

If reason and emphasis on the rational and the use of the rational faculties were deeply embedded in the Christian tradition of the European world, so, too, was the mystical. The other introductory verses of the Gospel According to St. John cast in a lyrical allegory the basically mystical quality of the coming of Christ as the Light sent to men to give them "power to become the sons of God" because they are born not merely of the will of the flesh "but of God." This same Light makes the Word flesh, to dwell among men, so that man might behold Christ's glory, "the glory as of the only begotten of the Father, full of grace and truth." This uneasy yoke — of God the Word and Christ the Light — has been borne by Christians throughout the ages, the Word always amenable to the operation of reason, the Light always elusive of reason, stirring great waves of emotional commitment and demanding of the believer a mystical rather than a rational comprehension of Christ. The root tension of the European world, the basic dualism of European culture, stems from the impossibility of ever adequately understanding God, existence, or the universe by mere reason or mere faith. Long after the secularization of European man, this dualism continues, and long after the last of the eruptions of Christian religious mysticism, eruptions of secular mysticism continue to disturb the European world.

On a more mundane plane, the European world claims as part of its heritage the rule of law. It could not be otherwise, for the European world was born in anarchy, in the dissolution of the Roman Empire and the inundation of barbarian hordes. Neither "anarchy" nor "barbarian" carry pejorative connotations here: the anarchy was the interregnum between the end of the effective rule of Rome and its laws and forms, and the beginning of the effective rule of barbarians bound together by their own legal bonds of primitive but viable law. Indeed, the most comprehensive system of law in the European world, summarized in the Emperor Justinian's *Institutes,* was a compilation of the laws of Rome, from the Republic to the end of the Empire, undertaken by an "Eastern" emperor, possibly of Slavonic origin, who was probably inspired by the example of barbarian kings and who borrowed freely from their compilations of primitive and Roman laws. The work of these barbarian kings is the clue to the concept of the rule of law, for they used law, both their own and the law of the peoples and cultures they conquered, to consolidate in governance the conquest of their arms. In the "Proem" to the *Institutes* Justinian strikes the right note in his assertion that majesty is "made glorious by arms, but [is] also armed with laws." The early barbarian kings, however, considered themselves above all law-givers, and the most pronounced attribute of kingship for their successors in the European world remained the power and authority to make law.

The marriage of the Christian faith and the rule of law was accomplished by the beginning of the second millennium of the Christian era. It was heralded in Justinian's compilation in the Roman concept of the law of nature. It was established in practice by several early Christian kings who sought to enforce in their courts the law of God. It was refined during the evolution of the law of the Church, the canon law of the Middle Ages, which drew heavily on Roman law as codified by Justinian. It reached fruition in the acceptance by medieval kings of the idea that they were under God and nature, bound by the laws of both and, by extension, bound even by their own laws, ideally if not always in reality, practically if not always theoretically.

Out of initial disorder, the king emerged as a law-giver invested with an almost priestly quality. The tribal chieftain of the barbarian horde became the converted priestlike king both of his people and of the people he conquered.

Tyranny appeared to be the greatest peril of the new kings, yet their power was not as great as their ambition or even as their conception of their role. Because of the continuing threat of barbarian invasions — the Vikings and the Magyars — and Moslem hostility, from the eighth through the ninth centuries, the kings could not defend their people or their territories without the creation of "mutual defense" arrangements with their most powerful subjects. Such arrangements were more pacts between nearly equal powers than between dutifully obedient subjects and their king. They constituted feudalism, which, though instituted for defense, carried with it the important corollary of responsibility for much of the implementation of law and justice. The feudatories constituted a barrier to kingly assertion of varying geographical and chronological effectiveness in western and central Europe. During the same period, the rise of the papacy, the evolution of an effective structure of ecclesiastical power centered on the Pope in Rome and exercised over the whole of the Western Church, raised another barrier to kingly assertion. The tyranny of kings was, for the moment at least, contained. By the time John of Salisbury wrote his *Policraticus*, in the middle of the twelfth century, his distinction between a prince (king) and a tyrant was accepted. In its strictly ecclesiastical form, the notion of the king's being under God and the law was never more cogently or more boldly asserted than in Pope Boniface VIII's bull *Unam Sanctam* of 1302. The power of the feudatories in the administration of law is illustrated by the account of the proceedings in an English feudal court typical of the fourteenth century. The description of life at Middleton also provides insight into the manorial system, the economic foundation of feudalism and the social organization of the majority of those under the rank of the feudatories.

The heritage of the European world cannot be summed up in a few pages; neither can it be illustrated by a few documents. Faith and law and their attributes, powers, rights, and obligations are the central strands of this heritage as the Middle Ages understood it. Yet in the early European world there was an "underworld" of serfs and peasants, of townsmen, of poor and ill-educated priests, of the vernacular tongues that in the later Middle Ages gained acceptance alongside the Latin of Church and state, of faith misunderstood, and of laws misapplied. Like most underworlds this one relied upon the overworld to give it voice. Seldom has the voice from below been so articulate, so poetic, so mov-

ing as that in *Piers the Ploughman,* spoken through the mastery of the
English vernacular of the fourteenth century by an obscure priest
named William Langland. The Christian faith and the rule of law are
the dominant motifs, and the allegory is worthy of the opening verses
of the Gospel According to St. John. Abundant learning and intimate
knowledge of the human condition of the age of war and plague,
deprivation, and repression inform its substance. But Piers's vision is
closer to the sixteenth century and the Reformation — to a tradition of
lay mysticism that began in the fourteenth century but peaked in the
sixteenth — than it is to the age of Boniface VIII and *Unam Sanctam:*
"All this makes me reflect on my dream — how the priest proved that
no pardon could compare with Do-well . . . and how, on Judgement
Day, Do-well will be received with honour, and exceed all the pardons
of St. Peter's Church."

In the Beginning . . .

*The Gospel According to St. John differs markedly from the other
three New Testament Gospels — Matthew, Mark, and Luke — which
agree much more among themselves in their portrayal of the life of
Christ than any of them do with John. Less "historical" than the
other three, John has the most complex literary structure and yet is the
most literarily refined. The author was perhaps John the Elder of
Ephesus (rather than the Apostle John), who did not know Christ personally, though he apparently had access to the reminiscences of someone who did know Christ. However, the scriptural authority of John's
Gospel has never been questioned. Perhaps its greatest significance is
that, unlike the other three Gospels, it presents the historic Christ
being transfigured into the Christ of Faith. Hence its popularity in
later ages. In 1576 the Council of Milan ordered that the first fourteen
verses of the Gospel According to St. John be read at the end of every
Mass in the Roman Catholic Church, in furtherance of the reform in
the Church following the Protestant Reformation.*

The Gospel According to St. John I:1–14

In the beginning was the Word, and the Word was with God, and the
Word was God.

The same was in the beginning with God.

All things were made by him; and without him was not any thing made that was made.

In him was life; and the life was the light of men.

And the light shineth in darkness; and the darkness comprehended it not.

There was a man sent from God, whose name was John.[1]

The same came for a witness, to bear witness of the Light, that all men through him might believe.

He was not that Light, but was sent to bear witness of that Light.

That was the true Light, which lighteth every man that cometh into the world.

He was in the world, and the world was made by him, and the world knew him not.

He came unto his own,[2] and his own received him not.

But as many as received him, to them gave he power to become the sons of God, even to them that believe on his name:

Which were born, not of blood, nor of the will of the flesh, nor of the will of man, but of God.

And the Word was made flesh, and dwelt among us (and we beheld his glory, the glory as of the only begotten of the Father), full of grace and truth.

The Law

Justinian, emperor first in Constantinople until he retook Rome from the barbarians in 536 A.D. *and restored the imperial power there, re-established something approaching the old Roman Empire after two decades of war against both barbarians and Persians. A great builder of public edifices, churches, and monasteries, within a year of his accession in 527, Justinian began the codification of the law of Rome by a commission under Tribonian, a member of his civil service. His* Codex *collected together all imperial legislation; the* Digest *was a critical edition of the writings of Roman jurists; the* Institutes *(533* A.D.*), teaching text for student use, was given the force of law by Justinian; the* Novellae *were new laws promulgated by Justinian himself. Altogether these works comprised the* Corpus Juris, *or Code of Laws. The* Corpus *has influenced all European and European-derived*

1 John the Baptist. — T. G. B.
2 That is, the Jews. — T. G. B.

legal systems (*Anglo-American common law included*) and furnishes
the basis of almost all the legal structures of continental Europe, Latin
America, and Japan.

This selection from the Institutes *consists of the Introduction and
part of the Law of Persons, which has no equivalent in our common
law tradition. The remaining books include the Law of Property, the
Law of Succession, the Law of Obligations, and the Law of Actions.*

The *Institutes* of Justinian

PROEM

In the Name of Our Lord Jesus Christ

The Emperor Caesar Flavius Justinianus; Conqueror of the Alamanni,
Goths, Franks, Germans, Antae, Alani, Vandals, Africans; Pious; Prosperous; Renowned; Victorious; Triumphant; Ever August; to young men
desirous of the law:

The Imperial Majesty should be not only made glorious by arms, but
also armed with laws, that war and peace alike may be well directed, and
that the Roman Emperor may not only be triumphant in battle, but also
by pursuing the paths of law may overcome the wicked designs of unprincipled men and be seen to be as much a scrupulous upholder of justice as victorious over conquered foes.

1. Both ends with untiring effort and unfailing foresight by God's
blessing we have attained. The valour of our arms barbarian nations
made subject to our sway have learnt to know. Africa and innumerable
other provinces, after so long an interval by the victories which God has
given us restored to our rule and Empire, bear witness to it. All nations
now are ruled by laws which we have issued or compiled.

2. For when we had reduced to splendid harmony the unordered mass
of imperial constitutions, we next extended our care to the immense
material of the ancient jurisprudence, and adventuring, so to say, into
mid ocean, by Heaven's favour completed a task, which might well have
been deemed hopeless.

3. This too by God's blessing accomplished, to the most eminent
Tribonian, master and ex-quaestor of our Sacred Palace together with the
illustrious Theophilus and Dorotheus, professors of law, who have given
many proofs of their ability, legal knowledge, and faithful discharge of
our orders, we have issued special directions by our authority and at our

From R. W. Lee, *The Elements of Roman Law*, 3d ed. (London, 1952), pp. 39–43, 54,
76–77. Reprinted by permission of Sweet & Maxwell Ltd.

instance to compile a book of Institutes, that so you may get your first notions of law not from ancient fables, but from the bright light of the imperial throne, and may hear and apprehend nothing useless, nothing out of place, but only what rests upon a solid basis of fact; thus, a thing to which former students attained only after four years' application — the reading of the imperial constitutions — you may now enter upon from the very beginning, being found worthy of the honour and the happiness of receiving your law from first to last from the mouth of the Emperor. 4. Accordingly, after the completion of the fifty books of the Digest or Pandects, in which with the help of the eminent Tribonian and other illustrious and learned men the whole of the old jurisprudence has been compiled, we have ordered the composition in four Books of these Institutes, destined to contain the elements of the whole science of law. 5. In these, a short account is given of the law of former days as well as of law which having been obscured by disuse has been brought into the light by our reforming hand. 6. These four Books, compiled from all the institutional works of ancient authors and in particular from the Institutions of our Gaius and from his book on "Daily Affairs" and many other commentaries, the three eminent men aforesaid have submitted for our approval. We have read and examined them, and have given them the force and effect of one of our constitutions.

7. Receive therefore earnestly and with eager attention these our laws and show yourselves so far advanced in your studies that you may be encouraged by the noble ambition of being able, when your training is complete, to undertake such functions of government as may be assigned to you in the different departments of our Empire.

Given at Constantinople on the eleventh day before the Kalends of December in the third consulate of the Emperor Justinian, Ever August [November 21, A.D. 533].

BOOK I

TITLE I. OF JUSTICE AND LAW

Justice is a set and constant purpose giving to every man his due.

1. Jurisprudence is the knowledge of things divine and human, the science of the just and the unjust.

2. So much being premised, since we are to explain what are the laws of the Roman People, it seems that the most convenient method will be to treat each subject in an easy simple way before proceeding to a careful and elaborate exposition. Otherwise, if from the very beginning we overload the mind of the student, still untrained and unequal to the burden, with a mass of various detail, one of two things will happen, either we shall deter him from the study of law, or, at the cost of much

toil and self-distrust, which so often discourages young men, we shall at last bring him to a point of attainment, which, led by an easier road, he might have reached more quickly, without great toil and want of confidence in his own powers.

3. The precepts of the law are these — to live honestly, not to harm another, to give every man his due. 4. The study of law has two branches, public and private. Public Law has regard to the constitution of the Roman State: Private Law is concerned with the interest of individuals. We are to speak of Private Law, which is of three kinds, being derived from natural precepts or from the precepts of universal law or from the precepts of the civil law.

TITLE II. OF THE LAW OF NATURE, UNIVERSAL LAW
AND THE CIVIL LAW

The law of nature is the law which nature has taught all animals. This law is not peculiar to the human race, but belongs to all living creatures, birds, beasts and fishes. This is the source of the union of male and female, which we called matrimony, as well as of the procreation and rearing of children; which things are characteristic of the whole animal creation.

1. The civil law is distinguished from universal law as follows. Every people which is governed by laws and customs uses partly a law peculiar to itself, partly a law common to all mankind. For the law which each people makes for itself is peculiar to itself, and is called the civil law, as being the law peculiar to the community in question. But the law which natural reason has prescribed for all mankind is held in equal observance amongst all peoples and is called universal law, as being the law which all peoples use. Thus the Roman People uses a law partly peculiar to itself, partly common to all mankind. What those laws are, we shall explain severally in proper sequence.

2. The civil law takes its name from the country to which it belongs. . . .

3. All our law is written or unwritten, according to the distinction made by the Greeks. The written law consists of statute (*lex*), *plebiscita*, *senatusconsulta*, enactments of the Emperors, the edicts of magistrates, the answers of men learned in the law. . . . 6. Further, what the Emperor has been pleased to command has the force of law since by the *lex regia* passed about his sovereignty the People has made over to him all its own sovereignty and power. Whatever, therefore, the Emperor has settled by letter or decided judicially or ordained by edict certainly has the force of a statute. All such expressions of the imperial will are called constitutions. Clearly some of these are personal and do not create a precedent to be followed, such not being the Emperor's intention. For example, a spe-

cial instance of reward or punishment or of relief not intended to create a precedent does not go beyond the person concerned. Other constitutions, being general in character, are undoubtedly binding on everyone. . . . 9. Unwritten law consists of rules approved by usage; for long-continued custom approved by the consent of those who use it imitates a statute. 10. So the civil law seems to be neatly distinguished as of two kinds. The distinction may be said to be derived from the institutions of two States, Athens and Lacedaemon. The Lacedaemonians maintained an oral tradition of the rules which they observed as laws, while the Athenians were the custodians of what they found written in their statute law.

11. The laws of nature which are observed amongst all peoples alike, being established by a divine providence, remain ever fixed and immutable, but the laws which each State makes for itself are frequently changed either by tacit consent of the people, or by a later statute.

12. The whole of our law relates either to persons, or to things, or to actions. Let us first consider persons; for it is of little use to know the law if we do not know the persons for whom the law was established.

Title III. of the Law of Persons

The principal divisions in the law of persons is that all men are either free or slaves.

1. Freedom, from which we get the description of men as free, is a man's natural capacity of doing what he pleases unless he is prevented by force or law. 2. Slavery is an institution of the *jus gentium* by which one man is made the property of another contrary to nature. 3. Slaves (*servi*) are so-called because military commanders order their captives to be sold, and so are used to preserve them alive (*servare*) instead of killing them. They are also called *mancipia* because they are taken from the enemy by the strong hand (*manu capiuntur*). 4. Slaves are either born slaves or made slaves. They are born of our female slaves. They are made slaves either by the *jus gentium*, that is by being taken captive, or by civil law, as when a free man upwards of twenty years of age suffers himself to be sold in order to share the price. 5. There is no difference in the condition of slaves. In the condition of free men there are many differences; for they are either born free (*ingenui*) or made free (*libertini*). . . .

Title VIII. of Persons sui juris and Persons alieni juris

There follows another division of the law of persons. For some persons are *sui juris*, others are *alieni juris*; and of these last some are in the power of parents, others in the power of masters. Let us consider then the persons who are *alieni juris*, for when we know who these are, we

shall understand at the same time who are *sui juris;* and first let us see
who are in the power of masters.

1. In the power of masters, then, are slaves. This power is created by
the *jus gentium,* for amongst all peoples it may be seen that masters have
over their slaves the power of life and death, and whatever is acquired
through a slave is acquired for the master. 2. But today no men subject
to our rule are allowed to do violence to their slaves without lawful
cause or beyond measure. For a constitution of the Emperor Antoninus
Pius directs that anyone who without cause kills his own slave is to be
punished just as much as if he had killed some other person's slave.
More than this, a constitution of the same Emperor restrains excessive
harshness of masters. For, being consulted by certain provincial governors
about slaves who fly for refuge to temples or to the statues of the Emperor, he directed that, if the masters appeared to have used intolerable
severity, they should be compelled to sell their slaves on fair conditions,
receiving the purchase price; and rightly so, for it is in the public interest
that a man should not misuse his property. These are the words of the
Emperor's rescript to Aelius Marcianus: "The power of masters over
their slaves should not be restricted, and no one should have his right
taken from him. But it is in the interest of masters that relief against
cruelty or starvation, or intolerable wrong, should not be denied to slaves
who justly invoke it. Do you, therefore, inquire into the grievances of
those of the establishment of Julius Sabinus who have fled to our statue,
and if you find that they have been treated with undue severity, or shame-
fully ill-used, order them to be sold on the terms that they are not to
revert to their master's power. And let Sabinus take notice, that if he
attempts to evade my decree, I will visit his offence with severe punishment."

TITLE IX. OF PATRIA POTESTAS

Children in lawful wedlock are in the power of parents. 1. Wedlock or
marriage is a union of male and female involving an undivided habit of
life. 2. The legal power which we have over our children is peculiar to
Roman citizens; for no other men have the power over their children
that we have. 3. The child born to you and to your wife is in your power,
also the child born to your son and his wife, that is your grandson and
granddaughter, and your great-grandchild and so forth. But a child born
to your daughter is not in your power, but in the power of the child's
father.

The Twelfth-Century Statesman

John of Salisbury (d. 1180), an English ecclesiastic, diplomat, philoso-
pher, historian, and poet, completed his Policraticus *in 1159. He stud-*
ied under Peter Abelard, the luminary-scholar of the great university
at Paris, and was secretary to the archbishop of Canterbury, and for a
time was intimately connected with both the papal administration and
the vigorous government of Henry II, one of the most able English
kings. He was exceptionally well educated for a twelfth-century cleric
and extraordinarily experienced in government. Policraticus, *a sophisti-*
cated medieval treatise on government, reflects both qualities. The
selection here is too short to indicate the breadth of treatment of Salis-
bury's book. It is drawn from Book 4, on the prince and the law.
Other books consider the administration of justice, the nature and
function of military service, and tyranny and tyrannicide (the latter
accepted as active resistance to a king who commands a Christian act
contrary to God's law). Ironically, John of Salisbury eventually was
called upon to practice the active resistance that he preached, although
it did not include tyrannicide. During the 1160's he played a leading
role in Archbishop Thomas Becket's resistance to Henry II's incursion
on ecclesiastical and clerical privileges. In 1170 he witnessed the cli-
mactic act of the drama, the murder of the archbishop at the high altar
in Canterbury Cathedral by knights moved to the act by some in-
temperate words of Henry against Thomas.

John of Salisbury's *Policraticus*

CHAPTER I. OF THE DIFFERENCE BETWEEN A PRINCE AND A TYRANT AND OF WHAT IS MEANT BY A PRINCE

Between a tyrant and a prince there is this single or chief difference, that the latter obeys the law and rules the people by its dictates, account-ing himself as but their servant. It is by virtue of the law that he makes good his claim to the foremost and chief place in the management of the affairs of the commonwealth and in the bearing of its burdens; and his elevation over others consists in this, that whereas private men are held responsible only for their private affairs, on the prince fall the burdens of

From *The Statesman's Book of John of Salisbury* (© 1928, 1956), ed. and trans. John Dickinson (New York, 1928), pp. 3–11. Reprinted by permission of Appleton-Century-Crofts, Educational Division, Meredith Corporation.

the whole community. Wherefore deservedly there is conferred on him, and gathered together in his hands, the power of all his subjects, to the end that he may be sufficient unto himself in seeking and bringing about the advantage of each individually, and of all; and to the end that the state of the human commonwealth may be ordered in the best possible manner, seeing that each and all are members one of another. Wherein we indeed but follow nature, the best guide of life; for nature has gathered together all the senses of her microcosm or little world, which is man, into the head, and has subjected all the members in obedience to it in such wise that they will all function properly so long as they follow the guidance of the head, and the head remains sane. Therefore the prince stands on a pinnacle which is exalted and made splendid with all the great and high privileges which he deems necessary for himself. And rightly so, because nothing is more advantageous to the people than that the needs of the prince should be fully satisfied; since it is impossible that his will should be found opposed to justice. Therefore, according to the usual definition, the prince is the public power, and a kind of likeness on earth of the divine majesty. Beyond doubt a large share of the divine power is shown to be in princes by the fact that at their nod men bow their necks and for the most part offer up their heads to the axe to be struck off, and, as by a divine impulse, the prince is feared by each of those over whom he is set as an object of fear. And this I do not think could be, except as a result of the will of God. For all power is from the Lord God, and has been with Him always, and is from everlasting. The power which the prince has is therefore from God, for the power of God is never lost, nor severed from Him, but He merely exercises it through a subordinate hand, making all things teach His mercy or justice. "Who, therefore, resists the ruling power, resists the ordinance of God," [1] in whose hand is the authority of conferring that power, and when He so desires, of withdrawing it again, or diminishing it. For it is not the ruler's own act when his will is turned to cruelty against his subjects, but it is rather the dispensation of God for His good pleasure to punish or chasten them. Thus during the Hunnish persecution, Attila, on being asked by the reverend bishop of a certain city who he was, replied, "I am Attila, the scourge of God." Whereupon it is written that the bishop adored him as representing the divine majesty. "Welcome," he said, "is the minister of God," and "Blessed is he that cometh in the name of the Lord," and with sighs and groans he unfastened the barred doors of the church, and admitted the persecutor through whom he attained straightway to the palm of martyrdom. For he dared not shut out the scourge of God, knowing that His beloved Son was scourged, and that the power of

---

[1] St. Paul's Epistle to the Romans XIII:2. — T. G. B.

this scourge which had come upon himself was as nought except it came from God. If good men thus regard power as worthy of veneration even when it comes as a plague upon the elect, who should not venerate that power which is instituted by God for the punishment of evil-doers and for the reward of good men, and which is promptest in devotion and obedience to the laws? To quote the words of the Emperor, "it is indeed a saying worthy of the majesty of royalty that the prince acknowledges himself bound by the Laws." [2] For the authority of the prince depends upon the authority of justice and law; and truly it is a greater thing than imperial power for the prince to place his government under the laws, so as to deem himself entitled to do nought which is at variance with the equity of justice.

CHAPTER II. WHAT THE LAW IS; AND THAT ALTHOUGH THE PRINCE IS NOT BOUND BY THE LAW, HE IS NEVERTHELESS THE SERVANT OF THE LAW AND OF EQUITY, AND BEARS THE PUBLIC PERSON, AND SHEDS BLOOD BLAMELESSLY

Princes should not deem that it detracts from their princely dignity to believe that the enactments of their own justice are not to be preferred to the justice of God, whose justice is an everlasting justice, and His law is equity. Now equity, as the learned jurists define it, is a certain fitness of things which compares all things rationally, and seeks to apply like rules of right and wrong to like cases, being impartially disposed toward all persons, and allotting to each that which belongs to him. Of this equity the interpreter is the law, to which the will and intention of equity and justice are known. Therefore Crisippus asserted that the power of the law extends over all things, both divine and human, and that it accordingly presides over all goods and ills, and is the ruler and guide of material things as well as of human beings. To which Papinian, a man most learned in the law, and Demosthenes, the great orator, seem to assent, subjecting all men to its obedience because all law is, as it were, a discovery, and a gift from God, a precept of wise men, the corrector of excesses of the will, the bond which knits together the fabric of the state, and the banisher of crime; and it is therefore fitting that all men should live according to it who lead their lives in a corporate political body. All are accordingly bound by the necessity of keeping the law, unless perchance there is any who can be thought to have been given the license of wrong-doing. However, it is said that the prince is absolved from the obligations of the law; but this is not true in the sense that it is lawful for

---

2 The Emperor Justinian, from his Code (I.14.4). See the preceding selection. — T. G. B.

him to do unjust acts, but only in the sense that his character should be such as to cause him to practice equity not through fear of the penalties of the law but through love of justice; and should also be such as to cause him from the same motive to promote the advantage of the commonwealth, and in all things to prefer the good of others before his own private will. Who, indeed, in respect of public matters can properly speak of the will of the prince at all, since therein he may not lawfully have any will of his own apart from that which the law or equity enjoins, or the calculation of the common interest requires? For in these matters his will is to have the force of a judgment; and most properly that which pleases him therein has the force of law, because his decision may not be at variance with the intention of equity. . . . The prince accordingly is the minister of the common interest and the bond-servant of equity, and he bears the public person in the sense that he punishes the wrongs and injuries of all, and all crimes, with even-handed equity. His rod and staff also, administered with wise moderation, restore irregularities and false departures to the straight path of equity. . . . His shield, too, is strong, but it is a shield for the protection of the weak, and one which wards off powerfully the darts of the wicked from the innocent. Those who derive the greatest advantage from his performance of the duties of his office are those who can do least for themselves, and his power is chiefly exercised against those who desire to do harm. Therefore not without reason he bears a sword, wherewith he sheds blood blamelessly, without becoming thereby a man of blood, and frequently puts men to death without incurring the name or guilt of homicide. . . .

CHAPTER III. THAT THE PRINCE IS THE MINISTER
OF THE PRIESTS AND INFERIOR TO THEM;
AND OF WHAT AMOUNTS TO FAITHFUL PERFORMANCE
OF THE PRINCE'S MINISTRY

This sword, then, the prince receives from the hand of the Church, although she herself has no sword of blood at all. Nevertheless she has this sword, but she uses it by the hand of the prince, upon whom she confers the power of bodily coercion, retaining to herself authority over spiritual things in the person of pontiffs. The prince is, then, as it were, a minister of the priestly power, and one who exercises that side of the sacred offices which seems unworthy of the hands of the priesthood. For every office existing under, and concerned with the execution of, the sacred laws is really a religious office, but that is inferior which consists in punishing crimes, and which therefore seems to be typified in the person of the hangman. . . . But if one who has been appointed prince has performed duly and faithfully the ministry which he has undertaken, as great honor and reverence are to be shown to him as the head excels in honor all the members of the body. Now he performs his ministry faithfully when he is mindful of his true status, and remembers that he bears the person of the *universitas* of those subject to him; and when he is fully conscious that he owes his life not to himself and his own private ends, but to others, and allots it to them accordingly, with duly ordered charity and affection. Therefore he owes the whole of himself to God, most of himself to his country, much to his relatives and friends, very little to foreigners, but still somewhat. He has duties to the very wise and the very foolish, to little children and to the aged. Supervision over these classes of persons is common to all in authority, both those who have care over spiritual things and those who exercise temporal jurisdiction. . . . And so let him be both father and husband to his subjects, or, if he has known some affection more tender still, let him employ that; let him desire to be loved rather than feared, and show himself to them as such a man that they will out of devotion prefer his life to their own, and regard his preservation and safety as a kind of public life; and then all things will prosper well for him, and a small bodyguard will, in case of needs, prevail by their loyalty against innumerable adversaries. For love is strong as death; and the wedge [3] which is held together by strands of love is not easily broken.

One Holy Catholic and Apostolic Church

Pope Boniface VIII (1294–1303) was the last of the great medieval popes, a worthy successor to Gregory VII (1073–1085) and Innocent III (1198–1216), who had tamed kings and emperors, built up the power of the papacy in Italy, and sought to raise the papacy above the temporal powers of Western Christendom. The bull Unam Sanctam *of 1302 was the most forthright assertion of papal temporal supremacy. It was also, for practical purposes, the last. The century that followed it witnessed increasing resistance of secular power to papal authority virtually everywhere in Europe. The year that followed it witnessed the agents of Philip IV of France bursting in on Boniface, taking him prisoner, and holding him for the last month of his life as a hostage of French temporal power. Two years later, his successor on the throne of St.*

---

[3] The formation of a soldierly bodyguard. — T. G. B.

*Peter became a client of the French king and moved to Avignon in
southern France. The papacy remained there for almost three-quarters
of a century, during the "Babylonian Captivity" of the heir of St. Peter,
"bound" not "binding." Nonetheless,* Unam Sanctam *summed up the
aspiration of the papacy, and in its allusion to the two swords, spiritual
and temporal, reiterated a concept of dualism in authority that was
not challenged in theory until the sixteenth century.*

Unam Sanctam, 1302

That there is one holy Catholic and apostolic Church we are im-
pelled by our faith to believe and to hold — this we do firmly believe and
openly confess — and outside of this there is neither salvation nor remission of sins, as the bridegroom proclaims in Canticles, "My dove, my un-
defiled is but one; she is the only one of her mother, she is the choice one
of her that bare her." The Church represents one mystic body, and of this
body Christ is the head; of Christ, indeed, God is the head. In it is one
Lord, and one faith, and one baptism. In the time of the flood there was
one ark of Noah, prefiguring the one Church, finished in one cubit, having
one Noah as steersman and commander. Outside of this all things upon
the face of the earth were, as we read, destroyed. This Church we venerate and this alone. . . . It is that seamless coat of the Lord, which was
not rent but fell by lot. Therefore, in this one and only Church there is
one body and one head — not two heads as if it were a monster — namely,
Christ and Christ's vicar, Peter and Peter's successor; for the Lord said
to Peter himself, "Feed my sheep." "My sheep," he said, using a general
term and not designating these or those sheep, so that we must believe
that all the sheep were committed to him. If, then, the Greeks, or others,
shall say that they were not intrusted to Peter and his successors, they
must perforce admit that they are not of Christ's sheep, as the Lord says
in John, "there is one fold, and one shepherd."

In this Church and in its power are two swords, to wit, a spiritual and
a temporal, and this we are taught by the words of the Gospel; for when
the apostles said, "Behold, here are two swords" (in the Church, namely,
since the apostles were speaking), the Lord did not reply that it was too
many, but enough. And surely he who claims that the temporal sword
is not in the power of Peter has but ill understood the word of our Lord
when he said, "Put up again thy sword into his place." Both the spiritual
and the material swords, therefore, are in the power of the Church, the

From *Readings in European History,* vol. 1, ed. J. H. Robinson (New York, 1904), pp.
346–48. Reprinted by permission of Ginn and Company.

latter indeed to be used for the Church, the former by the Church, the one by the priest, the other by the hand of kings and soldiers, but by the will and sufferance of the priest.

It is fitting, moreover, that one sword should be under the other, and the temporal authority subject to the spiritual power. For when the apostle said, "there is no power but of God: the powers that be are ordained of God," they would not be ordained unless one sword were under the other, and one, as inferior, was brought back by the other to the highest place. For, according to St. Dionysius, the law of divinity is to lead the lowest through the intermediate to the highest. Therefore, according to the law of the universe, things are not reduced to order directly and upon the same footing, but the lowest through the intermediate, and the inferior through the superior. It behooves us, therefore, the more freely to confess that the spiritual power excels in dignity and nobility any form whatsoever of earthly power, as spiritual interests exceed the temporal in importance. All this we see fairly from the giving of tithes, from the benediction and sanctification, from the recognition of this power and the control of these same things.

Hence, the truth bearing witness, it is for the spiritual power to establish the earthly power and judge it, if it be not good. Thus, in the case of the Church and the power of the Church, the prophecy of Jeremiah is fulfilled: "See, I have this day set thee over the nations and over the kingdoms," etc. Therefore, if the earthly power shall err, it shall be judged by the spiritual power; if the lesser spiritual power err, it shall be judged by the higher. But if the supreme power err, it can be judged by God alone and not by man, the apostles bearing witness, saying, The spiritual man judges all things, but he himself is judged by no one. Hence this power, although given to man and exercised by man, is not human, but rather a divine power, given by the divine lips to Peter, and founded on a rock for him and his successors in him (Christ) whom he confessed, the Lord saying to Peter himself, "Whatsoever thou shalt bind," etc.

Whoever, therefore, shall resist this power, ordained by God, resists the ordination of God, unless there should be two beginnings [i.e. principles], as the Manichaean imagines. But this we judge to be false and heretical, since, by the testimony of Moses, not in the *beginnings* but in the *beginning*, God created the heaven and the earth. We, moreover, proclaim, declare, and pronounce that it is altogether necessary to salvation for every human being to be subject to the Roman pontiff.

Given at the Lateran the twelfth day before the Kalends of December, in our eighth year, as a perpetual memorial of this matter.

The Manor Court

"The court holden at Middleton" in 1342 was entirely imaginary; the proceedings related were not, for this little manuscript tract of the mid-fourteenth century was to serve as a guide for holding just such a lord's manor court. "Middleton" can be taken as typical of English manorial courts, and, although differing in some details from the same jurisdiction in France and Germany, it illustrates the broad responsibility and considerable authority of the feudatory everywhere to render justice to his tenants, both serfs (bondmen) and freemen (franklins), to maintain order, and to implement both criminal and civil law among his tenants. The "frankpledges" referred to in the first paragraph were the freemen of the community responsible for the maintenance of good behavior among all the community's freemen. Presentment is made by the frankpledges as a jury, and trial of the facts in some instances is made by a jury of both freemen and bondmen. The very real lord for whose use this tract was compiled was the abbot of the great monastery of St. Alban's; The Church and its units were no less feudatories than the secular nobility.

Manorial Life at "Middleton"

Court holden at Middleton on Monday next after the feast of S. Nicholas in the sixteenth year of King Edward III [1342]. . . .

Then shall the steward make inquest by the frankpledges as to how the lord's franchise is maintained.

Whether the bailiff, reeve, hayward or any other of the servants behaveth himself ill in his office, and in each case how and in what.

Whether there be any voidance in the tenements of free or bond and what the lord shall have by their death by way of heriot or otherwise.

Whether any bond [man] be insufficient to hold the tenement that he holdeth; and tell us the reason.

Whether any bond [man] demiseth his land or part of it to any free man or other man without licence.

Whether any bond man hath betaken himself outside the franchise with his goods and his following; and whither.

Whether any bond man's unmarried daughter hath committed fornication and been convened in chapter, and what hath she given to the dean for her correction.

Whether any bond man or woman hath been charged in the chapter touching any thing other than marriage or testament.

From *The Court Baron*, ed. F. W. Maitland and W. P. Baildon, vol. 4 (London: Selden Society, 1891), pp. 101–06. Reprinted by permission of Seldon Society.

Whether any bond man's daughter hath been married without licence, and to whom, and what her father hath given with her in the way of goods.

Whether any bond man hath been ordained clerk [1] without leave.

Whether any bond man hath cut down oak or ash in his garden, unless it be to repair house, plough, or cart; and how much he hath taken.

And afterwards of all other matters which are to be presented for the lord.

Then they shall make presentment. The frankpledges say that Robert the reeve is always haunting fairs and taverns and that he is negligent in all his duties. Therefore be he removed. And P. of M. is at once elected in his stead, and is to be charged thus: "Thou shalt be loyal to thy lord and shalt loyally do all that to a reeve belongeth and loyally shalt thou charge thyself with all receipts and loyally discharge thyself with all lawful expenses to the best of thy power and knowledge. So help thee God and His saints." And then the said Robert shall be arrested and all his goods taken into the hand of the lord until he hath found good surety to answer his lord by lawful account for all his time, and if he can find no mainprise he shall be put in the stocks upon a pining-stool in the custody of his neighbours until he hath the grace of his lord, and besides this his goods shall be sold and the land that he holdeth shall be let out to another bond [man].

Also they say that Robert the parker doth not duly keep the park of the lord, for he giveth and selleth at his will beasts and wood [thus, for example,] a hart to the rector of A. Therefore command is given that he be attached by all his goods and kept safely until the lord shall [otherwise] ordain.

Also they say that in harvest time William the hayward hath been consenting with malefactors touching the lord's corn. Therefore be he in mercy; pledges, J. and A.; and further, be he removed.

Also they say that Walter the carter doth ill keep the lord's horses, for he stealeth the provender of the horses to the amount of one bushel. Therefore etc.

Also they say that Roger the sower defrauds the lord's land when sowing, for that by little and little he stealeth the seed, whereby he hath possessed himself of one bushel of corn, price 3 shillings. Therefore be he in mercy; pledges A. and B.; and further, be he removed.

Also they say that John the Franklain who held freely a virgate of land of the lord by the service of 5 shillings a year is dead, and that the lord shall have by way of heriot a cart-horse with bridle, saddle and sword. Also the lord shall have the wardship of John son and heir of the said John with all his land until he be of full age, and then he shall give a relief and do fealty in these words: "Hear this thou my lord! I John son and heir of [John] F. will be faithful and loyal to thee, and will bear

---

[1] Clergyman. — T. G. B.

faith to thee of the free tenement that I claim to hold of thee, and loyally will do to thee the customs and services that do I ought at the terms assigned therefor. So help me God and His saints."

Also they say that J. of B. who holdeth a messuage and a virgate of land in bondage is not sufficient to hold or maintain his land. Therefore be it seized into the lord's hand.

Also they say that Alice of C. who holds as above [i.e. in bondage] hath without the lord's licence demised and delivered half her land to John Clerk to plough and sow on the terms of receiving half the crop. Therefore be it seized into the lord's hand.

Also they say that M. of T. hath given rise to a legerwite.[2] Therefore be she in mercy; pledges, A. and B.

Roger W. giveth £3 for having entry into the messuage and virgate of land which his father held. Pledges, A. and B. And let him do the services which his father did. He shall do fealty thus: "Hear this my lord! I Roger will be faithful and loyal to thee, and faith to thee will bear of the tenement that I hold of thee in villanage, and will be justiciable by thee in body and chattels. So help me God and His saints."

Alice of B. found pledges A. and B. that for the future she will maintain her tenement and land like her neighbours. Therefore it is considered that she do rehave her land.

William of B. giveth the lord 20 shillings that he may not be the lord's reeve at C.

William of G. complaineth of J. B. in a plea of trespass — or, as the case may be, of land. Pledges to prosecute, A. and B.

Then shall the steward of the court command that Richard the late reeve do come to the bar, and that the beadle do proclaim that if anyone will complain against him for trespass or debt he shall do so at once since he is here present.

Master Robert of C. rector of the church of N. complaineth of Richard the last reeve that during his whole reeveship in contempt of God and Holy Church and to the heavy damage of the said rector hath he ill tithed all the goods of the lord which were tithable, to the damage of the said rector of 20 shillings.

The said Richard was arraigned of this and saith that he knoweth nothing of all these things that are charged against him, but that if there be any truth therein he was misled by his underlings to whom he trusted; and he prayeth that this be inquired. And the said rector doth the like.

Six free men and six born bondmen charged and sworn thereof say upon their oath that Richard is guilty of all these matters and of others which are not specified. Therefore command is given that the said [rector [3]] do seek the lord's favour, and further that the said Richard do

---

[2] The old Anglo-Saxon fine for fornication. — T. G. B.

[3] It must be the rector and not, as the MS. has it, Richard who is to seek the lord's

remain in the custody of the frankpledge until he shall have rendered an account.

Alice the widow complaineth of Richard late reeve, for that day by day he hath impounded her cow supposing and saying now that it was in the lord's corn, now that it was in the lord's pasture or his garden, until she gave him a half-mark for which she sold two quarters of wheat, which were then worth 8 shillings, and "other enormous things" he to her did to her damage 8 shillings, and "other enormous things" to her damage 20 shillings.

The said Richard being arraigned saith that never did he impound the cow of the said Alice taking from her a gift in order that she might be discharged [of the cow's trespass]; and he prays that this be inquired. And the said Alice doth the like.

The inquest touching this saith that the said Richard is guilty of the matter complained of. Therefore be he in mercy, and further it is considered that the said Alice do recover the said half-mark with the damages.

John of T. demands of Richard [the late] reeve 20 shillings which he oweth him for four quarters of wheat which he sold him for the lord's seed, and 10 shillings for pease bought of him. Richard confessed the debt etc. It is considered that all these plaintiffs do crave the lord's favour.

Taxers $\left\{ \begin{array}{l} \text{Richard} \\ \text{Phillip} \end{array} \right\}$ Total [of the amercements]

"Whatsoever Thou Shalt Bind"

As Boniface VIII states in Unam Sanctam, *quoting Christ's charge to St. Peter, "Whatsoever thou shalt bind," the great power of the Church was the power to pardon and save or to condemn and damn the Christian in the life to come. The machinery of ecclesiastical pardon was highly sophisticated by the time William Langland (d. circa 1400) wrote the* Vision of Piers the Ploughman. *Langland, a native of the rich farming area of England's western midlands, was a clergyman. About him little is known. From the* Vision, *however, a great deal can be learned about the Church, the state, society, and the condition of life in the Middle Ages. The next selection is among the most direct*

---

favour. Richard is a bondman, and having offended, all his chattels have been seized by his lord. Anyone, therefore, who has aught against Richard can get nothing out of him, but must crave a boon of the lord. See the last paragraph of this tract.

*and scathing of all the attacks on the apparatus of ecclesiastical par-
dons that the Middle Ages produced. Nothing like it was heard again
until Martin Luther attacked Tetzel, an indulgence-seller in Germany,
and challenged the whole system of ecclesiastical pardons and other
abuses in the Ninety-five Theses he nailed on the church door at Wit-
tenberg in 1517.*

Piers the Ploughman's Pardon

THE STORY. *Truth, who is likened here to a Pope granting men a Bull of
Indulgence, sends Piers a Pardon for his sins. And all Piers' helpers, that is,
those who work honestly in any calling, are to have a share in it. After
explaining how much pardon various callings are to have, the poet tells of
a priest who asks Piers to let him read it, and who finds that it is not a
pardon at all, but only a clause from the Athanasian Creed stating that
those who do well will go to Heaven, and those who do evil, to hell. Then
Piers tears the Pardon up in anger, and vows to give up farming and begin
a life of prayer and penance. There follows an argument between Piers and
the priest, the noise of which awakes the dreamer. Since then, he says, he
has often puzzled over the meaning of the dream, and has reached the
conclusion that to do well is more important for salvation than to gain
indulgences. So the Vision of Piers the Ploughman ends, and we are prepared for the search for Do-well.*

When Truth heard of these things, He sent a message to Piers telling
him to take his team of oxen and till the earth, and He granted him a
Pardon from guilt and punishment, both for himself and for his heirs
for ever. And He said that Piers must stay at home and plough the fields,
and whoever helped him to plough or plant or sow, or did any useful
work for him, would be included with him in the Pardon.

All kings and knights who defend Holy Church and rule their people
justly, have a pardon to pass lightly through Purgatory, and enjoy the
company of the patriarchs and prophets in Heaven.

And all truly consecrated Bishops who live up to their calling, so long
as they are well versed in both the Laws and preach them to the laity,
and do all in their power to convert sinners, are equal with the Apostles
(as Piers' Pardon shows), and will sit with them at the high table on
Judgment Day.

In the margin of the Bull, the merchants too had many years' indulgence, but none from guilt as well as punishment — the Pope would
never grant them that, for they will not keep Holy Days as the Church

From William Langland, *Piers the Ploughman*, Book 7, ed. and trans. J. F. Goodridge
(London, 1966), pp. 91–94, 96–97. The story summary is by Goodridge. Reprinted by
permission of Penguin Books Ltd. and J. F. Goodridge.

requires, and they swear "By my soul!" and "God help me!" against their conscience, in order to sell their wares.

But Truth sent the merchants a letter under His secret seal, telling them to buy up boldly all the best goods they could get, then sell them again, and use the profits to repair the hospitals and to help folk in trouble — to get the bad roads mended quickly and rebuild the broken bridges — to enable poor girls to marry or to enter nunneries — to feed the poor and the men in prisons — to send boys to school or apprentice them to a trade — and to assist Religious Orders and give them better endowments. "And if you will do these things," said Truth, "I myself will send you St Michael my Archangel when you die, so that no devil shall harm your souls or make you afraid; and he will ward off despair, and lead your souls in safety to meet my saints in Heaven."

The merchants were pleased with this, and many of them wept for joy, praising Piers from gaining them such an indulgence.

But the men of Law who plead at the bar were to receive the least pardon of all. For the Psalm denies salvation to those who take bribes, especially from innocent folk who suspect no guile: "He who taketh no bribes against the innocent." An advocate should do his utmost to help and plead for such poor folk, and princes and prelates should pay him for it — "Their wages shall be from kings and rulers." But I assure you, many of these Judges and jurymen would do more for their friend John than for the love of God himself. Yet if an advocate uses his eloquence on behalf of the poor, and pleads for the innocent and the needy, comforting them in their misfortunes without seeking gifts — if he explains the Law to them as he has learnt it, for the love of God, and does no man injury — he shall take no harm from the Devil when he dies, and his soul shall be safe. This is proved by the Psalm, "Lord, who shall dwell in Thy tabernacle."

For human intelligence is like water, air, and fire — it cannot be bought or sold. These four things the Father of Heaven made to be shared on earth in common. They are Truth's treasures, free for the use of all honest men, and no one can add to them or diminish them without God's will. So when, at the approach of death, the men of Law seek for indulgences, there is very little pardon for them if they have ever taken money from the poor for their counsel. You lawyers and advocates can be sure of this — blame St Matthew if I lie, for he gave me this proverb for you: "All things whatsoever ye would that men should do to you, do ye even so unto them."

But every labourer on earth who lives by his hands, who earns his own wages and gets them honestly, living in charity and obeying the Law, shall have for his humility the same absolution that was sent to Piers.

But beggars and tramps have no place in the Bull, unless they have an honest reason for begging. A man who begs without need is a swindler, and like the Devil, for he defrauds others who are really in need, and deceives men into giving against their will. For if the almsgiver knew the beggar was not in need, he would give his alms to someone who deserved it more, and help the most needy. Cato teaches this, and so does the author of the Scholastic Histories. "Take care whom you give alms to" — so Cato says. And this is Peter Comestor's advice: "Keep your alms in your hand until you have made sure whom you are giving them to."

Yet Gregory the Great,[1] who was a holy man, bade us give alms to all that ask, for the love of Him who gave us all things. "Do not choose whom you pity," he said, "and be sure not to pass over by mistake one who deserves to receive your gifts; for you never know for whose sake you are more pleasing to God." Nor do you ever know who is really in need — only God can know that. If there is any treachery, it is on the beggar's side, not on the giver's. For the giver is repaying God's gifts, and so preparing himself for death; but the beggar is borrowing, and running into debt, a debt which he can never repay, and for which Almighty God is his security; for only God can pay back the creditor, and pay him with interest. "Wherefore then gavest thou not my money into the bank, that at my coming I might have required mine own with usury."

So except in dire need, you tramps should avoid begging, for it is written that whoever has enough to buy bread, has all he needs, even if that is all he possesses. "He is rich enough who does not lack bread." Comfort yourselves, therefore, by reading the lives of the Saints, and profit by their example. The Scriptures strictly forbid begging, and condemn you in these words:

> I have been young, and now am old:
> And yet saw I never the righteous forsaken, nor his seed begging bread.

For your lives are bereft of charity, and you keep no law. Many of you do not marry the women you consort with; you mount and set to work, braying like wild beasts, and bring forth children who are branded bastards. Then you break their backs or their bones in childhood, and go begging with your offspring for ever after. There are more misshapen creatures among you beggars, than in all other professions put together! But be warned that on the day of your death, you will curse the time you were ever created men.

Not so the old men with white hair, who are weak and helpless, nor the women with child who cannot work, nor the blind and bedridden whose limbs are broken, nor the lepers, nor any such folk who bear their afflictions meekly: these shall have as full a pardon as the Ploughman himself. For out of love for their humility, our Lord has given them their purgatory and penance here on earth. . . .

So the priest and Perkin argued, and their noise awoke me. And I looked about, and saw the sun to the southwards, and found myself on

---

[1] Pope Gregory I, 590–604. — T. G. B.

the Malvern Hills, starving and penniless. So I went on my way, puzzling over my dream.

Since then, I have thought many times about this dream, and wondered if what I saw in my sleep were really true. And I have often felt anxious for Piers, and asked myself what sort of pardon it was with which he consoled the people, and how it was that the priest gainsaid it with a few clever words. . . .

All this makes me reflect on my dream — how the priest proved that no pardon could compare with Do-well, and thought Do-well surpassed indulgences, biennials, triennials,[2] and Bishops' Letters — and how, on Judgment Day, Do-well will be received with honour, and exceed all the pardons of St Peter's Church.

Yet the Pope has the power to grant men pardon, so that they may pass into Heaven without doing any penance. This is our belief; the theologians teach it: "And whatsoever thou shalt bind on earth shall be bound in Heaven: and whatsoever thou shalt loose on earth shall be loosed in Heaven."[3] And so I firmly believe (God forbid otherwise!) — that pardons, penances, and prayers do save souls, even if they have committed deadly sin seven times over. But I certainly think that to put one's trust in these Masses is not so sure for the soul as is Do-well.

So I warn all you rich men who trust in your wealth to have triennials said for you after your death, not to be bolder therefore to break the Ten Commandments. And especially you men in authority, Mayors and Judges — no doubt you are thought wise, and possess enough of the world's wealth to buy yourselves pardons and papal Bulls — but on that dreadful day when the dead shall rise and all men shall come before Christ to render up their accounts, then the sentence shall state openly how you led your lives, how well you kept God's laws, and everything that you have practised day by day. Then, you may have pardons or provincials' letters[4] by the sackful, and belong to the Fraternity of all the Four Orders,[5] and possess double or treble indulgences, but unless Do-well helps you, I would not give a peascod for all your pardons and certificates!

So I advise all Christians to pray to God, and to His Mother Mary, our mediator, for grace to do such works in this life, that after our death and on the Day of Judgement, Do-well may declare that we did as he commanded.

HERE ENDS WILLIAM'S VISION OF
PIERS THE PLOUGHMAN

---

2 Masses for the souls of the dead, during a period of two or three years. — T. G. B.
3 See *Unam Sanctam*. — T. G. B.
4 Letter of indulgence granted by the head of a monastic province or region. — T. G. B.
5 The four great orders of mendicant friars: Dominicans, Franciscans, Carmelites, and Augustinians. — T. G. B.

ECONOMIC CHANGE AND
THE EXPANSION OF EUROPE
Chapter 2

European civilization came of age about 1100. Its institutions, religious and secular, were well established by then. It was no longer threatened by barbarians and was able to take the offensive against its Moslem rival to the south and east. (The First Crusade had begun in 1095.) For the first time the European world began to know some measure of peace and stability, an opportunity for the luxury of arts and learning, and a chance to expand physical and spiritual horizons. The twelfth century experienced a proto-renaissance, a rediscovery of older learning and a novel boldness in the expression of knowledge and sentiment. Where for five centuries fortress-like monasteries had struggled to preserve the vestiges of knowledge threatened with extermination by infidels and ignorance, the twelfth century substituted schools and universities to impart and to advance knowledge. Art, architecture, and literature became freer, more open in form, more ethereal and less ascetic, lighter and more joyous. Confidence, maturity, and a sense of well-being characterized twelfth-century Europe.

The sense of well-being had a substantial material base. Beginning in the tenth century, the population of Europe began to increase because of the absence of great plagues, less destruction of human life by war and invasion, increased food supplies due to abundant land and a slow improvement in climate (principally a general warming in Europe north of the Alps) as well as to higher crop productivity resulting from new methods of farming. The twelfth and thirteenth centuries were particularly free of epidemic disease and famine. The general prosperity of agriculture — the basic economic endeavor of the age — underlay Europe's growing confidence.

Yet the future greatness of the Eurpoean world and its expansion beyond the confines of Europe depended upon trade, at best a secondary occupation in 1100. Beginning about 1000 and ending about 1300, commerce moved from the periphery of European endeavor to its center to become the most characteristic feature of the European economy, if still not its basis. This development depended upon the growth of towns, and the rapid expansion of sea trade. Towns provided the centers for commerce, the reservoirs of capital to undertake trade, and some industry requisite to working and finishing goods for commerce. Sea trade enabled the goods of the Near East and the Orient beyond to be transported in quantity, cheaply and relatively safely, to Europe. The great entrepôts of this trade were the Italian port towns, particularly Venice. From these towns developed the overland trade routes that linked trans-Alpine Europe in the north to Mediterranean Europe in the south. The great trade centers of Flanders (now Belgium) and the great fair-markets of northeastern France thrived on these overland routes, enriching not only the trade regions but the supply-and-market regions of the trade — England, Scandinavia, and Germany. By the end of the thirteenth century regular sea-trade routes were opened between the Italian centers and England and Flanders through the straits of Gibraltar.

Towns and trade did not fit into the predominant political and social organization of the epoch, feudalism and its agricultural infrastructure manorialism. Perhaps paradoxically, though, feudalism was in fact the prerequisite for the development of towns with sufficient internal freedom to develop their own institutions, regulations, social structures, and social dynamics for the conduct of commerce. Feudalism was localism enshrined in practice and theory. Civic particularism — city independence or even autonomy — was merely a derivative form of localism. Indeed, the development of trading towns between 1000 and 1300 was most rapid precisely in regions where feudalism was strongest and most resistant to kingly claims. Northern Italy is both the best illustration of this and the region of greatest urban and commercial growth. (See the first selection in Chapter Four for comments on the Italian towns in 1150.)

In about 1300, population growth began to level off. Increasing famine in the first half of the fourteenth century suggests that the population had reached the limits of its food supply. In midcentury the greatest natural disaster of the civilization struck — the Black Death. In a few years the bubonic plague, probably complemented by other diseases, wiped out one-third of the population of Europe as a whole and as much as three-fourths of the population in some regions. Boccaccio described the plague in Florence.

During the remainder of the fourteenth century depression, war, and civil disorder joined with plague and famine to threaten the extensive economic expansion Europe had experienced in the preceding three centuries.

The challenge was met principally by a resurgence of the private initiative and organization that constitute the roots of modern capital-ism. Entrepreneurs of Europe refined and elaborated techniques developed in the previous centuries of economic growth. Again Italian cities, particularly Florence and Genoa, showed the way.

By the second half of the fifteenth century, population and trade were once again on the upswing. This same period marked the beginning of the great era of overseas discoveries. The thirteenth century had opened trade with the inner continent of Asia as far as China. But this trade depended on overland transport and on non-European intermediaries; it was, consequently, expensive, time-consuming, dangerous, and ultimately unreliable. The Portuguese thrust down the west coast of Africa began in force in 1418 with Prince Henry the Navigator's annual expeditions and reached India with Vasco da Gama in 1499. Within six years after da Gama's voyage the trade was considered profitable enough to induce a German printer in Nuremberg — a city that had close commercial relations with Portugal — to print a brochure of news, practical advice, and fantasy about the sea route from Lisbon to India.

Columbus' bold venture to the west and the New World in 1492 ultimately determined the direction, the means, and the ends of the new age of European expansion. The direction became transoceanic, not coastwise, across the trackless sea with all that this required in technological advances in shipbuilding and navigation. It led toward a vast brace of continents with which there had been no previous contact and on which exploitation and colonization (with African slaves as well as Europeans), rather than trade, would yield the greatest profit and from which gold and silver would pour into Europe for more than two centuries with enormous effects on the European economy and the relations of European states. Trade with eastern Asia meant trade with established societies and political entities; trade with the Americas meant trade with European colonists. Europe's outposts of empire in the Spanish and Portuguese New World proved the most lasting of the extensions of the European world beyond its birth limits. But without an advanced technology, the extension would have been short-lived. The man whose name was given to the New World, Amerigo Vespucci, duly noted that "the natives rushed down and shot many arrows; but we then had little fear of them. We replied with two bombard-shots . . . ," as he and his companions escaped from Curaçao, the Island of the Giants, in 1499. Giants with bows were no match for little Europeans with big guns, great ships, and inordinate ambition.

The Black Death

Giovanni Boccaccio (1313–1375), Florentine diplomat, intimate of the great early Renaissance scholar Petrarch, was the first eminent master of Italian prose. His Decameron, *one hundred little novels or stories, was published in 1353. It has provided plots, stories, modes of style, and situations for countless writers since, beginning with Boccaccio's English contemporary Chaucer.*

Renaissance writers were not frightened of hyperbole and were seldom averse to drawing men and events larger than life, but the plague beggared fiction in its immensity and terror. There is no exaggeration in Boccaccio's depiction of the plague and its effects on Florentine men and women in 1348.

Description of the Plague in *The Decameron*

I say, then, that the years of the beatific incarnation of the Son of God had reached the tale of one thousand three hundred and forty-eight, when in the illustrious city of Florence, the fairest of all the cities of Italy, there made its appearance that deadly pestilence, which, whether disseminated by the influence of the celestial bodies, or sent upon us mortals by God in His just wrath by way of retribution for our iniquities, had had its origin some years before in the East, whence, after destroying an innumerable multitude of living beings, it had propagated itself without respite from place to place, and so, calamitously, had spread into the West.

In Florence, despite all that human wisdom and forethought could devise to avert it, as the cleansing of the city from many impurities by officials appointed for the purpose, the refusal of entrance to all sick folk, and the adoption of many precautions for the preservation of health; despite also humble supplications addressed to God, and often repeated both in public procession and otherwise, by the devout; towards the beginning of the spring of the said year the doleful effects of the pestilence began to be horribly apparent by symptoms that shewed as if miraculous.

Not such were they as in the East, where an issue of blood from the nose was a manifest sign of inevitable death; but in men and women alike it first betrayed itself by the emergence of certain tumours in the groin or the armpits, some of which grew as large as a common apple, others as an egg, some more, some less, which the common folk called gavoccioli. From the two said parts of the body this deadly gavocciolo soon began to propagate and spread itself in all directions indifferently;

From Giovanni Boccaccio, *The Decameron*, trans. J. M. Rigg (London, 1903), pp. 5–9, 11–12.

after which the form of the malady began to change, black spots or livid making their appearance in many cases on the arm or the thigh or elsewhere, now few and large, now minute and numerous. And as the gavocciolo had been and still was an infallible token of approaching death, such also were these spots on whomsoever they shewed themselves. Which maladies seemed to set entirely at naught both the art of the physician and the virtues of physic; indeed, whether it was that the disorder was of a nature to defy such treatment, or that the physicians were at fault — besides the qualified there was now a multitude both of men and of women who practised without having received the slightest tincture of medical science — and, being in ignorance of its source, failed to apply the proper remedies; in either case, not merely were those that recovered few, but almost all within three days from the appearance of the said symptoms, sooner or later, died, and in most cases without any fever or other attendant malady.

Moreover, the virulence of the pest was the greater by reason that intercourse was apt to convey it from the sick to the whole, just as fire devours things dry or greasy when they are brought close to it. Nay, the evil went yet further, for not merely by speech or association with the sick was the malady communicated to the healthy with consequent peril of common death; but any that touched the clothes of the sick or aught else that had been touched or used by them, seemed thereby to contract the disease.

So marvellous sounds that which I have now to relate, that, had not many, and I among them, observed it with their own eyes, I had hardly dared to credit it, much less to set it down in writing, though I had had it from the lips of a credible witness.

I say, then, that such was the energy of the contagion of the said pestilence, that it was not merely propagated from man to man, but, what is much more startling, it was frequently observed, that things which had belonged to one sick or dead of the disease, if touched by some other living creature, not of the human species, were the occasion, not merely of sickening, but of an almost instantaneous death. Whereof my own eyes (as I said a little before) had cognisance, one day among others, by the following experience. The rags of a poor man who had died of the disease being strewn about the open street, two hogs came thither, and after, as is their wont, no little trifling with their snouts, took the rags between their teeth and tossed them to and fro about their chaps; whereupon, almost immediately, they gave a few turns, and fell down dead, as if by poison, upon the rags which in an evil hour they had disturbed.

In which circumstances, not to speak of many others of a similar or even graver complexion, divers apprehensions and imaginations were engendered in the minds of such as were left alive, inclining almost all of them to the same harsh resolution, to wit, to shun and abhor all contact with the sick and all that belonged to them, thinking thereby to make each his own health secure. Among whom there were those who thought that to live temperately and avoid all excess would count for much as a preservative against seizures of this kind. Wherefore they banded together, and, dissociating themselves from all others, formed communities in houses where there were no sick, and lived a separate and secluded life, which they regulated with the utmost care, avoiding every kind of luxury, but eating and drinking very moderately of the most delicate viands and the finest wines, holding converse with none but one another, lest tidings of sickness or death should reach them, and diverting their minds with music and such other delights as they could devise. Others, the bias of whose minds was in the opposite direction, maintained, that to drink freely, frequent places of public resort, and take their pleasure with song and revel, sparing to satisfy no appetite, and to laugh and mock at no event, was the sovereign remedy for so great an evil: and that which they affirmed they also put in practice, so far as they were able, resorting day and night, now to this tavern, now to that, drinking with an entire disregard of rule or measure, and by preference making the houses of others, as it were, their inns, if they but saw in them aught that was particularly to their taste or liking; which they were readily able to do, because the owners, seeing death imminent, had become as reckless of their property as of their lives; so that most of the houses were open to all comers, and no distinction was observed between the stranger who presented himself and the rightful lord. Thus, adhering ever to their inhuman determination to shun the sick, as far as possible, they ordered their life. In this extremity of our city's suffering and tribulation the venerable authority of laws, human and divine, was abased and all but totally dissolved, for lack of those who should have administered and enforced them, most of whom, like the rest of the citizens, were either dead or sick, or so hard bested for servants that they were unable to execute any office; whereby every man was free to do what was right in his own eyes. . . .

Some again, the most sound, perhaps, in judgment, as they were also the most harsh in temper, of all, affirmed that there was no medicine for the disease superior or equal in efficacy to flight; following which prescription a multitude of men and women, negligent of all but themselves, deserted their city, their houses, their estates, their kinsfolk, their goods, and went into voluntary exile, or migrated to the country parts, as if God in visiting men with this pestilence in requital of their iniquities would not pursue them with His wrath wherever they might be, but intended the destruction of such alone as remained within the circuit of the walls of the city; or deeming, perchance, that it was now time for all to flee from it, and that its last hour was come.

Of the adherents of these divers opinions not all died, neither did all escape; but rather there were, of each sort and in every place, many that sickened, and by those who retained their health were treated after the example which they themselves, while whole, had set, being everywhere left to languish in almost total neglect. Tedious were it to recount, how citizen avoided citizen, how among neighbours was scarce found any that shewed fellow-feeling for another, how kinsfolk held aloof, and never met, or but rarely; enough that this sore affliction entered so deep into the minds of men and women, that in the horror thereof brother was forsaken by brother, nephew by uncle, brother by sister, and oftentimes husband by wife; nay, what is more, and scarcely to be believed, fathers and mothers were found to abandon their own children, untended, unvisited, to their fate, as if they had been strangers. Wherefore the sick of both sexes, whose number could not be estimated, were left without resource but in the charity of friends (and few such there were), or the interest of servants, who were hardly to be had at high rates and on unseemly terms, and being, moreover, one and all, men and women of gross understanding, and for the most part unused to such offices, concerned themselves no further than to supply the immediate and expressed wants of the sick, and to watch them die; in which service they themselves not seldom perished with their gains. In consequence of which dearth of servants and dereliction of the sick by neighbours, kinsfolk and friends, it came to pass — a thing, perhaps, never before heard of — that no woman, however dainty, fair or well-born she might be, shrank, when stricken with the disease, from the ministrations of a man, no matter whether he were young or no, or scrupled to expose to him every part of her body, with no more shame than if he had been a woman, submitting of necessity to that which her malady required; wherefrom, perchance, there resulted in after time some loss of modesty in such as recovered. Besides which many succumbed, who with proper attendance, would, perhaps, have escaped death; so that, what with the virulence of the plague and the lack of due tendance of the sick, the multitude of the deaths, that daily and nightly took place in the city, was such that those who heard the tale — not to say witnessed the fact — were struck dumb with amazement. Whereby, practices contrary to the former habits of the citizens could hardly fail to grow up among the survivors. . . . What need we add, but (reverting to the city) that such and so grievous was the harshness of heaven, and perhaps in some degree of man, that, what with the fury of the pestilence, the panic of those whom it spared, and their consequent neglect or desertion of not a few of the stricken in their need, it is believed without any manner of doubt, that between March and the ensuing July upwards of a hundred thousand human beings lost their lives within the walls of the city of Florence, which before the deadly visitation would not have been supposed to contain so many people! How many grand palaces, how many stately homes, how many splendid residences, once full of retainers, of lords, of ladies, were now left desolate of all, even to the meanest servant! How many families of historic fame, of vast ancestral domains, and wealth proverbial, found now no scion to continue the succession! How many brave men, how many fair ladies, how many gallant youths, whom any physician, were he Galen, Hippocrates, or Aesculapius himself, would have pronounced in the soundest of health, broke fast with their kinsfolk, comrades and friends in the morning, and when evening came, supped with their forefathers in the other world! . . .

Florentines Contract "In the Name of God and of Profit"

The three parties to this contract of partnership were all from junior branches of the great ruling family of Florence — the Medici. The contract establishes a shop for the sale of the superior wool cloth produced in Florence under the Gild of Wool Manufacturers (the Arte di Lana). The contract is typical of those used in northern Italian cities for some centuries before and after this period. It sets up a trading company of limited duration (three years in this case), with profit and loss proportional to the original investment and with the junior partner (Giovenco di Giuliano) responsible for much of the routine business without further remuneration and with restrictions on his business activity outside the company. The agreement was fair, flexible, and workable — provided the partners trusted each other. But, then, the mark of business from the beginning was mutual trust in the name of profit, and the extensive credit structure that made medieval trade possible put a high premium on trustworthiness.

Article of Association Involving Giovenco di Giuliano de' Medici, Giovenco d'Antonio de' Medici, and Bernardo d'Antonio de' Medici, All of Florence

†*In the name of God, Amen, the first day of June, 1434.*

Be it known to whomsoever shall see or read the present contract made the year and month mentioned above, that it is declared in the name of God and of profit, that Bernardo d'Antonio de' Medici on the one part, and Giovenco d'Antonio de' Medici on another part, and Giovenco di Giuliano [de' Medici] on the other part, all three Florentine citizens and

From *Florentine Merchants in the Age of the Medici*, ed. Gertrude Richards (Cambridge, Mass., 1932), pp. 236–39. Reprinted by permission of Harvard University Press.

merchants, have made this present new Company under the *Arte di Lana,* in the *Convento* of San Martino, with this pact and condition and agreement that thus they make a partnership. That is:

In the first place, they are agreed that the capital of the said Company shall be, and must be, 4000 gold florins, and that this shall be contributed in cash within twelve months from now in this wise: the said Bernardo d'Antonio [shall put therein] 2200 florins; the said Giovenco d'Antonio [shall put therein] 1500 florins; and the above-said Giovenco di Giuliano shall put therein 300 for the said term of one year, as stated above, so that in all the sum [shall be] 4000 gold florins. Each one shall put in the above-said amount for the time mentioned, and whosoever shall fail to put in the stated sum within one year for the use of the said Company shall be obliged to make good to the said Company [with interest at] ten per cent of his account at the beginning of the year, according to what he has lacked.

And the said Giovenco di Giuliano promises his person and assistance and service and usefulness to the said Company and traffic under the *Arte di Lana,* and [he promises] to go to the looms and to other places generally at other times, always in whatever place is necessary, without other provision or salary. And the said Bernardo and Giovenco d'Antonio are not held to any such service in the said shop more than they give voluntarily during the said time. And if it pleases Giovenco d'Antonio to withdraw himself [from the firm] for any reason during the said time, that such absence is possible, providing that it appears to Bernardo d'Antonio and to Giovenco di Giuliano that it is possible; and that such salary [as he may receive] shall be paid into the said shop and Company.

And they are agreed that the said shop and traffic under the *Arte di Lana* shall be conducted in the *Convento* of San Martino in Florence and that the name of this Company shall be Bernardo d'Antonio de' Medici and Company with this sign that appears here on the side. This Company is agreed that they commence and are bound to commence on the 1st day of June, 1434, and are to continue for the next three years and that this contract terminates the 1st day of June, 1437, and at that time the said sign shall remain with the said Bernardo d'Antonio.

And they are agreed that the profit which our Lord God concedes through His mercy and grace will be divided in this manner: that is, that Bernardo d'Antonio shall draw on the basis of 1800 florins and Giovenco d'Antonio shall draw on the basis of 1300 florins, and Giovenco di Giuliano shall draw on the basis of 900 florins; and similarly during this time if any damage occurs, which God forbid, [each shall contribute on this basis]; and also each may draw out [his share] of their [joint] profits at any time, and at each withdrawal there shall be a balancing of accounts.

And they are agreed that Giovenco di Giuliano de' Medici may draw for his needs 4 florins the month, and similarly Bernardo d'Antonio may draw, and similarly Giovenco d'Antonio may draw, as their necessities demand, such money without paying any costs; and that whoever draws more, must restore the lack at 10 per cent the florin at the beginning of the year.

And they are agreed that the said Giovenco di Giuliano may not carry on or have carried on any other business or service to another traffic outside of this firm under any [condition] on the pain of paying 200 florins in gold, and if he does so engage, he must pay the said sum to the said Bernardo d'Antonio and Giovenco d'Antonio who may force him if he breaks this agreement. And furthermore, if he engages in any outside enterprise, whether he pays this fine or not, the said Bernardo d'Antonio and Giovenco d'Antonio may claim whatever profits or salary he has made, and he shall be responsible for whatever damages [may be incurred in this other business].

And they are agreed that the said Bernardo and Giovenco d'Antonio may manufacture or engage in other traffic of any sort in Florence or out of Florence.

And they are agreed that if any of the said Company shall hold in that Company any amount of money above the original capital, they may receive for it 8 florins the hundred as interest, but that this money may not be put into the Company without consent of all members thereof. And it [the interest] is to be paid from the time when it is desposited as if on interest with a third person, and such money may be withdrawn whenever its owner wishes, providing the others agree.

And they are agreed that the said Giovenco di Giuliano shall not engage any credits outside the business without the express permission of the said Bernardo and Giovenco d'Antonio or at least one or the other of them; and that in case he so does, the fact shall be entered against his account for the day; and the said Giovenco shall not be permitted to extend credit or make any guarantees for the said Company for a sum exceeding 20 florins without permission of both of the senior partners, and that any violation of the above shall incur a fine of 100 florins for each offense.

And they are agreed that when the termination of this Company shall draw near, and if any one of the partners does not wish to continue or reconfirm the traffic, in such case the one or the other must speak; and if he gives six months' notice, the firm shall be discontinued. The said Giovenco di Giuliano shall be obligated to stay in the shop until all the *panni* [1] and samples have been restored to the stock of the said shop. And within two months Bernardo and Giovenco must have cancelled all debts so that within such time they shall be free of all obligations; and the stock shall be divided among them in this proportion: To Bernardo, 1800 florins in gold; to Giovenco d'Antonio, 1300 florins in gold; to Giovenco di Giuliano, 900 florins in gold. And the merchandise shall be divided among them, each receiving according to his share. And whoso-

1 Cloths. — T. G. B.

ever of the partners has taken goods on good security, must pay in money for what is outstanding.

And similarly, if through the given time it should please our Lord God to call to Himself any one of the said Company (which may God in His mercy forbid), the said Company shall be terminated and the division of the property shall follow the above-mentioned terms.

From Lisbon to Calicut

Until the sixteenth century, German investment in the Orient trade flowed through the Italian ports because of their virtual monopoly of it. Portuguese exploration culminating in Da Gama's voyage to India in 1499, however, swung German and all northern European business attention toward Lisbon, and by 1505 several German trade houses, including the great Fugger combine, had established Lisbon offices. It is likely that the following selection, printed as a pamphlet in Nuremberg, was a promotional brochure published by German traders — quick to seize a commercial opportunity — to attract capital and customers to the sea trade with the Orient via Lisbon. It is not detailed enough to be a rutter (sailing directions), and its rosy enthusiasm for gain suggests that it is an early precursor of Madison Avenue advertising techniques.

The Right Way to Sail from Lisbon to Calicut Mile by Mile, 1505

This report sets forth the right way, mile by mile, to sail from Lisbon to Calicut. It also explains how the king of Portugal has of recent date requisitioned many galleys and ships in order to conquer new countries and islands, seeking to reach India by way of Calicut. These orders, as will be printed hereafter in this account, are to be carried out by his captain, and mention is also made of very newsworthy items.

This sphere according to Ptolemy's description of the earth will teach and inform the reader, pointing out marvelous things concerning the location of countries as to their latitudes and longitudes. The illustration below [1] also contains all the recorded matters of newly discovered islands

From *From Lisbon to Calicut* (© 1956 by the University of Minnesota), ed. John Parker, trans. Alvin E. Prottengeier (Minneapolis, 1956), pp. 27–32, 35–38. Reprinted by permission of the University of Minnesota Press, Minneapolis.

[1] Sketch not reproduced. John Parker's excellent notes to the text are given in a condensed form to clarify the text. — T. G. B.

and countries which have been recently discovered and which have been unknown for a long time to the philosophers. One finds in this sketch indicated by points and single letters also the cities of Nuremberg, Lisbon, and Calicut.

Now on the journey from Lisbon to Kalenkuth (Calicut) one travels setting forth from Lisbon to the Konnarien (Canary Islands). They are located 300 miles from Lisbon; thence one proceeds to Kabawerd (Cape Verde), another 200 miles.[2] There water is taken on board ship, and then it sails across the great gulf to the Kabedespranza (Cape of Good Hope), a distance of 120 miles. No land is found lying in between, and from Cape Verde on one encounters the black people. From the Cape of Good Hope it is a distance of 40 miles until one reaches water at Sand Prasz (St. Braz). There the natives go without clothes except for the barest covering to conceal their private parts.

Setting forth from St. Braz to Zappal (Sofala) the distance is 225 miles, and from there to Mansawick (Mozambique) another 135 miles. Likewise from Mozambique to Mellina (Malindi) one travels 100 miles, and from there one sails across the great gulf, a distance of 40 miles to Agendina (Anjediva). Again from Anjediva to Canuare (Cananor) are another 33 miles. There ginger grows quite abundantly, and from there it is another 12 miles to Calicut. From Calicut it is 35 miles to Gudschin (Cochin); there our ships load all kinds of spices.

Again from Cochin it is 25 miles to Collan (Quilon); there live many who believe in the teachings of St. Paul. At this point some ships also load cargo. Again from there to Mellacka (Malacca) is a distance of 700 miles. Here cloves and nutmeg are abundant.

Furthermore, it is reported that on the 19th day of November (1505) there sailed from Lisbon to India two caravels and one ship which are to carry out the purpose as is set forth in the following. At first, namely, they are to ascertain whether it is now possible at all times to travel from Lisbon to India, even though they embarked at a time less favorable than usual.[3]

And in the second place, if they should call at all ports on the entire coast in the direction of Sant Thoma (St. Thomas Island) down as far as the Cape of Good Hope, would they find some sources of sweet water

2 If these "miles" are converted to Portuguese leagues of four miles each, some of the distances given approach correctness. The errors in the distance between Cape Verde and the Cape of Good Hope, and from Malindi to Anjediva, are so great as to indicate typographical errors.

3 Sailing from Lisbon for India in November was a radical departure from usual practice, since all of the previous fleets, except the first expedition of Da Gama, had sailed in March or April. This enabled them to take advantage of the southwest monsoon which blew from Africa toward India in the late summer months. The three ships mentioned here were those sent out under the command of Cyde Barbudo and Pedro Coresma by King Manuel.

along the route. And if it should happen that they find sweet water then the King will have all fleets load an additional 400 quintals of spices.[4] For, at all events, they must take on sweet water at Calicut in order to have a sufficient supply until they reach Cababerd (Cape Verde). However, on their way to Calicut they must stop at Mansabigk (Mozambique). Likewise, they are supposed to visit each and every island and harbor along the sea to inquire what has happened to the two large ships which went there with the fleet and have been lost sight of as of this present year of 1505, and which are the largest ships which have belonged to the fleet. Hence they want to search all the sea ports to see whether they might have perished, or perhaps might have run aground and are unable to regain the sea.[5] In the latter event they are to take the sailors along on board ship together with the best cargo contained in the ship. And should they not find them, which God forbid, then they should be gone three years and should search in India and everywhere, and thereafter take on cargo of spices, as other ships do.

Another item of information to be reported is the fact that the great fleet of over twenty ships will sail to India.[6] That will take place in April 1506. For this purpose several ships are being well equipped, and they are to be guided in their conduct by the following directives. Some shall be gone for six years and some for three years, and should God prosper them in this mission, then they shall recondition the ships on land with all that is needed in the best manner as may be required. Thereafter they should sail with the captain who will be called the admiral, and who had been in India prior to the past two voyages and has been in command of the whole distance from Calicut to Kayl.[7] These he will seek to conquer: indeed he intends to sail to Ylla Hasserland, an island which he will conquer, perhaps, if he be able.[8] After that he will sail to Scharmarttar (Sumatra), which is an island, the largest to be found in the world, and is located not far from the mainland of the country of Mossa.[9]

If they should then conquer all of these islands, afterwards they want

---

[4] The quintal and bahar were the common units for measuring spices. A quintal was slightly in excess of one hundred pounds, and a bahar consisted of four quintals and six pounds.

[5] The ships being sought were from two previous fleets.

[6] This is a reference to the fleet sent out on April 18, 1506, under the general command of Tristão da Cunha. Five of the twenty-one ships, however, were commanded by Afonso de Albuquerque.

[7] This is a reference to Afonso de Albuquerque. Albuquerque had made one previous trip to India, in 1503. The region of Albuquerque's operations was from Calicut to Quilon, and there is no indication in the *Commentaries* of Albuquerque that he went as far to the southeast as Caell. It is probable that the author confused Quilon with Caell.

[8] Ylla Hasserland refers to the island of Socotra near Arabia.

[9] Probably Tenasserim, a region of the Malay Peninsula.

to sail to Mellicka (Malacca), and there they expect to load the ships with precious cargo, and thereupon they will seek to return home.[10] For this enterprise they will require seven years. But what his reward will be is not known to me. Also he is a valiant man, and is well to do in material goods. Moreover, he is a man above forty years of age, and one estimates his wealth to embrace approximately five kingdoms which he is reputed to have won in India. Moreover, he had previously been a poor nobleman. Hence it is supposed, should God prosper him together with his crew and give him good fortune on his journey and provide him with bountiful goods, he might be enriched by 300,000 crowns, for he is a more intrepid hero than the king has at his court among all his captains. He is also spoken of as a hero on the high seas.

Likewise it is also made a matter of public information that news has recently reached Lisbon that the Venetians are intending to send many people to Mellacka in Arabia via Alexandria to offer assistance to the Sultan.[11] These men are to serve as carpenters and other skilled craftsmen which are required there in order to build ships. And they intend to make galleys and have in mind to do great harm to the Portuguese in India. For the large fleet which has come from India has burned, to be sure, fourteen large ships intended for the King of Calicut. These were all laden with spices, and the same spices would all have come to the Venetians. Therefore the latter do not wish to tarry, and want to aid the Sultan to build other ships.

But the Portuguese have little faith in this venture, since Arabia and the coast of that side of Africa have little or no wood. It is all sandy desert, and as one report goes, they will be unable to accomplish anything in the way of shipping by sea, for there is no wood available.

It is also to be observed how all spices grow in India. Pepper grows like grapes in clusters, just as do elderberries. At times they bring to Lisbon green peppers just as they come from the tree. Cinnamon quills come also from large trees resembling the willow tree growing here. They have leaves which are broader than those of the willow tree, and when the time comes the cinnamon bark is peeled off and is dried. That is cinnamon bark, and afterwards the tree must stand two years until it grows a new bark again. This is the characteristic of the cinnamon.

Likewise, the greatest part of ginger is found to grow at Kandinor (Cananor), not far from Calicut. This is at times also imported to Lisbon; it consists of roots, and has leaves like wide-bladed grass. I have seen it, to be sure.

Also, the buds of cloves and nutmeg blossoms are obtained from

---

10 The Portuguese reached Malacca in 1509 when Diogo Lopez de Sequeira arrived there only to be denied the right to trade, and some of his crew were held as hostages. Albuquerque's expedition to Malacca, foreseen here, was undertaken from Goa in 1511.

11 Mellacka here must refer to Mecca. [Its seaport was Jiddah. — T. G. B.]

Malacca which is located 700 miles beyond Calicut. How this spice grows even they do not know. From there is also obtained the largest supply of drugs and precious gems. Pearls are also sought in an island located in the Persian Gulf. It is called Armasa (Ormuz). They are also sought at a place called Kayl (Caell) located on the continent. From there they bring many strange things, such as oriental rugs, also dogs and cats which have under their tails aromatic organs. If one seeks to extract these from them, then one must make them angry.[12] Also large cocoa nuts are imported from there; they are called *metzen* and are good to eat. Several cats have also come with the large fleet. They are called cats of Alcaldy,[13] from which is extracted under their tails a pleasant smelling substance called zedoary.[14]

Amerigo in America

Amerigo Vespucci (1451–1512) was a Florentine agent in Cadiz, Spain, of the Florentine commercial house of the Medici when he decided to go to sea with various Spanish voyages of discovery to the New World beginning in 1497. The following account is of the voyage of Alonzo de Ojeda in 1499 along the coast of Venezuela and the outlying islands, which was the first discovery of the mainland of the Western Hemisphere. Vespucci's role on the voyage was secondary, but his capacity for self-advertisement (if not for accuracy) by the written word made it "his" voyage. His accounts of the voyages were published in 1507 by a German geographer who suggested that the new lands be called "America." Vespucci made significant contributions to cartography on later voyages in 1505 and 1507, but his account of his voyage of 1499 caught the public imagination. It remains one of the most impressive descriptions of early discovery.

[12] These "dogs and cats" are a reference to the musk deer, an animal native to Tibet, the Himalayan region, Siberia, and western China. This animal is about twenty inches high and from the standpoint of size, could be confused with a dog or cat. Its distinguishing feature is a sac on its abdomen, containing a gland which secrets a substance with an odor more persistent and more penetrating than any other known substance. This secretion was much sought after for medicinal uses and for perfumery.

[13] Hence we may be justified in interpreting "cats of Alcaldy" as civet cats coming from Chaldaea or possibly from Arabia, either country being well within the geographical province of our text. The civet cat, like the musk deer, secretes a substance useful for perfumery.

[14] In this the author is badly misinformed. Zedoary is not an animal product, but the product of a plant native to India and China whose rootstocks were used in medicine.

The Second Voyage to America
of Amerigo Vespucci, 1499

As regards the second voyage, what I saw in it most worthy of mention is as follows: We left the port of Cadiz, with three ships, on the 16th of May 1499, and shaped our course direct for the Cape Verde islands, passing in sight of the island of Grand Canary; and we navigated until we reached an island which is called the island of Fuoco. Here we got in our supplies of wood and water, and thence shaped our course to the south-west. In forty-four days we came in sight of a new land, and we judged it to be the mainland, continuous with that of which mention has already been made. This land is within the Torrid Zone, and beyond the equinoctical line on the south side, over which the Pole rises from the meridian 5°, beyond every climate. It is distant from the said islands by the S.W. wind [1] 500 leagues. We found the day and night to be equal, because we arrived on the 27th of June, when the sun is near the tropic of Cancer. We found this land to be all drowned, and full of very great rivers. At first we did not see any people. We anchored our ships and got our boats out, going with them to the land, which, as I have said, we found to be full of very large rivers, and drowned by these great rivers. There we tried in many directions to see if we could enter; and owing to the great waters and rivers, in spite of so much labour, we could not find a place that was not inundated.

We saw, along the rivers, many signs of the country being inhabited; but having ascertained that we could not enter from this part, we determined to return to the ships, and to try another part. We weighed our anchors, and navigated between the east south-east, coasting along the land, which trended southwards, and many times we made forty leagues, but all was time lost. We found on this coast that the current of the sea had such force that it prevented us from navigating, for it ran from south to north. The inconvenience was so great for our navigation that, after a consultation, we decided upon altering the course to north, and we made good such a distance along the land, that we reached a most excellent port, formed by a large island, which was at the entrance.[2] Within, a very large haven was formed.

In sailing along the island to enter it we saw many people, and we steered our ships so as to bring them up where the people were seen, which was nearly four leagues more towards the sea. Sailing in this way we had seen a canoe, which was coming from seaward, with many people

From *The Letters of Amerigo Vespucci*, vol. 90, ed. C. R. Markham (London: Hakluyt Society, 1894), pp. 21–24, 27, 29–30.

1 He uses the word "wind" for rhumb or course.
2 Trinidad and the Gulf of Paria.

on board. We determined to overhaul her, and we went round with our ships in her direction, so that we might not lose her. Sailing towards the canoe with a fresh breeze, we saw that they had stopped with their oars tossed — I believe, with wonder at the sight of our ships. But when they saw that we were gaining upon them, they put down their oars, and began to row towards the land. As our company came in a fast-sailing caravel of forty-five tons, we got to windward of the canoe, and when it seemed time to bear down upon her, the sheets were eased off so as to come near her; and as the caravel seemed to be coming down upon her, and those on board did not wish to be caught, they pulled away to leeward, and, seeing their advantage, they gave way with their oars to escape. As we had our boats at the stern well manned, we thought we should catch the canoe. The boats chased for more than two hours, and at last the caravel made another tack, but could not fetch the canoe. As the people in the canoe saw they were closely pressed by the caravel and the boats, they all jumped into the sea, their number being about seventy men; the distance from the shore being nearly two leagues. Following them in the boats, during the whole day, we were unable to capture more than two, all the rest escaping on shore. Only four boys remained in the canoe, who were not of their tribe, but prisoners from some other land. They had been castrated, and were all without the virile member, and with the scars fresh, at which we wondered much. Having taken them on board, they told us by signs that they had been castrated to be eaten. We then knew that the people in the canoe belonged to a tribe called *Cambali*, very fierce men who eat human flesh. We came with the ship, towing the canoe astern, approaching the land, and anchored at a distance of half a league. We saw a great number of people on the beach, so we went on shore with the boats, taking with us the two men we had captured. When we came near all the people fled into the wood. So we released one of our prisoners, giving him many signs that we wanted to be their friends. He did what we wanted very well, and brought back all the people with him, numbering about 400 men and many women, and they came unarmed to the boats. A good understanding was established with them; we released the other prisoner, sent to the ships for their canoe, and restored it to them. This canoe was twenty-six *paces* long, and two *braccia* [3] in width, all dug out of a single tree, and very well worked. When they had hauled it up and put it in a secure place, they all fled, and would not have anything more to do with us; which seemed a barbarous act, and we judged them to be a faithless and ill-conditioned people. We saw a little gold, which they wear in their ears.

. . . [Having visited another island of "brutish" natives, which "offered no profit," they departed] and went to another island. We found that this

---

[3] That is, 65 feet long and 4 feet wide. The *braccio* was an Italian measure equal to about 2 feet; a *pace* was about 30 inches. — T. G. B.

other island was inhabited by very tall people. We landed to see whether there was any fresh water, and not thinking it was inhabited, as we had not seen anyone, we came upon very large foot-marks in the sand, as we were walking along the beach. We judged that if the other measurements were in proportion to those of their feet, they must be very tall. Going in search, we came into a road which led inland. There were nine of us. Judging that there could not be many inhabitants, as the island was small, we walked over it to see what sort of people they were. When we had gone about a league we saw five huts, which appeared to be uninhabited, in a valley, and we went to them. But we only found five women, two old, and three children of such lofty stature that, for the wonder of the thing, we wanted to keep them. When they saw us they were so frightened that they had not the power to run away. The two old women began to invite us with words, and to set before us many things, and took us into a hut. They were taller than a large man who may well be tall, such as was Francesco degli Albizi, but better proportioned. Our intention was to take the young girls by force, and to bring them to Castille as a wonderful thing. While we were forming this design there entered by the door of the hut as many as thirty-six men, much bigger than the women, and so well made that it was a rare thing to behold them. They, in like manner, put us into such a state of perturbation that we rather wished we were on board, than having dealings with such people. They carried very large bows and arrows, and great clubs with knobs. They talked among themselves in a tone as if they wished to destroy us. Seeing ourselves in such danger, we made various suggestions one to another. Some proposed that we should attack them in the hut, and others said that it would be better to do so outside, while others advised that we should not take any action until we saw what the natives were going to do. We at last agreed to go out of the hut, and walk away in the direction of the ships as if nothing had happened, and this we did. Having taken our route to return to the ships, they also came along behind us at a distance of about a stone's-throw, talking among themselves. I believe they had not less fear of us than we of them; for sometimes we stopped to rest, and they did so also without coming nearer. At last we came to the beach, where the boats were waiting for us. We got in, and, when we were some way from the shore, the natives rushed down and shot many arrows; but we then had little fear of them. We replied with two bombard-shots, more to frighten them than to do them harm. They all fled into the woods, and so we took leave of them, thankful to escape after a dangerous adventure. They all went naked like the others. We called this island *the Island of the Giants,* by reason of their stature.[4]
. . . [After visiting other islands, including one yielding "exceedingly

[4] Curaçao.

good" pearls] we departed, and, for the sake of obtaining many things of which we were in need, we shaped a course for the island of *Antiglia*,[5] being that which Christopher Columbus discovered a few years ago. Here we took many supplies on board, and remained two months and seventeen days. Here we endured many dangers and troubles from the same Christians who were in this island with Columbus. I believe this was caused by envy; but to avoid prolixity, I will refrain from recounting what happened. We departed from the said island on the 22nd of July, and after a voyage of a month and a half, we entered the port of Cadiz on the 8th of September,[6] being my second voyage. God be praised.

[5] Hispaniola (Haiti–Dominican Republic).
[6] These dates are inaccurate; the date of arrival at Cadiz was about February 1500.

THE RENAISSANCE
Chapter 3

The Renaissance was art — not merely in the sense that much of its creative energy went into works of art, but in the sense that its distinguishing characteristic throughout was a self-conscious channeling of knowledge and skill toward a creative end. This assertion demands close, critical attention. The key to it is "self-conscious." To be of the "Renaissance" required an awareness of renascence, of the rebirth of a life-style distinguishable from that of the Middle Ages, which, whether secular or religious, was derived from the narrow castellated and cloistered perspective of the early Middle Ages, at best tinged with the broader horizons of the twelfth century. Renaissance men were not the first creative and articulate Europeans, but they were the first to be entirely sensible of their creativity and at times were as much enamored of themselves as creators as of the products of their creativity. In short, the Renaissance life-style emphasized subjective rather than objective criteria for understanding, endeavor, and even belief.

This shift made its impact felt in the arts and sciences with its assertion that the study of man (humanism) was the proper object of man's creative urge. The Renaissance "universal man" was not so much a man who could do, or even know, everything, but a man who knew himself. The "universal man" was what all men should aspire to be, and, although they were impatient of failure, Renaissance men had enough tolerance bred by the clash of self-esteems to accept fairly readily each man's claim to his "universality." *Virtù* was the sign of a "universal man": manly self-assertion, self-aggrandizement, self-advertisement, self-confidence. Still, amid all the arrogance and the brutal competitiveness of the Renaissance life-style there was tremendous optimism, belief in the improvement of man and perhaps of the human condition, and plain unbounded enthusiasm.

The problem that bedevils our understanding of the Renaissance is the historian's predilection to see the past in strictly defined epochs, each internally integrated, distinct from preceding and succeeding periods, causally connected with the preceding and effectually connected with the succeeding. Thus, the "Renaissance" often appears as the elegant meat sandwiched between the dry crust of the "medieval" and the yeasty slice of the "modern." In fact, the Renaissance must be savored by itself, removed from its intermediacy, appreciated for its uniqueness. The Renaissance makes most sense if it is considered an aberration in medieval development, sprung from the vitality of the northern Italian communities and carried with all the other merchandise of the era across the Alps to the burgeoning towns of northern France, the Low Countries, the Rhineland, and even London. In its native northern Italy, it was an almost universal phenomenon by the fifteenth century, setting styles and giving tone to all aspects of life. In its trans-Alpine manifestation, the Renaissance remained a limited, virtually rootless endeavor of a handful of intellectuals and a larger group of artists, who, because of the techniques in painting and sculpture of the southern Renaissance, were able to undertake a more complete adaptation of southern modes than of ideas. Nowhere did the Renaissance in its ideational substance survive the first half of the sixteenth century, for it became one of the early victims of the ideological conflict called the Reformation. It did survive, however, in material form: in indelible works of art, in the fruits of its scholarship, in the evocation of the ancient Classical world of Greece and Rome, and in an irrepressible spirit of humanistic commitment that reinforced the secular urge in Europe in the aftermath of the Reformation's excesses of religiosity.

The discerning and appreciative eye most readily grasps the Renaissance in art and architecture; for our purposes literary evidence will have to suffice. The Renaissance ideal of *virtù* dictated an emphasis on education that was not narrow or technical but brought exposure to the classics of Greece, Rome, and the early Church, mathematics, some science, music, and religion (though not necessarily theology). What is remarkable is that despite the manly quality of *virtù* (the root of the word itself is Latin for man, *vir*), the educational concept was readily extended to women, with little distinction between studies suitable for men and women, and to ends Leonardo Bruni makes clear. What was to be done by men with their education was another matter, and in this *virtù* asserted itself. Benvenuto Cellini — goldsmith, sculptor, autobiographer, and fearless warrior — by his own depiction exuded *virtù* in art and craft, brawling, dealing, and warfare, the last being a wholly acceptable and all too common arena for *virtù* in the Renaissance. Machiavelli (see Chapter Four) later turned Renaissance education and Classical learning to statecraft and political theory. Michelangelo, the greatest of all Renaissance artists, a true "universal man" in virtuosity, like Cellini and countless other artists, owed less to formal education than to a long and laborious apprenticeship in crafts. Florence was productive of such commanding figures precisely because of the excellence of its craft shops. The soaring individuality of Renaissance artists was inculcated in the craft-apprenticeship as fully as in the idealized pedagogy laid down by Leonardo Bruni.

The Renaissance of northern humanism was more low key than the Italian version. As practiced by the luminous Erasmus of Rotterdam, Lefèvre d'Étaples, and Sir Thomas More, it was called "Christian humanism" because it sought to apply Classical learning to the purification and reform of the Church and the deepening of the faith. It possessed its own arrogance and self-assertive individuality, however, as the briefest reading of Erasmus indicates. But at base Christian humanism contained a deep humility. Perhaps it required the shadow of the scaffold to bring it out in such strength as that manifested in More's *Dialogue of Comfort Against Tribulation*. But by then, the Renaissance humanist More was indistinguishable from the fifteen centuries of Christian martyrs who preceded him or from the martyrs, Catholic and Protestant, who would succeed him. The terrible irony is that More was destroyed by King Henry VIII, who, learned, hailed by Erasmus, and full of *virtù*, was the most perfect Renaissance prince the age produced. The Renaissance did not survive the Reformation.

A Classical Education
for a Young Lady

Leonardo Bruni d'Arezzo (1369–1444) addressed his tractate "Of Studies and Letters" to Baptista, daughter of the Count of Urbino, at about the time of her marriage to Galeazzo Malatesta in 1404. It is probably the earliest Renaissance tract on the education of women, and it was merely the first of many exhortations to women to make themselves intellectually worthy of their spouses, full of virtù, and to provide the environment to raise sons full of virtù.

Leonardo Bruni d'Arezzo: Concerning the Study of Literature: A Letter Addressed to the Illustrious Lady Baptista Malatesta

I am led to address this Tractate to you, Illustrious Lady, by the high repute which attaches to your name in the field of learning; and I offer it, partly as an expression of my homage to distinction already attained, partly as an encouragement to further effort. Were it necessary I might urge you by brilliant instances from antiquity: Cornelia, the daughter of Scipio, whose Epistles survived for centuries as models of style; Sappho, the poetess, held in so great honour for the exuberance of her poetic art; Aspasia, whose learning and eloquence made her not unworthy of the intimacy of Socrates. Upon these, the most distinguished of a long range of great names, I would have you fix your mind; for an intelligence such as your own can be satisfied with nothing less than the best. You yourself, indeed, may hope to win a fame higher even than theirs. For they lived in days when learning was no rare attainment, and therefore they enjoyed no unique renown. Whilst, alas, upon such times are we fallen that a learned man seems well-nigh a portent, and erudition in a woman is a thing utterly unknown. For true learning has almost died away amongst us. True learning, I say: not a mere acquaintance with that vulgar, threadbare jargon which satisfies those who devote themselves to Theology, but sound learning in its proper and legitimate sense, viz., the knowledge of realities — Facts and Principles — united to a perfect familiarity with Letters and the art of expression. Now this combination we find in Lactantius, in Augustine, or in Jerome; each of them at once a great theologian and profoundly versed in literature. But turn from them to their successors of to-day: how must we blush for their ignorance of the whole field of Letters!

This leads me to press home this truth — though in your case it is unnecessary — that the foundations of all true learning must be laid in the sound and thorough knowledge of Latin: which implies study marked by a broad spirit, accurate scholarship, and careful attention to details. Unless this solid basis be secured it is useless to attempt to rear an enduring edifice. Without it the great monuments of literature are unintelligible, and the art of composition impossible. . . .

You may naturally turn first to Christian writers, foremost amongst whom, with marked distinction, stands Lactantius, by common consent the finest stylist of the post-classical period. Especially do I commend to your study his works, "*Adversus falsam Religionem,*" "*De via Dei,*" and

From *Vittorino de Feltre and Other Humanist Educators: Essays & Versions,* ed. W. H. Woodward (Cambridge, 1897), pp. 123–29, 132–33. Reprinted by permission of Cambridge University Press.

"De opificio hominis." After Lactantius your choice may lie between Augustine, Jerome, Ambrose, and Cyprian; should you desire to read Gregory of Nazianzen, Chrysostom, and Basil, be careful as to the accuracy of the translations you adopt.[1] Of the classical authors Cicero will be your constant pleasure: how unapproachable in wealth of ideas and of language, in force of style, indeed, in all that can attract in a writer! Next to him ranks Vergil, the glory and the delight of our national literature. Livy and Sallust, and then the chief poets, follow in order. The usage of these authors will serve you as your test of correctness in choice of vocabulary and of constructions. . . .

But the wider question now confronts us, that of the subject matter of our studies, that which I have already called the realities of fact and principle, as distinct from literary form. Here, as before, I am contemplating a student of keen and lofty aspiration to whom nothing that is worthy in any learned discipline is without its interest. But it is necessary to exercise discrimination. In some branches of knowledge I would rather restrain the ardour of the learner, in others, again, encourage it to the uttermost. Thus there are certain subjects in which, whilst a modest proficiency is on all accounts to be desired, a minute knowledge and excessive devotion seem to be a vain display. For instance, subtleties of Arithmetic and Geometry are not worthy to absorb a cultivated mind, and the same must be said of Astrology. You will be surprised to find me suggesting (though with much more hesitation) that the great and complex art of Rhetoric should be placed in the same category. My chief reason is the obvious one, that I have in view the cultivation most fitting to a woman. To her neither the intricacies of debate nor the oratorical artifices of action and delivery are of the least practical use, if indeed they are not positively unbecoming. Rhetoric in all its forms — public discussion, forensic argument, logical fence, and the like — lies absolutely outside the province of woman.

What Disciplines then are properly open to her? In the first place she has before her, as a subject peculiarly her own, the whole field of religion and morals. The literature of the Church will thus claim her earnest study. Such a writer, for instance, as St. Augustine affords her the fullest scope for reverent yet learned inquiry. Her devotional instinct may lead her to value the help and consolation of holy men now living; but in this case let her not for an instant yield to the impulse to look into their writings, which, compared with those of Augustine, are utterly destitute of sound and melodious style, and seem to me to have no attraction whatever.

1 Augustine, Jerome, Ambrose, and Cyprian were Latin Fathers. Since their works were written in Latin, they could be read in the original. Gregory of Nazianzen, Chrysostom, and Basil were Greek Fathers, and their works had to be read in translation. At this stage of the Renaissance, Greek was not yet common equipment for the budding scholar. — T. G. B.

Moreover, the cultivated Christian lady has no need in the study of this weighty subject to confine herself to ecclesiastical writers. Morals, indeed, have been treated of by the noblest intellects of Greece and Rome. What they have left to us upon Continence, Temperance, Modesty, Justice, Courage, Greatness of Soul, demands your sincere respect. You must enter into such questions as the sufficiency of Virtue to Happiness; or whether, if Happiness consist in Virtue, it can be destroyed by torture, imprisonment or exile; whether, admitting that these may prevent a man from being happy, they can be further said to make him miserable. Again, does Happiness consist (with Epicurus) in the presence of pleasure and the absence of pain: or (with Xenophon) in the consciousness of uprightness: or (with Aristotle) in the practice of Virtue? These inquiries are, of all others, most worthy to be pursued by men and women alike; they are fit material for formal discussion and for literary exercise. Let religion and morals, therefore, hold the first place in the education of a Christian lady.

But we must not forget that true distinction is to be gained by a wide and varied range of such studies as conduce to the profitable enjoyment of life, in which, however, we must observe due proportion in the attention and time we devote to them.

First amongst such studies I place History: a subject which must not on any account be neglected by one who aspires to true cultivation. For it is our duty to understand the origins of our own history and its development; and the achievements of Peoples and of Kings.

For the careful study of the past enlarges our foresight in contemporary affairs and affords to citizens and to monarchs lessons of incitement or warning in the ordering of public policy. From History, also, we draw our store of examples of moral precepts.

In the monuments of ancient literature which have come down to us History holds a position of great distinction. We specially prize such authors as Livy, Sallust and Curtius; and, perhaps even above these, Julius Caesar; the style of whose Commentaries, so elegant and so limpid, entitles them to our warm admiration. Such writers are fully within the comprehension of a studious lady. For, after all, History is an easy subject: there is nothing in its study subtle or complex. It consists in the narration of the simplest matters of fact which, once grasped, are readily retained in the memory.

The great Orators of antiquity must by all means be included. Nowhere do we find the virtues more warmly extolled, the vices so fiercely decried. From them we may learn, also, how to express consolation, encouragement, dissuasion or advice. If the principles which orators set forth are portrayed for us by philosophers, it is from the former that we learn how to employ the emotions — such as indignation, or pity — in driving home their application in individual cases. Further, from oratory we derive our store of those elegant or striking turns of expression which are used with so much effect in literary compositions. Lastly, in oratory we find that wealth of vocabulary, that clear easy-flowing style, that verve and force, which are invaluable to us both in writing and in conversation.

I come now to Poetry and the Poets — a subject with which every educated lady must shew herself thoroughly familiar. For we cannot point to any great mind of the past for whom the Poets had not a powerful attraction. Aristotle, in constantly quoting Homer, Hesiod, Pindar, Euripides and other poets, proves that he knew their works hardly less intimately than those of the philosophers. Plato, also, frequently appeals to them, and in this way covers them with his approval. If we turn to Cicero, we find him not content with quoting Ennius, Accius, and others of the Latins, but rendering poems from the Greek and employing them habitually. Seneca, the austere, not only abounds in poetical allusions, but was himself a poet; whilst the great Fathers of the Church, Jerome, Augustine, Lactantius and Boethius, reveal their acquaintance with the poets in their controversies and, indeed, in all their writings. Hence my view that familiarity with the great poets of antiquity is essential to any claim to true education. For in their writings we find deep speculations upon Nature, and upon the Causes and Origins of things, which must carry weight with us both from their antiquity and from their authorship. Besides these, many important truths upon matters of daily life are suggested or illustrated. All this is expressed with such grace and dignity as demands our admiration. For example, how vividly is the art of war portrayed in Homer: the duties of a leader of men: the chances of the field: the varying temper of the host! Wise counsel, too, is not wanting, as when Hector upbraids Aeneas for too rashly urging the pursuit. Would, indeed, that in our own day our captains would deign to profit by this ancient wisdom, to the security of the commonwealth and the saving of valuable lives! . . .

But I am ready to admit that there are two types of poet: the aristocracy, so to call them, of their craft, and the vulgar, and that the latter may be put aside in ordering a woman's reading. A comic dramatist may season his wit too highly: a satirist describe too bluntly the moral corruption which he scourges: let her pass them by. Vergil, on the other hand, Seneca, Statius, and others like them, rank with the noblest names, and may, nay must, be the trusted companions of all who aspire to be called cultivated.

To sum up what I have endeavoured to set forth. That high standard of education to which I referred at the outset is only to be reached by one who has seen many things and read much. Poet, Orator, Historian, and the rest, all must be studied, each must contribute a share. Our learning thus becomes full, ready, varied and elegant, available for action or for discourse in all subjects. But to enable us to make effectual use of what we know we must add to our knowledge the power of expression. These two sides of learning, indeed, should not be separated: they afford mutual aid and distinction. Proficiency in literary form, not accompanied by broad acquaintance with facts and truths, is a barren attainment; whilst information, however vast, which lacks all grace of expression, would seem to be put under a bushel or partly thrown away. Indeed, one may fairly ask what advantage it is to possess profound and varied learning if one cannot convey it in language worthy of the subject. Where, however, this double capacity exists — breadth of learning and grace of style — we allow the highest title to distinction and to abiding fame. If we review the great names of ancient literature, Plato, Democritus, Aristotle, Theophrastus, Varro, Cicero, Seneca, Augustine, Jerome, Lactantius, we shall find it hard to say whether we admire more their attainments or their literary power.

But my last word must be this. The intelligence that aspires to the best must aim at both. In doing so, all sources of profitable learning will in due proportion claim your study. None have more urgent claim than the subjects and authors which treat of Religion and of our duties in the world; and it is because they assist and illustrate these supreme studies that I press upon your attention the works of the most approved poets, historians and orators of the past.

Virtù on the Battlements of Rome, 1527

The man of virtù found war one outlet for his energies, and Renaissance men made major contributions to the development of strategy, tactics, arms, and logistics. The French invasion of Italy in 1494 began a general war between France and Spain and their allies and satellites — a war that lasted for two-thirds of a century. On the battlefields of Italy siege warfare was perfected, cannon was first effectually used in field warfare, handguns began to challenge the pike as the infantryman's weapon. The states of Europe, especially Spain and its famous tercios (infantry soldiers), developed an effective infantry, trained, tactically disciplined, and well handled in battle. Mercenaries were still more common than any other type of soldier, but Machiavelli enunciated clearly the notion of a citizen-soldiery in the Classical Roman ideal, and the Spanish tercios came very close to the ideal.

Benvenuto Cellini (1500–1571) was a major sculptor and metal worker of the Renaissance; he was a minor soldier. This account of his artillery prowess on the walls of the Pope's castle of San Angelo against the Spanish army in 1527 is characteristic of his braggadocio. It also depicts the siege warfare of the era with great fidelity.

Cellini as Artilleryman

This tale of my sore-troubled life I write,
  To thank the God of nature, who conveyed
  My soul to me, and with such care hath stayed
  That divers noble deeds I've brought to light.
'Twas He subdued my cruel fortune's spite:
  Life glory virtue measureless hath made
  Such grace worth beauty be through me displayed
  That few can rival, none surpass me quite.
Only it grieves me when I understand
  What precious time in vanity I've spent —
  The wind it beareth man's frail thoughts away.
Yet, since remorse avails not, I'm content,
  As erst I came, welcome to go one day,
  Here in the Flower of this fair Tuscan land.

. . . Having got into the castle in this way, I attached myself to certain pieces of artillery, which were under the command of a bombardier called Giuliano Fiorentino. Leaning there against the battlements, the unhappy man could see his poor house being sacked, and his wife and children outraged; fearing to strike his own folk, he dared not discharge the cannon, and flinging the burning fuse upon the ground, he wept as though his heart would break, and tore his cheeks with both his hands. Some of the other bombardiers were behaving in like manner; seeing which, I took one of the matches, and got the assistance of a few men who were not overcome by their emotions. I aimed some swivels and falconets [1] at points where I saw it would be useful, and killed with them a good number of the enemy. Had it not been for this, the troops who poured into Rome that morning, and were marching straight upon the castle, might possibly have entered it with ease, because the artillery was doing them no damage. I went on firing under the eyes of several cardinals and lords, who kept blessing me and giving me the heartiest encouragement. In my enthusiasm I strove to achieve the impossible; let it suffice that it was I who saved the castle that morning, and brought the other bombardiers back to their duty.

During the course of my artillery practice, which I never intermitted through the whole month passed by us beleaguered in the castle, I met

From *The Life of Benvenuto Cellini*, ch. 34, ed. John Addington Symonds, 4th ed. (London, 1896), pp. 67–75.
[1] Small swivel cannons. — T. G. B.

with a great many very striking accidents, all of them worthy to be related. But since I do not care to be too prolix, or to exhibit myself outside the sphere of my profession, I will omit the larger part of them, only touching upon those I cannot well neglect, which shall be the fewest in number and the most remarkable. The first which comes to hand is this: Messer Antonio Santacroce had made me come down from the Angel, in order to fire on some houses in the neighbourhood, where certain of our besiegers had been seen to enter. While I was firing, a cannon shot reached me, which hit the angle of a battlement, and carried off enough of it to be the cause why I sustained no injury. The whole mass struck me in the chest and took my breath away. I lay stretched upon the ground like a dead man, and could hear what the bystanders were saying. Among them all, Messer Antonio Santacroce lamented greatly, exclaiming: "Alas, alas! we have lost the best defender that we had." Attracted by the uproar, one of my comrades ran up; he was called Gianfrancesco, and was a bandsman, but was far more naturally given to medicine than to music. On the spot he flew off, crying for a stoop of the very best Greek wine. Then he made a tile red-hot, and cast upon it a good handful of wormwood; after which he sprinkled the Greek wine; and when the wormwood was well soaked, he laid it on my breast, just where the bruise was visible to all. Such was the virtue of the wormwood that I immediately regained my scattered faculties. I wanted to begin to speak, but could not; for some stupid soldiers had filled my mouth with earth, imagining that by so doing they were giving me the sacrament; and indeed they were more like to have excommunicated me, since I could with difficulty come to myself again, the earth doing me more mischief than the blow. However, I escaped that danger, and returned to the rage and fury of the guns, pursuing my work there with all the ability and eagerness that I could summon. . . .

While I was at work upon that diabolical task of mine, there came from time to time to watch me some of the cardinals who were invested in the castle; and most frequently the Cardinal of Ravenna and the Cardinal de' Gaddi. I often told them not to show themselves, since their nasty red caps gave a fair mark to our enemies. From neighbouring buildings, such as the Torre de' Bini, we ran great peril when they were there; and at last I had them locked off, and gained thereby their deep ill-will. I frequently received visits also from the general, Orazio Baglioni, who was very well affected toward me. One day while he was talking with me, he noticed something going forward in a drinking-place outside the Porta di Castello, which bore the name of Baccanello. This tavern had for sign a sun painted between two windows, of a bright red colour. The windows being closed, Signor Orazio concluded that a band of soldiers were carousing at table just between them and behind the sun. So he said to me: "Benvenuto, if you think that you could hit that wall an ell's breadth from the sun with your demi-cannon here, I believe you would be doing a good stroke of business, for there is a great commotion there, and men of much importance must probably be inside the house." I answered that I felt quite capable of hitting the sun in its centre, but that a barrel full of stones, which was standing close to the muzzle of the gun, might be knocked down by the shock of the discharge and the blast of the artillery. He rejoined: "Don't waste time, Benvenuto. In the first place, it is not possible, where it was standing, that the cannon's blast should bring it down; and even if it were to fall, and the Pope himself was underneath, the mischief would not be so great as you imagine. Fire, then, only fire!" Taking no more thought about it, I struck the sun in the centre, exactly as I said I should. The cask was dislodged, as I predicted, and fell precisely between Cardinal Farnese and Messer Jacopo Salviati. It might very well have dashed out the brains of both of them, except that just at that very moment Farnese was reproaching Salviati with having caused the sack of Rome, and while they stood apart from one another to exchange opprobrious remarks, my gabion fell without destroying them. . . . Of Farnese I shall say nothing here, because it will appear in its proper place how well it would have been if I had killed him.

I pursued my business of artilleryman, and every day performed some extraordinary feat, whereby the credit and the favour I acquired with the Pope [2] was something indescribable. There never passed a day but what I killed one or another of our enemies in the besieging army. On one occasion the Pope was walking around the circular keep, when he observed a Spanish Colonel in the Prati; he recognised the man by certain indications, seeing that this officer had formerly been in his service; and while he fixed his eyes on him, he kept talking about him. I, above by the Angel, knew nothing of all this, but spied a fellow down there, busying himself about the trenches with a javelin in his hand; he was dressed entirely in rose-colour; and so, studying the worst that I could do against him, I selected a gerfalcon which I had at hand; it is a piece of ordnance larger and longer than a swivel, and about the size of a demi-culverin. This I emptied, and loaded it again with a good charge of fine powder mixed with the coarser sort; then I aimed it exactly at the man in red, elevating prodigiously, because a piece of that calibre could hardly be expected to carry true at such a distance. I fired, and hit my man exactly in the middle. He had trussed his sword in front, for swagger, after a way those Spaniards have; and my ball, when it struck him, broke upon the blade, and one could see the fellow cut in two fair halves. The Pope, who was expecting nothing of this kind, derived great pleasure and amazement from the sight, both because it seemed to him impossible that one should aim and hit the mark at such a distance, and also because the

[2] Clement VII. — T. G. B.

man was cut in two, and he could not comprehend how this should happen. He sent for me, and asked about it. I explained all the devices I had used in firing; but told him that why the man was cut in halves, neither he nor I could know. Upon my bended knees I then besought him to give me the pardon of his blessing for that homicide; and for all the others I had committed in the castle in the service of the Church. Thereat the Pope, raising his hand, and making a large open sign of the cross upon my face, told me that he blessed me, and that he gave me pardon for all murders I had ever perpetrated, or should ever perpetrate, in the service of the Apostolic Church. When I left him, I went aloft, and never stayed from firing to the utmost of my power; and few were the shots of mine that missed their mark. My drawing, and my fine studies in my craft, and my charming art of music, all were swallowed up in the din of that artillery; and if I were to relate in detail all the splendid things I did in that infernal work of cruelty, I should make the world stand by and wonder. But, not to be too prolix, I will pass them over. Only I must tell a few of the most remarkable, which are, as it were, forced in upon me.

To begin then: pondering day and night what I could render for my own part in defence of Holy Church, and having noticed that the enemy changed guard and marched past through the great gate of Santo Spirito, which was within a reasonable range, I thereupon directed my attention to that spot; but, having to shoot sideways, I could not do the damage that I wished, although I killed a fair percentage every day. This induced our adversaries, when they saw their passage covered by my guns, to load the roof of a certain house one night with thirty gabions, which obstructed the view I formerly enjoyed. Taking better thought than I had done of the whole situation, I now turned all my five pieces of artillery directly on the gabions, and waited till the evening hour, when they changed guard. Our enemies, thinking they were safe, came on at greater ease and in a closer body than usual; whereupon I set fire to my blow-pipes. Not merely did I dash to pieces the gabions which stood in my way; but, what was better, by that one blast I slaughtered more than thirty men. In consequence of this manoeuvre, which I repeated twice, the soldiers were thrown into such disorder, that being, moreover, encumbered with the spoils of that great sack, and some of them desirous of enjoying the fruits of their labour, they oftentimes showed a mind to mutiny and take themselves away from Rome. However, after coming to terms with their valiant captain, Gian di Urbino, they were ultimately compelled, at their excessive inconvenience, to take another road when they changed guard. It cost them three miles of march, whereas before they had but half a mile. Having achieved this feat, I was entreated with prodigious favours by all the men of quality who were invested in the castle. This incident was so important that I thought it well to relate it, before finishing the history of things outside my art, the which is the real object of my writing: forsooth, if I wanted to ornament my biography with such matters, I should have far too much to tell. . . .

The Patriarch
of Christian Humanism

Geert Geerts (1466?–1536), better known by his self-assumed sobriquet Desiderius Erasmus, was a remarkable man in the age of remarkable men. To call him the patriarch of Christian humanism barely does him justice and does no injustice to the early patriarchs, or bishops, of the Church whose lives of piety and learning he never tired of holding up as the model of Christian manhood. He bears comparison with St. Paul himself. Like Paul he wrote ceaselessly (over three thousand letters survive) to exhort and sustain the faithful. Moreover, his enemy was not far different from St. Paul's — unbelief, corruption, sloth, divisiveness, and ignorance among Christians within the Church and the brutality and senseless destructiveness of secular power bent to greed and pride.

Christian humanists everywhere looked to Erasmus for leadership and moral support. His circle reached to the limits of the western world. A Dutchman, he lived all over Europe — in Germany, France, Italy, the Low Countries, and England. His wit, learning, enthusiasm, and a rare facility to combine acerbity and graciousness in such measure as seldom to offend and often to persuade won the respect even of those little disposed to accept his notions of reform. His essential moderateness and equableness prevented him from joining the Protestant crusade, with which he had so much in common, and from lending his enormous literary talents to Catholic reaction, which he could not help but understand even if he did not sympathize with it.

Erasmus' Praise of Folly (1511; see the letter to Thomas More that follows) remains his greatest work. He himself saw his 1516 edition of the Greek text with Latin translation of the New Testament as his memorial (letter to Servatius), and though it was soon submerged in the biblical scholarship spawned by the Reformation it established his scholarly reputation with his contemporaries. His letter to Martin Dorpius catches the free spirit of the humanist critic. That rejecting monastic life addressed to Servatius, a former fellow-monk and now prior of the Augustinian monastery at Steyn in which Erasmus had become a monk and a priest, is a self-revealing portrait of great poignancy.

Erasmus to Thomas More

When of late days I was returning from Italy to England, being unwilling to waste the whole time that I had to spend on horseback in illiterate talk, I sometimes preferred either to think over some of our common studies, or to enjoy the recollection of the friends, no less amiable than learned, that I had left here. Of these, my More, you were among the first I called to mind, being wont to enjoy the remembrance of you in your absence, as I had, when you were present, enjoyed your company, than which I protest I have never met with anything more delightful in my life. Therefore, since at any rate something had to be done, and the occasion did not seem suited for serious meditation, I chose to amuse myself with the Praise of Folly. What Pallas,[1] you will say, put that idea into your head? Well, the first thing that struck me was your surname of More, which is just as near the name of *Moria* or Folly, as you are far from the thing, from which by general acclamation you are remote indeed. In the next place I surmised, that this playful production of our genius would find special favour with you, disposed as you are to take pleasure in jests of this kind, — jests, which, I trust, are neither ignorant nor quite insipid, — and generally in society, to play the part of a sort of Democritus;[2] although for that matter, while from the unusual clearness of your mind you differ widely from the vulgar, still such is your incredible sweetness and good nature, that you are able to be on terms of fellowship with all mankind, and are delighted at all hours to be so. You will therefore not only willingly receive this little declamation, as a memento of your comrade, but will adopt and protect it, as dedicated to you and become not mine, but yours. For censors will perhaps be found who may complain, that these trifles are in some parts more frivolous than becomes a theologian, and in others more aggressive than consists with Christian modesty, and will exclaim that we are bringing back the old Comedy, or the Satire of Lucian, and seizing everything by the teeth. But those who are offended by the levity and drollery of the subject should consider, that this is no new precedent of mine, the same thing having been done over and over again by great authors. . . .

But when a writer censures the lives of men without reflecting on anyone by name, I would ask whether he does not appear as a teacher and adviser rather than a detractor. And pray, how many names can I accuse myself of mentioning? Besides he who passes over no class of mankind is evidently angry with no individual, but with every vice; and therefore if any one shall be found to cry out that he is hit, he will either betray

From *The Epistles of Erasmus*, vol. 2, ed. and trans. Francis Morgan Nichols (London, 1904), pp. 1–4.

[1] The Greek goddess Pallas Athene, daughter of Zeus, who presided over the moral and intellectual side of life. — T. G. B.

[2] The Greek philosopher, fifth century B.C., dubbed "the Laughing Philosopher" for his merry and playful disposition. — T. G. B.

his consciousness, or at any rate his fear. St. Jerome [3] used this kind of writing with much more freedom and bitterness, sometimes not sparing to mention names; while we altogether avoid names, and so temper our pen, that the intelligent reader may easily see that we have sought rather to amuse than to wound. For we have not followed Juvenal's example,[4] nor made acquaintance anywhere with the hidden sink of wickedness, but have endeavoured to pass under review not so much what is shocking as what is ridiculous. Finally, if there is anyone not appeased by these arguments, he may at any rate recollect that it is an honour to be blamed by Folly, and as we have made her the speaker, we were bound to preserve the consistency of the character. But what need have I to suggest such arguments to an accomplished advocate like you, who are able to plead with the greatest skill even causes that are not the best. Farewell, most eloquent More, and defend your *Moria* [5] with all your might.

From the country, 9 June [1510].

Erasmus to Servatius

Most gracious Father, your letter, after having been tossed about by a great many hands, has reached mine at last, now that I have left England. It has indeed given me incredible pleasure inasmuch as it still breathes your old affection for me. I will answer it briefly, writing, as I do, on a journey, and will address myself to the main questions about which you write. . . .

Different persons have different aptitudes. By my bodily constitution I was always impatient of fasting, and when once awake, I could not sleep again for some hours. My mind was absorbed in the pursuit of Letters, for which in that profession there is no use; so that I do not doubt that, if my life had been free, I might have been counted, not only among the happy part of mankind, but even among the good. When, however, I saw that I was quite unfit for the kind of life, which I had undertaken, not voluntarily but by compulsion, nevertheless since it is regarded by the public opinion of our age as an act of impiety for a man to abandon the calling which he has once adopted, I had made up my mind to accept with patience this part of my unhappiness as well as others. For you know how unfortunate I have been in many respects,

---

3 A Latin Father of the Church (340?–420), biblical scholar, and translator of the Bible into Latin, the "Vulgate," accepted as the authoritative translation throughout the Middle Ages. Erasmus published a commentary on St. Jerome as well as a new translation of the New Testament. — T. G. B.

4 Roman lawyer (died c. 140) and satirizer of vice (rather too explicitly portrayed for Erasmus' moral sensibilities). — T. G. B.

5 That is, "folly." — T. G. B.

From *The Epistles of Erasmus*, vol. 2, ed. and trans. Francis Morgan Nichols (London, 1904), pp. 141–44, 146–51.

but I think this more grievous than anything else, that I was thrust into that kind of life from which I was most averse both in mind and body; in mind, because I shrank from ceremonies and was fond of liberty; in body, because even if I had liked the plan of life ever so much, my constitution was not adapted for such trials.

Some one will perhaps object, that I had my year of probation as they call it, and was of ripe age. Ridiculous! to expect that a lad in his seventeenth year, especially one brought up in study, should know himself, a great thing even in an old man! Though indeed for my own part I did not approve the life from the first, much less after I had tasted it, but was ensnared by the reasons I have mentioned. I admit that a really good man will live well in any kind of life; neither do I deny that I was myself inclined to great vices, but without my nature being so corrupt that I might not have been led aright, if I had had a suitable director, whose religion was Christianity and not a Jewish superstition. Meantime I have looked to see in what kind of life I should be least bad, and I think it is that which I have followed. I have lived among sober persons, and in literary pursuits, which have turned my thoughts from many vices. I have been able to pass my time with men who really savour of Christ, and by whose conversation I have become a better man.

I do not boast of my books, which perhaps you despise. But many persons confess that they have been made, not only more learned, but better by reading them. The love of money never affected me. Neither am I in the least degree moved by the vanity of fame. I was never a slave to pleasures, though I did not escape some stain. Drunkenness and intemperance I have always avoided. Whenever I have thought of rejoining your society, I have been reminded of the jealousy of many, the contempt of all, of conversations how cold, how silly, how utterly without any savour of Christ! of feasts how secular! in fact, of a whole system of life, *in which, if you take away what they call the ceremonies, I know not what is left that one would choose.* And lastly I have thought of the weakness of my constitution, increased by age and sickness and labours, which would prevent my satisfying you, while I should kill myself. I have been for several years subject to the Stone, a serious and fatal disease. For some years I have drunk nothing but wine, and am obliged to be careful in the choice of it on account of my sickness. I cannot be indifferent as to food or climate. For this disease, frequently recurring, makes the strictest regimen necessary; and I know the Dutch climate, I know your mode of living, not to speak of morals. Therefore, if I had returned, I should only have brought trouble to you, and death to myself.

But you perhaps think it a great happiness to die among your brethren. That is a sort of persuasion which imposes not only upon you, but on almost all. We rest our religion upon place, dress, food, or some trifling ceremonies. We think it is all over with one who changes a white coat for a black, wears a hat instead of a cowl, or occasionally shifts his locality. I venture to say, that *the greatest bane of Christian piety has arisen out of these so called religions,*[1] although it was perhaps a pious zeal that first introduced them. The authority of Popes, often too easy and indulgent, has come to their aid. For what is *more foul or more impious* than these religions when they are lax? And if you turn to those that are commended and even most commended, I know not what image of Christ you will find, *unless you can so regard some cold Jewish ordinances.* It is on these they pride themselves, and on the strength of these they judge and despise others. How much more in accordance with the sentiment of Christ, to regard the whole world as one household, or as it were one convent, to think of all mankind as our brethren or fellow Canons, to hold the sacrament of baptism as the highest order of religion, and not to look where a man lives, but how well he lives. . . .

I will now say something about my books. I think you have read the *Enchiridion,* by which not a few confess themselves to have been inflamed to a love of piety. I claim no merit of my own, but rejoice with Christ, if by his gift through my means any good has been done. I do not know whether you have seen the Book of Adages, as it has been printed by Aldus. It is not a theological work, but one that is useful for every branch of learning, and cost me incalculable nights of toil. I have published a book on Copiousness of matter and language, which I dedicated to my friend Colet, a useful work for persons preparing to preach, though such studies are scorned by those who despise all good Letters. During the last two years, beside other employments, I have corrected the Epistles of Jerome, distinguishing with dagger-marks the spurious additions, and illustrating the obscure passages with notes. I have also corrected the New Testament from the collation of ancient Greek manuscripts, and annotated more than a thousand places, not without profit to theologians. I have begun a commentary on the Epistles of St. Paul, which I shall finish, when I have published what I have already mentioned. For I have resolved to give up my life to Sacred Literature. These are the things to which I devote my hours of leisure and of work; persons of consideration say that I have a capacity for them which others have not; for your kind of life I have no capacity. I have associated with many grave and learned persons, both here [2] and in Italy and France, and have never found any who advised me to return to you, or considered that to be the better course. Even your own predecessor, Nicolas Werner of happy memory, was wont to dissuade me from doing so, advising me rather to attach myself to some bishop, and adding, that he knew both my disposition and the character of his poor brethren; these were the words he used in the vernacular tongue. In the condition of life in which I am now, I see what to avoid; but what I should rather follow, I do not see. . . .

1 That is, monastic orders. — T. G. B.
2 England; Calais, where Erasmus wrote this letter, was an English enclave in France. — T. G. B.

I have explained to you the whole scheme of my life, and what my ideas are. I am quite ready to change even this mode of life, if I see anything better. But I do not see what I can do in Holland. I know I shall not find either the climate or the food agree with me; and I shall draw all eyes upon me. I shall return old and grey to the place I left when young; I shall return an invalid. I shall be exposed to the contempt of the lowest people after being accustomed to be honoured by the greatest. I shall exchange my studies for drinking parties. And whereas you promise your assistance in finding me a place where I may live, as you say, with a good income, I cannot think what that can be, unless you would quarter me upon some convent of nuns, where I should be a servant to women, after having declined to serve Archbishops and Kings. I do not stick about income, having no anxiety to be rich, but only to have as much fortune as is needed for my health and literary leisure, so that I may not be a burden to anyone. As to these matters I should like to talk with you in person, for one cannot do so by letter either in comfort or safety. Yours, though sent by the surest messengers, has gone so far astray, that unless I had happened to come to this castle, I should never have seen it, and I received it after it had already been read by many others. Please therefore do not write any secret matter, unless you know where I am, and have a very sure messenger. I am now on my way to Germany, that is to Basel, for the purpose of publishing my lucubrations; and in the winter I may perhaps be at Rome. On my way back I will arrange for having an interview somewhere; but now the summer is almost gone, and the journey before me is long. . . .

I received your letter, written on the third day after Easter, on the 7th of July. I beg you will not omit in your prayers to commend my health to Christ. If I were sure that He would be better served by my returning to your society, I would start on my journey this very day.

Farewell, my once sweetest companion, and now my reverend Father.

From the Castle of Hammes by Calais,
the 8th of July, [1514].

Erasmus to Dorpius

With regard to a different kind of studies, I admit that what you [1] write is true, and that a person dissenting does no harm to an author, and even in many cases does good. But in this case one who dissents does

From *The Epistles of Erasmus*, vol. 2, ed. and trans. Francis Morgan Nichols (London, 1904), pp. 500–01.

[1] Martin Dorpius was a professor at the new, humanist-influenced, university of Louvain in Belgium. In 1514 he had doubts about the propriety of Erasmus' translating the New Testament. More had patched up the quarrel between Dorpius and Erasmus, which is the subject of the first paragraph of this letter. — T. G. B.

not so much show his own superior learning, as that his adversary is not
a Christian; and even if he does not intend that himself, still the person
attacked is lowered in the opinion of an ignorant public, and a handle
is given to the most perverse class of people, who are fed or grow great
by the misfortunes of others. I never had any suspicion of your own
intention, but perhaps I had a better knowledge of human character, and
considered the circumstances of the case more deeply than you did. If any
people are distressed at our agreement, let us do our best, my Dorpius,
to increase their sorrow; as they do not deserve to be happy, who rejoice
at the misfortunes of their neighbours. There is no reason for you to be
frightened by rumours; no one on earth is less disturbed by them than
myself. Those who wish well to Erasmus will readily extend their love
to Dorpius, if they perceive that you are heartily my friend. I received
two letters from More yesterday, and before two days are over, the messenger will take mine in return, in which I will add what you wish; indeed I had already written something about the good terms we are on,
before I received any hint from you.

I am invited to France by letters from several persons with splendid
promises, and that in the King's name; but I am not disposed to trust
myself again on the stage. My inclination demands retirement; and the
age I have reached, or rather my state of health, also compels me to keep
quiet.

Peter Gillis received your greeting with pleasure, and lovingly returns
his own. If you have anything for England, send it at once, and we will
attend to it. You will greet over and over again in my name Joannes
Atensis, who is praised by every one and yet never praised enough. Farewell.

Antwerp, 21 February, [1517].

The Christian Humanist's
"Short Temporal Death
Patiently Taken" for God

*Sir Thomas More (1478–1535) as a Christian humanist is best known
for his* Utopia *(1516), a dialogue that contrasted the Europe of his day
with a mythical island of peace and prosperity set in the New World.*
Utopia *is justly famous as an outstanding work of the northern Renaissance, second only to Erasmus'* Praise of Folly *in the firmament of
Christian humanism. It is not to belittle it to point out that* Utopia
*was the product of an aspiring lawyer, politician, and man of letters
in search of recognition in the dazzling Renaissance climate of the*

early reign of Henry VIII of England. Excessive wit, a certain acerbity, a touch of condescension, and a fondness for belaboring a point mark Utopia.

A Dialogue of Comfort Against Tribulation (1534) is another matter. It was written in prison by a man who, having stood at the pinnacle of office, wealth, and power, had become poor and powerless, awaiting condemnation to death for treasonous contumacy of his king. More's profound conviction that he could not forswear his allegiance to the Pope as the only head of the Holy Catholic Church brought the former lord chancellor to his "short temporal death" under the ax on July 6, 1535. A Dialogue of Comfort *is a series of meditations on the Passion of Christ, climaxing in a triumph over fear and death in the joy of deliverance. It has wit — muted, sad perhaps — Vincent in his last speech twice uses the word "more" as a pun on "More." Vincent represents More's beloved daughter Margaret; the uncle, Antony, is More himself; "the Turk" is an allegorical representation of Henry VIII as the archenemy of Christendom, the Turkish Sultan.*

In 1518, More had written, "the King has virtue and learning and . . . I see His Majesty increase in all the good and really kingly qualities." The tragedy of More's death is that neither he nor Henry had changed; both — the Christian humanist and the Renaissance prince — had no choice in the age of ideological confrontation but to play their roles to the end. Both the men and their roles were "Renaissance," but the roles were no longer compatible.

More's *Dialogue of Comfort Against Tribulation*

The Consideration of the painful Death of Christ is sufficient to make us content to suffer painful Death for his sake.

Surely, cousin, as I said before, in bearing the loss of worldly goods, in suffering of captivity, thraldom, and imprisonment, and in the glad sustaining of worldly shame, that if we would in all these points deeply ponder the sample of our Saviour himself, if it were of itself alone sufficient to encourage every kind Christian man and woman, to refuse none of all those calamities for his sake. So say I now for painful death also, that if we could and would with due compassion conceive in our minds a right imagination and remembrance of Christ's bitter painful passion, of the many sore bloody strokes that the cruel tormentors with rods and whips gave him upon every part of his holy tender body, the scornful

From Thomas More, *A Dialogue of Comfort Against Tribulation*, last chapter (London, 1897), pp. 312–14, 316, 318–20.

crown of sharp thorns beaten down upon his holy head, so strait and so deep, that on every part his blessed blood issued out and streamed down his lovely limbs drawn and stretched out upon the cross, to the intolerable pain of his forbeaten and sore beaten veins and sinews, new feeling with the cruel stretching and straining pain, far passing any cramp in every part of his blessed body at once: then the great long nails cruelly driven with hammers through his holy hands and feet, and in this horrible pain lift up and let hang with the peise of all his body, bearing down upon the painful wounded places, so grievously pierced with nails, and in such torment (without pity, but not without many despites) suffered to be pined and pained the space of more than three long hours, till himself willingly gave up unto his Father his holy soul: after which yet to shew the mightiness of their malice, after his holy soul departed, they pierced his holy heart with a sharp spear, at which issued out the holy blood and water whereof his holy sacraments have inestimable secret strength: if we would, I say, remember these things in such wise, as would God we would, I verily think and suppose that the consideration of his incomparable kindness could not in such wise fail to inflame our key-cold hearts, and set them on fire in his love, that we should find ourself not only content, but also glad and desirous, to suffer death for his sake, that so marvellous lovingly letted not to sustain so far passing painful death for ours.

Would God we would here to the shame of our cold affection again toward God, for such fervent love, and inestimable kindness of God toward us: would God we would, I say, but consider what hot affection many of these fleshly lovers have borne, and daily do bear those upon whom they doat! How many of them have not letted to jeopard their lives, and how many have willingly lost their lives indeed without either great kindness shewed them before (and afterward, you wot well, they could nothing win), but even that it contented and satisfied their mind, that by their death their lover should clearly see how faithfully they loved? The delight whereof, imprinted in their phantasy, not assuaged only, but counterpeised also (they thought) all their pain. Of these affections with the wonderful dolorous effects following thereon, not only old written stories, but over that I think in every country Christian and heathen both, experience giveth us proof enough. And is it not then a wonderful shame for us for the dread of temporal death, to forsake our Saviour that willingly suffered so painful death, rather than he would forsake us, considering that beside that he shall for our suffering so highly reward us with everlasting wealth? Oh! if he that is content to die for her love, of whom he looketh after for no reward, and yet by his death goeth from her, might by his death be sure to come to her, and ever after in delight and pleasure to dwell with her: such a lover would not let here to die for her twice. And how cold lovers be we then unto God, if rather than die for him once we will refuse him and forsake him for ever that both died for us before, and hath also provided that if we die here for him, we shall in heaven everlastingly both live and also reign with him. For, as St. Paul saith, if we suffer with him, we shall reign with him. How many Romans, how many noble courages of other sundry countries have willingly given their own lives, and suffered great deadly pains, and very painful deaths for their countries, and the respect of winning by their deaths the only reward of worldly renown and fame? And should we then shrink to suffer as much for eternal honour in heaven and everlasting glory? The devil hath some also so obstinate heretics that endure wittingly painful death for vain glory: and is it not more than shame, that Christ shall see his Catholics forsake his faith, rather than suffer the same for heaven and very glory? Would God, as I many times have said, that the remembrance of Christ's kindness in suffering his passion for us, the consideration of hell that we should fall in by forsaking of him, the joyful meditation of eternal life in heaven, that we shall win with this short temporal death patiently taken for him, had so deep a place in our breast, as reason would they should, and as (if we would do our devoir toward it, and labour for it, and pray therefor) I verily think they should. . . .

And therefore, cousin, let us well consider these things, and let us have sure hope in the help of God, and I then doubt not but that we shall be sure, that as the prophet saith, the truth of his promise shall so compass us with a pavice, that of this incursion of this midday devil, this Turk's persecution, we shall never need to fear. For either if we trust in God well, and prepare us therefor, the Turk shall never meddle with us, or else if he do, harm shall he none do us, but instead of harm, inestimable good. Of whose gracious help wherefore should we so sore now despair, except we were so mad men as to ween, that either his power or his mercy were worn out already, when we see so many a thousand holy martyrs by his holy help suffered as much before, as any man shall be put to now? Or what excuse can we have by the tenderness of our flesh, when we can be no more tender than were many of them, among whom were not only men of strength, but also weak women and children. And sith the strength of them all stood in the help of God, and that the very strongest of them all was never able of himself, and with God's help the feeblest of them all was strong enough to stand against all the world, let us prepare ourself with prayer, with our whole trust in his help, without any trust in our own strength; let us think thereon and prepare us in our minds thereto long before; let us therein conform our will unto his, not desiring to be brought unto the peril of persecution (for it seemeth a proud high mind to desire martyrdom) but desiring help and strength of God, if he suffer us to come to the stress, either being sought, formed, or brought out against our wills, or else being by his commandment (for the comfort of our cure) bounden to abide, let us fall to fasting, to prayer, to almsdeed in time, and give that unto God that may be taken from us.

When we feel us too bold, remember our own feebleness. When we feel us too faint, remember Christ's strength. In our fear, let us remember Christ's painful agony, that himself would (for our comfort) suffer before his passion, to the intent that no fear should make us despair. And ever call for his help, such as himself list to send us, and then we need never to doubt, but that either he shall keep us from the painful death, or shall not fail to strength us in it, that he shall joyously bring us to heaven by it. And then doth he much more for us, than if he kept us from it.

We should not, I ween, cousin, need much more in all this whole matter, than that one text of St. Paul,[1] if we would consider it well. For surely, mine own good cousin, remember that if it were possible for me and you alone, to suffer as much trouble, as the whole world doth together all, that were not worthy of itself to bring us to the joy which we hope to have everlastingly. And therefore I pray you let the consideration of that joy put out all worldly trouble out of your heart, and also pray that it may do the same in me. And even thus will I, good cousin, with these words make a sudden end of my whole tale, and bid you farewell. For now I begin to feel myself somewhat weary.

VINCENT. Forsooth, good uncle, this is a good end: and it is no marvel though you be waxen weary. For I have this day put you to so much labour, that saving for the comfort that yourself may take of your time so well bestowed, and for the comfort that I have myself taken, and more shall, I trust, for your good counsel given; else would I be very sorry to have put you to so much pain. But now shall our Lord reward and recompense you therefor, and many shall, I trust, pray for you. For to the intent that the more may take profit by you, I purpose, uncle, as my poor wit and learning will serve me, to put your good counsel in remembrance, not in our language only, but in the Almaine [2] tongue too. And thus praying God to give me and all other that shall read it, the grace to follow your good counsel therein, I shall commit you to God.

ANTONY. Sith you be minded, cousin, to bestow so much labour thereon, I would it had happed you to fetch the counsel at some wiser man that could have given you better. But better men may set more things, and better also, thereto. And in the meantime, I beseech our Lord to breathe of his Holy Spirit into the reader's breast, which inwardly may teach him in heart, without whom, little availeth all that all the mouths of the world were able to teach in men's ears. And thus, good cousin, farewell, till God bring us together again, either here, or in heaven! Amen!

---

1 "The passions of this time be not worthy of the glory that is to come, which shall be showed in us." Epistle of Paul to the Romans VIII:18.
2 German. — T. G. B.

THE POLITICS
OF THE RENAISSANCE
Chapter 4

For much of the fourteenth, all of the fifteenth, and the first two or three decades of the sixteenth centuries the independent states of Italy were a microcosm of European statecraft. Characteristically, the microcosm was somewhat in advance of the greater entity that included it, in both the practice of and the theory about statecraft. The significant fact is that by 1530 Europe as a whole had caught up with Italy, if not passed it, and Italian statecraft had become the accepted mode of European statecraft. Italy paid a terrible price for its preeminence: it was the battleground of Europe, where the new techniques of diplomacy and war were tried out where they were learned, on the spot.

The Italian microcosm was composed of independent city-states, nominally subject to the Holy Roman emperor in the north; the Papal States in the middle; and the kingdom of Naples (with Sicily) in the south. The kingdom of Naples was the least developed economically and culturally, though it was a unified kingdom and suffered less from internal chaos than the northern city-states. Naples-Sicily, however, was too closely linked with the French and Spanish royal houses for comfort in atomized Italy. The Papal States were the home fief of the Pope, a territorial entity as well as the seat of the Catholic Church, and successive popes played international politics with all the Italian states and the three external powers with interests in Italy — the emperor and the houses of France and Spain.

The northern Italian city-states emerged from a long rivalry between the Pope and the emperor that had divided the northern nobility and then the non-noble merchant oligarchies of the towns, who used the rivalry to escape the control of the noble feudatories who were the lords of the towns. As the towns grew in size and wealth through trade, the oligarchies became more powerful, the noble feudatories' suzerainty became more nominal, and the party identifications of the rivalry —

Ghibelline (pro-emperor) and Guelph (pro-Pope) — became merely labels for oligarchic factions vying for power within the towns. By the thirteenth century independence from external control was completed, some of the city-states had emerged as republics, and the rest, though technically duchies or marquisates, were in fact autonomous. In the process, each city's oligarchy had extended its sway over the surrounding countryside of the city's territory, which became the food supplier for the mercantile city-state.

A continuous involvement of every city in a two-front rivalry time and again broke into open warfare. The external front was trade competition, often outright trade war accompanied occasionally by actual military aggression and invasion. The internal front was a repeated challenge to the oligarchy's control by the shopkeepers and craftsmen of the city and sometimes by the mass of wage earners, with numerous rebellions, insurrections, and even revolutions. The cities were either ungovernable or governable only by militarily supported despotism. Even despotism did not last long. The military captain (*condottiere*) summoned to save an oligarchic faction in power sometimes overthrew it, only to be driven out himself by a broadly based insurrection that, in succeeding, merely established another oligarchy. Machiavelli's skepticism about the durability of any system — monarchy, oligarchy, or democracy — had its basis in fact.

The survival of the city-states against the external enemy depended upon careful diplomacy, and the first regularly undertaken continuous diplomacy in Europe was among the city-states. By the fifteenth century the protective device of the small states was balance-of-power politics, alliances of small states to outweigh and deter a great state, such as the alliance of Florence and Milan with Naples against Venice. Against the internal threat nothing availed except statecraft capable of winning the allegiance of the populace to the governing power. By the fifteenth century, wise rulers had learned that public works and beautification programs, tax reform, and the promotion of business brought material benefits, thereby lessening the chance of insurrection. Such programs also stimulated the inherent civic pride of the city-states, which — even if it did not always provide a sure defense against external enemies — at least tended to support internal order. Pride was fierce. It increased independence, and it was intimately involved with internal politics.

The death knell of the golden age of the Italian city-states was sounded in 1494 when Charles VIII of France, in connivance with Milan, invaded Italy to assert a tenuous claim to the throne of Naples. A military alliance of other states, hastily gotten together, took up the challenge, and in seeking assistance from outside brought Spain into Italy. For two-thirds of a century Italy was the battleground for a great dynastic rivalry between France and Spain (the latter later including the Empire). A Florentine historian such as Guicciardini might well catalog the horrors brought by the Italian wars. Another development overtook the localism of which the Italian city-states were the finest examples: the advent of the monarchical nation-state. Both France and Spain in the late fifteenth century made large steps toward becoming national entities under strong monarchs (though still weak monarchies) at the expense of the feudatories. The development was even further advanced in England during the reign of Henry VII. The next three centuries of European history turned almost entirely on the new powers and their development, rivalries, and expansion.

Civic Pride in the
Northern Italian City-States

Otto, Bishop of Freising (1114?–1158) was a warm supporter of the emperor, as well he might have been, since he was the grandson of Emperor Henry IV and uncle of Frederick Barbarossa (whose reign he set out to chronicle). His bias is evident in his remarkably searching description of the Italian city-states within the Empire, written about 1150. The proclivity of the city-states to call in foreign assistance was already evident, presaging the fatal error of Milan in 1494.

Giovanni Villani (1280?–1348), in his chronicle history of Florence, wrote from a pro-papal point of view. Yet his accuracy is remarkable, and in the first part of the excerpt given here he illuminates the civic factionalism common to all the city-states. The "White" and "Black" parties might earlier have been called Ghibellines and Guelphs. In any event, Pope Boniface VIII intervened in the dispute in 1301, calling in a French nobleman to crush the Whites and put in the Blacks. Villani's regret that the suppression of the Whites exiled Florence's greatest citizen, Dante, was genuine.

In 1472, during the age of Lorenzo de' Medici, "the Magnificent," Benedetto Dei might well have bragged to a rival Venetian merchant of Ficino's Platonic Academy, of Luca and Andrea della Robbia, and of the other artists of Florence's last great age. That he chose to brag of the wealth and trade of Florence was not emphasis misplaced, for they supported all the rest.

The Northern Italian Cities in the Age of Frederick Barbarossa, c. 1150

[The Lombards after their arrival in Italy] gradually laid aside their fierce barbarian customs and intermarried with the natives. Thus their children have derived from the mothers' race, and from the character of the country and the climate, something of Roman culture and civilization, and retain the elegance and refinement of Latin speech and manner.

In the government of the cities and in the management of civil affairs they also imitate the skill of the ancient Romans. Furthermore they love liberty so well that, to guard against the abuse of power, they choose to be ruled by the authority of consuls rather than by princes. They are divided into three classes, namely, "captains," vavasors, and the people. To prevent the growth of class pride, the consuls are chosen from each class in turn, and, for fear that they may yield to the lust of power, they are changed nearly every year.

It has come to pass that almost the whole country belongs to the cities, each of which forces the inhabitants of her territory to submit to her sway. One can hardly find, within a wide circuit, a man of rank or importance who does not recognize the authority of his city. . . . In order that there shall be no lack of forces for tyrannizing over their neighbors, the cities stoop to bestow the sword-belt and honorable rank upon youths of inferior station, or even upon laborers in despised and mechanical trades, who, among other peoples, are shunned like the pest by those who follow the higher pursuits. To this practice it is due that they surpass all other cities of the world in riches and power; and the long-continued absence of their ruler across the Alps [1] has further contributed to their independence.

In one respect they are unmindful of their ancient nobility and betray their barbarian origin; for, although they boast of living under law, they do not obey the law. They rarely or never receive their ruler submissively, although it is their duty to show him willing and respectful obedience. They do not obey the decrees that he issues by virtue of his legal powers, unless they are made to feel his authority by the presence of his great army. Although, in a civilized state, the citizens should submit to law, and only an enemy should be coerced by force, yet they often greet with hostility him whom they ought to receive as their own gracious prince, when he comes to demand his own.

This situation brings double evil on the state. The prince's attention is

From *Readings in European History*, vol. 1, ed. J. H. Robinson (New York, 1904), pp. 303–05. Reprinted by permission of Ginn and Company.

1 The emperor. — T. G. B.

occupied with gathering together an army to subdue the townsmen, and the citizens, though forced to obey the prince, waste their resources in the struggle. The fault, in such a case, lies wholly in the insolence of the people; the prince, who has acted under necessity, should be absolved before God and man.

Among all these cities Milan has become the leading one. . . . It must be regarded as more powerful than any of the others, in the first place, on account of its size and its multitude of brave men, and, secondly, because it has brought the two neighboring cities of Como and Lodi under its sway. Led on by Fortune's smiles, as is the way of this fleeting world, Milan has become so puffed up with pride that she has dared not only to incur the enmity of her neighbors, but, fearing not even the majesty of the emperor himself, she has recently courted his anger. . . .

Dante's Florence, 1300

39. HOW THE CITY OF FLORENCE WAS DIVIDED AND BROUGHT TO SHAME BY THE SAID WHITE AND BLACK PARTIES [1300].

In the said time, our city of Florence was in the greatest and happiest state which had ever been since it was rebuilt, or before, alike in greatness and power and in number of people, forasmuch as there were more than 30,000 citizens in the city, and more than 70,000 men capable of arms in the country within her territory; and she was great in nobility of good knights, and in free populace, and in riches, ruling over the greater part of Tuscany; whereupon the sin of ingratitude, with the instigation of the enemy of the human race, brought forth from the said prosperity pride and corruption, which put an end to the feasts and joyaunce of the Florentines. For hitherto they had been living in many delights and dainties, and in tranquillity and with continual banquets; and every year throughout almost all the city on the first day of May, there were bands and companies of men and of women, with sports and dances. But now it came to pass that through envy there arose factions among the citizens; and one of the chief and greatest began in the sesto of offence, to wit of Porte San Piero, betwen the house of the Cerchi, and the Donati; on the one side through envy, and on the other through rude ungraciousness. The head of the family of the Cerchi was one M. Vieri dei Cerchi, and he and those of his house were of great affairs, and powerful, and with great kinsfolk, and were very rich merchants, so that their company was among the largest in the world; these were luxurious, inoffensive, uncul-

From *Villani's Chronicle,* ed. P. H. Wicksteed, trans. Rose E. Selfe (London, 1906), pp. 323–27, 448–50. Reprinted by permission of Archibald Constable and Co. Ltd.

tured and ungracious, like folk come in a short time to great estate and power. The head of the family of the Donati was M. Corso Donati, and he and those of his house were gentlemen and warriors, and of no superabundant riches, but were called by a gibe the Malefami.[1] Neighbours they were in Florence and in the country, and while the one set was envious the other stood on their boorish dignity, so that there arose from the clash a fierce scorn between them, which was greatly inflamed by the ill seed of the White and Black parties from Pistoia. . . . And the said Cerchi were the heads of the White party in Florence, and with them held almost all the house of the Adimari, save the branch of the Cavicciuli; all the house of the Abati, . . . a great part of the Tosinghi, . . . part of the house of the Bardi, and part of the Rossi, and likewise some of the Frescobaldi, and part of the Nerli and of the Mannelli, and all the Mozzi, . . . all those of the house of the Scali, and the greater part of the Gherardini, all the Malispini, and a great part of the Bostichi and Giandonati, of the Pigli, and of the Vecchietti and Arrigucci, and almost all the Cavalcanti, which were a great and powerful house, and all the Falconieri which were a powerful house of the people. And with them took part many houses and families of popolani, and lesser craftsmen, and all the Ghibelline magnates and popolani; and by reason of the great following which the Cerchi had, the government of the city was almost all in their power. On the side of the Blacks were all they of the house of the Pazzi, who may be counted with the Donati as the chiefs, and all the Visdomini and all the Manieri and Bagnesi, and all the Tornaquinci, and the Spini and the Bondelmonti, and the Gianfigliazzi, Agli, and Brunelleschi, and Cavicciuli, and the other part of the Tosinghi; all the part that was left of all the Guelf houses named above, for those which were not with the Whites held on the contrary with the Blacks. And thus from the said two parties all the city of Florence and its territory was divided and contaminated. . . .

136. CONCERNING THE POET DANTE ALIGHIERI OF FLORENCE [1325].

In the said year 1321, in the month of July, Dante Alighieri, of Florence, died in the city of Ravenna, in Romagna, having returned from an embassy to Venice in the service of the lords of Polenta, with whom he was living; and in Ravenna, before the door of the chief church, he was buried with great honour, in the garb of a poet and of a great philosopher. He died in exile from the commonwealth of Florence, at the age of about fifty-six years. This Dante was a citizen of an honourable and ancient family in Florence, of the Porta San Piero, and our neighbour; and his exile from Florence was by reason that when M. Charles of

---

1 "The Notorious." — T. G. B.

Valois, of the House of France, came to Florence in the year 1301 and banished the White party, as has been afore mentioned at its due time, the said Dante was among the chief governors of our city, and pertained to that party, albeit he was a Guelf; and, therefore, for no other fault he was driven out and banished from Florence with the White party; and went to the university at Bologna, and afterwards at Paris, and in many parts of the world. This man was a great scholar in almost every branch of learning, albeit he was a layman; he was a great poet and philosopher, and a perfect rhetorician alike in prose and verse, a very noble orator in public speaking, supreme in rhyme, with the most polished and beautiful style which in our language ever was up to his time and beyond it. . . . And he wrote the [Divine] Comedy, wherein, in polished verse, and with great and subtle questions, moral, natural, astrological, philosophical, and theological, with new and beautiful illustrations, comparisons, and poetry, he dealt and treated in 100 chapters or songs, of the existence and condition of Hell, Purgatory and Paradise as loftily as it were possible to treat of them, as in his said treatise may be seen and understood by whoso has subtle intellect. It is true that he in this Comedy delighted to denounce and to cry out after the manner of poets, perhaps in certain places more than was fitting; but may be his exile was the cause of this. . . . This Dante, because of his knowledge, was somewhat haughty and reserved and disdainful, and after the fashion of a philosopher, careless of graces and not easy in his converse with laymen; but because of the lofty virtues and knowledge and worth of so great a citizen, it seems fitting to confer lasting memory upon him in this our chronicle, although, indeed, his noble works, left to us in writing, are the true testimony to him, and are an honourable report to our city.

Lorenzo the Magnificent's Florence, 1472

Florence is more beautiful and five hundred forty years older than your Venice. We spring from triply noble blood. We are one-third Roman, one-third Frankish, and one-third Fiesolan. . . . We have round about us thirty thousand estates, owned by noblemen and merchants, citizens and craftsmen, yielding us yearly bread and meat, wine and oil, vegetables and cheese, hay and wood, to the value of nine hundred thousand ducats in cash, as you Venetians, Genoese, Chians, and Rhodians who come to buy them know well enough. We have two trades greater than any four of yours in Venice put together — the trades of wool and silk. Witness the Roman court and that of the King of Naples, the Marches and Sicily, Constantinople and Pera, Broussa and Adrianople, Salonika

From *Florentine Merchants in the Age of the Medici,* ed. Gertrude Richards (Cambridge, Mass., 1932), pp. 44–46. Reprinted by permission of Harvard University Press.

and Gallipoli, Chios and Rhodes, where, to your envy and disgust, in all of those places there are Florentine consuls and merchants, churches and houses, banks and offices, and whither go more Florentine wares of all kinds, especially silken stuffs and gold and silver brocades, than from Venice, Genoa, and Lucca put together. Ask your merchants who visit Marseilles, Avignon, and the whole of Provence, Bruges, Antwerp, London, and other cities where there are great banks and royal warehouses, fine dwellings, and stately churches; ask those who should know, as they go to fairs every year, whether they have seen the banks of the Medici, the Pazzi, the Capponi, the Buondelmonti, the Corsini, the Falconieri, the Portinari and the Ghini,[1] and a hundred of others which I will not name, because to do so I should need at least a ream of paper. You say we are bankrupt since Cosimo's death.[2] If we have had losses, it is owing to your dishonesty and the wickedness of your Levantine merchants, who have made us lose thousands of florins; it is the fault of those with well-known names who have filled Constantinople and Pera with failures, whereof our great houses could tell many a tale. But though Cosimo is dead and buried, he did not take his gold florins and the rest of his money and bonds with him into the other world, nor his banks and store-houses, nor his woolen and silken cloths, nor his plate and jewelry; but he left them all to his worthy sons and grandsons, who take pains to keep them and to add to them, to the everlasting vexation of the Venetians and other envious foes whose tongues are more malicious and slanderous than if they were Sienese. . . . Our beautiful Florence contains within the city in this present year two hundred seventy shops belonging to the wool merchants' guild, from whence their wares are sent to Rome and the Marches, Naples and Sicily, Constantinople and Pera, Adrianople, Broussa and the whole of Turkey. It contains also eighty-three rich and splendid warehouses of the silk merchants' guild, and furnishes gold and silver stuffs, velvet, brocade, damask, taffeta, and satin to Rome, Naples, Catalonia, and the whole of Spain, especially Seville, and to Turkey and Barbary. The principal fairs to which these wares go are those of Genoa, the Marches, Ferrara, Mantua, and the whole of Italy; Lyons, Avignon, Montpelier, Antwerp, and London. The number of banks amounts to thirty-three; the shops of the cabinet-makers, whose business is carving and inlaid work, to eighty-four; and the workshops of the stone-cutters and marble workers in the city and its immediate neighborhood, to fifty-four. There are forty-four goldsmiths' and jewelers' shops, thirty gold-beaters, silver wire-drawers, and a wax-figure maker.[3] . . . Go through all

---

[1] The Bank of the Medici and their partners at Milan.

[2] Cosimo de' Medici, the founder of Medici power in Florence, died in 1464. — T. G. B.

[3] This was at that time a profitable industry, as such images were used in all churches.

the cities of the world, nowhere will you ever be able to find artists in wax equal to those we now have in Florence, and to whom the figures in [the church of] the Nunziata can bear witness. Another flourishing industry is the making of light and elegant gold and silver wreaths and garlands, which are worn by young maidens of high degree, and which have given their names to the artist family of Ghirlandaio. Sixty-six is the number of the apothecaries' and grocer shops; seventy that of the butchers, besides eight large shops in which are sold fowls of all kinds, as well as game and also the native wine called Trebbiano, from San Giovanni in the upper Arno Valley; it would awaken the dead in its praise.

The New Politics

The Prince (1513) immortalized Niccolò Machiavelli the theorist and "Machiavelli" as a synonym for ruthless political cunning. His continuing influence on political theory, however, owes hardly less to his Discourses on the First Ten Books of Titus Livy, begun before The Prince and completed after it. In this long commentary on a Roman historian, Machiavelli undertakes a systematic analysis of governmental structures in historical context, apparently weighted toward the experience of ancient Rome but incorporating a great deal of astute consideration of Machiavelli's own experience, as a Florentine civil servant, of recent Italian history.

The selection that follows introduces the three "good" forms of government — monarchy, aristocracy, democracy — and the three "bad" forms — tyranny, oligarchy, anarchy. The latter three are virtually alter egos of the former three, and all are pernicious because the "good" are too short-lived and the "bad" are inherently evil. The cyclical pattern of change from one to another with an implicit dialetic in operation, not the grimness of Machiavelli's conclusion, makes this model arresting. In the pattern, the single monarch-become-tyrant is overthrown by a more numerous aristocracy, which in becoming an oligarchy is in turn overthrown by the most numerous democracy. If Machiavelli did not see democracy as the ultimate form of government, later political theorists, including Marx, did. In fact, the short selection below is particularly rich in the devices with which political theorists continued to deal for another two centuries after Machiavelli: the "state of nature," "mixed monarchy" (monarchy, aristocracy, and democracy existing together), the "just ruler," and "checks and balances." For the moment, Machiavelli had postulated a dynamic model of gov-

ernment in which the state and its preservation, without respect to the form of government, are the objects of statecraft in theory and in practice. On the threshold of creating the modern nation-state, European rulers far beyond Italy found Machiavelli's distillation and blend of Classical Roman history and contemporary Italian history a strong brew.

Machiavelli: Of the Various Kinds of Government, and to Which of Them the Roman Commonwealth Belonged

I forego all discussion concerning those cities which at the outset have been dependent upon others, and shall speak only of those which from their earliest beginnings have stood entirely clear of all foreign control, being governed from the first as pleased themselves, whether as republics or as princedoms.

These as they have had different origins, so likewise have had different laws and institutions. For to some at their very first commencement, or not long after, laws have been given by a single legislator, and all at one time; like those given by Lycurgus to the Spartans; while to others they have been given at different times, as need rose or accident determined; as in the case of Rome. That republic, indeed, may be called happy, whose lot has been to have a founder so prudent as to provide for it laws under which it can continue to live securely, without need to amend them; as we find Sparta preserving hers for eight hundred years, without deterioration and without any dangerous disturbance. On the other hand, some measure of unhappiness attaches to the State which, not having yielded itself once for all into the hands of a single wise legislator, is obliged to recast its institutions for itself; and of such States, by far the most unhappy is that which is furthest removed from a sound system of government, by which I mean that its institutions lie wholly outside the path which might lead it to a true and perfect end. For it is scarcely possible that a State in this position can ever, by any chance, set itself to rights; whereas another whose institutions are imperfect, if it have made a good beginning and such as admits of its amendment, may in the course of events arrive at perfection. It is certain, however, that such States can never be reformed without great risk; for, as a rule, men will accept no new law altering the institutions of their State, unless the necessity for such a change be demonstrated; and since this necessity cannot arise without danger, the State may easily be overthrown before the new order of

From Niccolò Machiavelli, *Discourse on the First Decade of Titus Livius*, ch. 2, trans. N. H. Thomson (London, 1883), pp. 11–16.

things is established. In proof whereof we may instance the republic of Florence, which was reformed in the year 1502, in consequence of the affair of Arezzo, but was ruined in 1512, in consequence of the affair of Prato.[1]

Desiring, therefore, to discuss the nature of the government of Rome, and to ascertain the accidental circumstances which brought it to its perfection, I say, as has been said before by many who have written of Governments, that of these there are three forms, known by the names Monarchy, Aristocracy, and Democracy, and that those who give its institutions to a State have recourse to one or other of these three, according as it suits their purpose. Other, and, as many have thought, wiser teachers, will have it, that there are altogether six forms of Government, three of them utterly bad, the other three good in themselves, but so readily corrupted that they too are apt to become hurtful. The good are the three above named; the bad, three others dependent upon these, and each so like that to which it is related, that it is easy to pass imperceptibly from the one to the other. For a Monarchy readily becomes a Tyranny, an Aristocracy an Oligarchy, while a Democracy tends to degenerate into Anarchy. So that if the founder of a State should establish any one of these three forms of Government, he establishes it for a short time only, since no precaution he may take can prevent it from sliding into its contrary, by reason of the close resemblance which, in this case, the virtue bears to the vice.

These diversities in the form of Government spring up among men by chance. For in the beginning of the world, its inhabitants, being few in number, for a time lived scattered after the fashion of beasts; but afterwards, as they increased and multiplied, gathered themselves into societies, and, the better to protect themselves, began to seek who among them was the strongest and of the highest courage, to whom, making him their head, they rendered obedience. Next arose the knowledge of such things as are honourable and good, as opposed to those which are bad and shameful. For observing that when a man wronged his benefactor, hatred was universally felt for the one and sympathy for the other, and that the ungrateful were blamed, while those who showed gratitude were honoured, and reflecting that the wrongs they saw done to others might be done to themselves, to escape these they resorted to making laws and fixing punishments against any who should transgress them; and in this way grew the recognition of Justice. Whence it came that afterwards, in choosing their rulers, men no longer looked about for the strongest, but for him who was the most prudent and the most just.

---

[1] The reforms of 1502 were intended to give greater stability to Florentine government, principally by making life appointment of the chief magistrate, who was given the right to propose laws to the governing signory of the republic. Machiavelli enjoyed some influence in the reformed government. In 1512, the Medici entered Florence with Spanish troops and reestablished their power, virtually a dictatorship. — T. G. B.

But, presently, when sovereignty grew to be hereditary, and no longer elective, hereditary sovereigns began to degenerate from their ancestors, and, quitting worthy courses, took up the notion that princes had nothing to do but to surpass the rest of the world in sumptuous display, and wantonness, and whatever else ministers to pleasure; so that the prince coming to be hated, and therefore to feel fear, and passing from fear to infliction of injuries, a tyranny soon sprang up. Forthwith there began movements to overthrow the prince, and plots and conspiracies against him, undertaken not by those who were weak, or afraid for themselves, but by such as being conspicuous for their birth, courage, wealth, and station, could not tolerate the shameful life of the tyrant. The multitude, following the lead of these powerful men, took up arms against the prince, and, he being got rid of, obeyed these others as their liberators; who, on their part, holding in hatred the name of sole ruler, formed themselves into a government; and at first, while the recollection of past tyranny was still fresh, observed the laws they themselves made, and postponing personal advantage to the common welfare, administered affairs both publicly and privately with the utmost diligence and zeal. But this government passing, afterwards, to their descendants who, never having been taught in the school of Adversity, knew nothing of the vicissitudes of Fortune, these not choosing to rest content with mere civil equality, but abandoning themselves to avarice, ambition, and lust, converted, without respect to civil rights, what had been a government of the best into a government of the few; and so very soon met with the same fate as the tyrant.

For the multitude loathing its rulers, lent itself to any who ventured, in whatever way, to attack them; when some one man speedily arose who with the aid of the people overthrew them. But the recollection of the tyrant and of the wrongs suffered at his hands being still fresh in the minds of the people, who therefore felt no desire to restore the monarchy, they had recourse to a popular government, which they established on such a footing that neither king nor nobles had any place in it. And because all governments inspire respect at the first, this government also lasted for a while, but not for long, and seldom after the generation which brought it into existence had died out. For, suddenly, liberty passed into license, wherein neither private worth nor public authority was respected, but, every one living as he liked, a thousand wrongs were done daily. Whereupon, whether driven by necessity, or on the suggestion of some wiser man among them and to escape anarchy, the people reverted to a monarchy from which, step by step, in the manner and for the causes already assigned, they came round once more to license. For this is the circle revolving within which all States are and have been governed; although in the same State the same forms of Government rarely repeat themselves, because hardly any State can have such vitality as to pass through such a cycle more than once, and still hold together.

For it may be expected that in some season of disaster, when a State must always be wanting in prudent counsels and in strength, it will become subject to some neighbouring and better-governed State; though assuming this not to happen, it might well pass for an indefinite period from one of these forms of government to another.

I say, then, that all these six forms of government are pernicious — the three good kinds, from their brief duration; the three bad, from their inherent badness. Wise legislators, therefore, knowing these defects, and avoiding each of these forms in its simplicity, have made choice of a form which shares in the qualities of all the first three, and which they judge to be more stable and lasting than any of them separately. For where we have a monarchy, an aristocracy, and a democracy existing together in the same city, each of the three serves as a check upon the other.

The Italian Balance of Power Fails

Francesco Guicciardini (1483–1540), like Machiavelli, was a Florentine with the sensibilities of an all-Italian patriot. His enormous project of writing the history of Italy from the eve of the French invasion of 1494 climaxed a life spent in the service of the papacy and Florence and was motivated by his desire that "from the understanding of these events, so diverse and grave, all men will be able to draw many useful lessons both for themselves and for the public good." For him as for Machiavelli, careful historical exploration uncovered the well-springs of change, man.

The alliance structure described by Guicciardini eroded rapidly in the early 1490's. Milan feared a preemptive attack by Naples and made cause with Charles VIII of France, who had imperial ambitions and saw the assertion of his tenuous claim to Naples as the first step toward realizing them.

Guicciardini's *History of Italy*

CHAPTER 1

I propose to relate what past in our Memory in *Italy*, since the *French*, invited by our own Princes, came with powerful Armies, and interrupted her Repose: A Subject, full of melancholy Events; and of such Calamities, as the Almighty is wont, in his Displeasure, to inflict on wretched Mor-

From Francesco Guicciardini, *The History of Italy,* vol. 1, trans. Austin Parke Goddard (London, 1753), pp. 1–5, 8–10, 124–33.

tals, for their Impieties and Wickedness. From the Knowledge of so many, so various, and so important Incidents, every one may draw Instructions of some sort or other, conducive both to his own, and to the Publick Good. By numberless Examples, it will evidently appear, that human Affairs are as subject to Change and Fluctuation, as the Waters of the Sea, agitated by the Winds: And likewise, how pernicious often to themselves, and ever to their People, are the precipitate Measures of our Rulers, when actuated only by the Allurement of some vain Project, or present Pleasure and Advantage. Such Princes never allow themselves Leisure to reflect on the Instability of Fortune; but, perverting the Use of that Power, which was given them to do good, become the Authors of Disquiet and Confusion, by their Misconduct and Ambition.

'Ere I proceed to give my Reader an Account of the Troubles in *Italy,* together with the Causes from whence so many Evils were deriv'd; it will not be improper to observe, that our Calamities affected us with so much the greater Terror and Sensibility, as the Minds of Men were perfectly at Ease, and the Country, at that Time, in a State of profound Peace and Tranquillity. It is certain, that for above a thousand Years back (at which Period, the Roman Empire, weaken'd by a Change of her antient Institutions, began to fall off from that Pitch of Grandeur, to the attaining of which, the most incredible Virtue and good Fortune had equally contributed) *Italy* had at no Time enjoy'd a State of such compleat Prosperity and Repose, as in the Year 1490; and some Time before and after.

The People too had taken Advantage of this Halcyon Season, and been busied in cultivating all their Lands, as well Mountains as Vallies; and being under no Foreign Influence, but govern'd by their own Princes, *Italy* not only abounded with Inhabitants and Riches, but grew renown'd for the Grandeur and Magnificence of her Sovereigns; for the Splendor of many noble and well-built Cities; for the Seat and Majesty of Religion; and for a Number of great Men, learned in all Arts and Sciences. She had also no small Share of Military Glory, according to the Knowledge and Practice of Arms in those Days.

An happy Concurrence of Causes had preserv'd her in this flourishing Condition. Amongst the rest, common Fame ascribed no small Share, to the Virtue and active Spirit of *Lorenzo de Medici:* A Citizen of such distinguished Merit in the State of *Florence,* that the whole Affairs of that Republick were conducted, as he thought proper to advise or direct. And it was, indeed, to the Prudence of her Councils, the Happiness of her Situation, and her Opulency, that this Common-Wealth chiefly owed her Power and Influence. . . .

There was then the same Inclination for Peace in *Ferdinando, Lodovico,* and *Lorenzo;* [1] partly from the same, and partly from different

---

[1] Ferdinand of Aragon, King of Naples; Lodovico Sforza, uncle of the Duke of Milan and the real power in Milan; Lorenzo de' Medici of Florence. — T. G. B.

Motives: So that a Confederacy many Years before contracted, in the Name of *Ferdinando,* King of *Naples, Giov. Galeazzo,* Duke of *Milan,* and the Republick of *Florence,* for the mutual Defence of each other's Dominions, was with Ease corroborated and confirm'd.

This League, of some Years standing, as I observ'd, but interrupted by various Accidents, was renew'd for Twenty-five Years, in 1480, and acceded to by all the inferior Powers of *Italy.* The chief Design of the contracting Parties was to keep down the Power of the *Venetians;* who were superior to any of the Confederates separately, but not able to cope with them when united.

Their Senate seem'd to consider themselves, and acted, as a Body, that had little or no Connection with the other People of *Italy:* Widening every Breach, and cherishing and fomenting Discord amongst them, in hopes of attaining, by these Means, the Sovereignty of *Italy.* The whole Tenor of their Councils and Conduct manifested their Design: But it appear'd most plainly, when, upon the Death of *Philippo Maria Visconti,* Duke of *Milan,* they attempted, under the plausible Pretence of preserving the Liberties of the *Milanese,* to make themselves Masters of that Dutchy: And in a more recent Instance, when with open Violence they endeavour'd to seize the Dukedom of *Ferrara.*

This Confederacy produced the intended Effect, so far as to restrain the Ambition of the *Venetians;* but it did not unite the Confederates, in a sincere and solid Friendship among themselves. Their Envy and Emulation of each other, made them watchful of every Motion, and jealous of every Measure, that they conceiv'd might any way encrease the Power or Credit of their Neighbours. Nevertheless, this did not make the Peace less secure: On the contrary, it created a most ardent Impatience in them all, to quench immediately those Sparks, which, if neglected, might break out into a general Conflagration.

This was then the State of Affairs; these were the Foundations for the Tranquillity of *Italy;* so connected, and counterpois'd, that there was not only no Appearance of a present Change, but the most discerning Person cou'd not devise, by what Counsels, Accidents, or Powers, such a Peace cou'd be disturb'd. . . .

CHAPTER 9

Charles [2] was now come to *Vienne* in *Dauphine;* and could neither be dissuaded from going personally into *Italy,* by the Intreaties of his whole Kingdom; nor retarded by the Want of Money: There not being, at that Time, a Sufficiency for the present Exigencies, without pawning, and that for no considerable Sum, the Jewels that had been sent him by the Duke

---

[2] Charles VIII of France. — T. G. B.

of *Savoy,* the Marchesana of *Monferrato,* and some other Noblemen of his own Kingdom. All the Money of the Finances, and what *Lodovico* [3] had lent him, had partly been expended in fitting out his Fleet (on which great Dependance had been laid) and the rest inconsiderately dissipated at *Lyons* amongst his Favourites: Nor could he, easily, procure a fresh Supply. For, in those Days, Princes were not accustom'd to extort Money from their Subjects, as they have since been taught to do, by Avarice and Ambition, without any Regard to human or divine Laws.

In this Disorder, and on so slender a Foundation, *Charles* undertook this important War; hurry'd on rather by Impetuosity and Rashness, than guided by Prudence and Counsel.

But, as it often happens at the Entrance upon the Execution of great and hazardous Exploits, how maturely soever projected, that Difficulties, unforeseen, are apt to arise: So now, when the Army was in Motion towards the *Alps,* a sudden Murmur spread over the Camp; some complaining of the common Difficulties, attending such an Expedition; others, of the Prefidiousness of the *Italians;* and, above all, of the late Treachery of *Lodovico Sforza;* against whom they were, perhaps, the more exasperated, because they had heard a Sum of Money expected from him was not arrived: And, as is generally the Case, when the proposed Advantages of an Expedition become doubtful, those who earnestly advised it, would willingly retract: So now, the Bishop of St. *Malό,* chief Promoter, with several others, who had been most sanguine, alarmed at such unexpected Clamours, appeared undetermined. This affected the Courtiers, and the King himself, to such a Degree, that immediate Orders were given to the Army not to proceed. The Rumour of which being spread, several Officers, who had already set out, returned back, supposing the War to be at an End: And, it was thought, that would have been the Case, if the Cardinal of St. *Piero in Vincola,*[4] fatal Instrument then, before, and after, of all the Calamities of *Italy,* had not interposed, and with the Authority and Vehemence of his Speech, melted the almost frozen Spirits of the Army, and brought the King back to his former Resolution.

He not only refreshed the King's Memory with the Motives which had induced him to engage in this Enterprize, but laid also before him the Infamy and Scorn which would arise, if so noble a Design was not carried into Execution.

"To what Purpose, said he, has your Majesty weakened your Frontiers, by giving up the Province of *Artois?* For what reason have you open'd a Door to the King of *Spain* to enter your Kingdom, by parting with the *Roussillon,* to the great Dissatisfaction of your People? Such important Concessions were never made by Princes, but to free themselves from the

---

[3] Lodovico Sforza of Milan. — T. G. B.
[4] Giuliano della Rovere, afterward Pope Julius II (1503–1513). — T. G. B.

utmost Dangers; or with a View of getting much more than an Equivalent: Wherefore, as your Majesty cannot pretend to have been in any Danger, you must appear to the World, to have purchased nothing but Shame, and that at a dear Rate. What new Difficulties have arisen? What new Dangers have been discovered since the Publication of this Enterprize? On the contrary, are not the Hopes of Victory considerably encreased, by the Disappointment of your Enemies in every thing they have undertaken? For the *Arragonian* Fleet, after making a vain Attempt on *Porto Venere*, is retired to *Livorno*, which has secur'd the City of *Genoa;* the Enemy having neither Land or Sea Forces sufficient to attack it: And a few of your Troops, posted in *Romagna*, have been able to prevent *Ferdinando* from advancing into *Lombardy*. What a Panick, then, must your Adversaries be seized with, when they hear you have passed the *Alps?* What Tumults will arise? With what Terror will the Pope be affected, when, from his Palace, he views the Arms of the *Colonnese* at the Gates of *Rome?* How confounded *Piero de Medici*, when abandoned by his Relations, and by the *Florentines*, who love the *French*, and are desirous of recovering their Liberties infringed by him? Your Majesty can meet with no sort of Opposition, till you arrive on the Frontiers of the Kingdom of *Naples*. Besides, on your Approach, you will diffuse a general Terror; and nothing else will be seen but Tumult, Flight, and Rebellion. Can there be any Apprehension of a Want of Money? None surely: For as soon as the Sound of your thundering Artillery is heard in *Italy*, the *Italians* will strive who can bring most Money:[5] And, besides, if any petty State should offer to resist, the Riches which would accrue from their Overthrow would be sufficient to maintain the Army. For the *Italians* being accustomed rather to a Shew of, than a real War, are not in a Condition to resist the intrepid Valour of the *French*. What sudden Fears then? What Confusion? What Dreams? What Shadows of Danger have possessed your Royal Breast? What is become of that Magnanimity which induced you, a few Days since, to assert, that you could make yourself Master of *Italy*, tho' all the *Italian* Powers were combined against you? He desired he would consider, that Things now were gone too far for his Majesty to recede; since his Dominions were alienated, Ambassadors admitted, dismissed, and dispatched; the Expences and Preparations made; his Intentions publick, and he come in Person so near the Foot of the *Alps*. The State of his Affairs was now such, that altho' the Expedition were to appear hazardous, it could not be avoided; there being no Medium, in his present Situation, between Glory and Infamy, Flight and Triumph; or his being reputed the Greatest, or Lowest of Monarchs. Why, then, should he hesitate one Moment to proceed, and gather the Fruits of those Victories already prepared for him?". . .

---

[5] French artillery was the best of the age. — T. G. B.

The 9th of *September,* 1494, *Charles* arrived at *Asti;* bringing with him into *Italy* the Seeds of innumerable Calamities, horrible Events, and Confusions: For from this Passage derived their Origin, not only Changes of Dominions, Subversion of Kingdoms, Desolation of Countries, Destruction of Cities, and cruel Slaughters; but also new Fashions, new Customs, new and bloody Ways of making War, and Diseases, unknown in those Days: Besides, the Foundation and Arts of Government, which connected the Union of our Princes, have been ever since so unhinged, that they could never after be reinstated; so that a Door was left open for barbarous Nations to invade and oppress us. And, that our Shame may not be lessen'd by the Merits of the Author of our Miseries, it must be owned, that altho' he was fortunate in being born Heir to so powerful a Kingdom, yet he was no ways favoured by Nature either in Body or Mind.

Charles, from his Youth, was of a weak and infirm Constitution; short and ugly; had indeed some Sprightliness and Majesty in his Eyes; but his Limbs were so disproportioned, that he had rather the Appearance of a Monster than a Man. He was not only exceeding illiterate, but hardly knew the Names of the Letters: A Soul aspiring after Dominion, but no ways capable of it. He was ever imposed upon by his Courtiers; with whom he knew not how to preserve either Majesty or Authority. Indolent in every thing that required Trouble; and what he undertook was conducted with little Prudence or Judgment: If he had any thing in him commendable, it was yet farther from Virtue than Vice: For he had an Inclination to Glory, but then he acted rashly, and without Counsel. He was liberal, but profusely so, without Measure or Distinction; steady, sometimes, in his Resolutions; but more through Obstinacy than Firmness; and what was in him called Goodness, deserved rather the Name of Pusillanimity.

Henry VII of England: A New-Style Monarch

By a successful invasion and a pitched battle, in August, 1485, Henry VII, founder of the Tudor dynasty, ended three decades of dynastic war between the contending royal houses of Lancaster and York and their feudal supporters. Richard III (York) was killed in battle, and Henry moved to consolidate his victory by winning his kingdom. An Italian contemporary of Guicciardini, a clergyman and papal agent in England from 1502, Polydore Vergil (1470?–1555), wrote a history of

England that is particularly valuable for its account of the reign of
Henry VII (1485–1509).

Henry VII did not create a new style of monarchy. He used existing
institutions and extended accepted powers to curb the feudatories and
to restore order in England. Above all, he founded and maintained the
dynasty that would transform England into a modern nation-state.

Polydore Vergil's *Anglia Historia*

We have described . . . what Richard [III] did after the death of
Edward [V], and the revolt of the nobles as well as the destruction of
Richard himself. After Henry [VII] had obtained power, from the very
start of his reign he then set about quelling the insurrections. Accordingly, before he left Leicester, he despatched Robert Willoughby to
Yorkshire with instructions to bring back Edward, the fifteen-year-old
earl of Warwick, sole survivor of George duke of Clarence, whom Richard
had held hitherto in the castle called Sheriff Hutton. For indeed, Henry,
not unaware of the mob's natural tendency always to seek changes, was
fearful lest, if the boy should escape and given any alteration in circumstances, he might stir up civil discord. Having made for the castle without
delay, Robert received the boy from the commander of the place and
brought him to London, where the wretch, born to misery, remained in
the Tower until his death, as will be recounted elsewhere. Detained in
the same fortress was Elizabeth, elder daughter of King Edward, whom
Richard had kept unharmed with a view to marriage. To such a marriage
the girl had a singular aversion. Weighed down for this reason by her
great grief she would repeatedly exclaim, saying, "I will not thus be
married, but, unhappy creature that I am, will rather suffer all the torments which St. Catherine is said to have endured for the love of Christ
than be united with a man who is the enemy of my family." This girl too,
attended by noble ladies, was brought to her mother in London. Henry
meanwhile made his way to London like a triumphing general, and in
the places through which he passed was greeted with the greatest joy by
all. Far and wide the people hastened to assemble by the roadside, saluting him as king and filling the length of his journey with laden tables
and overflowing goblets, so that the weary victors might refresh themselves. But when he approached the capital, the chief magistrate (whom
they call the "mayor") and all the citizens came forth to meet him and
accompanied him ceremoniously as he entered the city: trumpeters went
in front with the spoils of the enemy, thundering forth martial sounds.
In this manner Henry came, after all his toils, to his kingdom, where he

From *The Anglia Historia of Polydore Vergil, A.D. 1485–1537*, book 74, ed. and trans.
Denys Hay (London: Camden Society, 1950), pp. 3, 5, 11, 143, 145, 147. Reprinted by
permission of the Council of the Royal Historical Society and Denys Hay.

was most acceptable to all. After this he summoned a parliament, as was the custom, in which he might receive the crown by popular consent. His chief care was to regulate well affairs of state and, in order that the people of England should not be further torn by rival factions, he publicly proclaimed that (as he had already promised) he would take for his wife Elizabeth daughter of King Edward and that he would give complete pardon and forgiveness to all those who swore obedience to his name. Then at length, having won the good-will of all men and at the instigation of both nobles and people, he was made king at Westminster on 31 October and called Henry, seventh of that name. These events took place in the year 1486 [*sic*] after the birth of our Saviour.

Thus Henry acquired the kingdom, an event of which foreknowledge had been possible both many centuries earlier and also soon after his birth. For 797 years before, there came one night to Cadwallader, last king of the Britons (as we have recorded in the third book of this history), some sort of an apparition with a heavenly appearance; this foretold how long afterwards it would come to pass that his descendants would recover the land. This prophecy, they say, came true in Henry, who traced his ancestry back to Cadwallader. The same prediction was made to Henry in his childhood by Henry VI (as we have pointed out in the life of Edward). But we must return to the task we have begun. As soon as he was crowned the king created his uncle Jasper, to whom he was much indebted, Duke of Bedford; Thomas Stanley he made earl of Derby, Giles Daubeney lord Daubeney, Robert Willoughby lord of Broke; and he ennobled many others. To others he restored their ranks and estates. Upon yet others he bestowed public office or further preferment; or enriched them with gifts of money, according to his estimate of their services to him. Furthermore, he redeemed and recalled home Thomas marquis of Dorset and John Bourchier lord Fenewary, who (as we said in the life of Richard) had both been left behind in Paris as sureties or bondsmen for the money which had been advanced there as a loan. Likewise he summoned to his side John Morton, bishop of Ely, from Flanders. To his mother Margaret, a most worthy woman whom no one can extol too much or too often for her sound sense and holiness of life, Henry allotted a share in most of his public and private resources, thus easing her declining years. Henry, moreover, was the first English king to appoint retainers, to the number of about two hundred, to be a bodyguard: these he incorporated in his household so that they should never leave his side; in this he imitated the French kings so that he might thereafter be better protected from treachery. These things having been done, the king, so that he might deserve equally well of both his friends and his enemies, at once granted his pardon for past offences to all of whatever party who swore allegiance to him. He then took in marriage Elizabeth, daughter of Edward, a woman indeed intelligent above all others, and equally beautiful. It is legitimate to attribute this to divine intervention, for plainly by it all things which nourished the two most ruinous factions were utterly removed, by it the two houses of Lancaster and York were united and from the union the true and established royal line emerged which now reigns. . . .

After Henry had well regulated his affairs in London he set out for York, in order to keep in obedience the folk of the North, savage and more eager than others for upheavals. He halted his journey at Lincoln, where he kept the feast of Easter. While he lingered here, he was informed that Francis lord Lovell, together with Humphrey Stafford, had disappeared from sanctuary at Colchester, but no one could say for certain where they had gone. Treating the matter as of small account the king made (as he had planned to do) for York. But he was no sooner there than the whole town was suddenly filled with the news that Francis Lovell had assembled a large number of troops in Yorkshire itself, a little beyond the castle of Middleham, and was to march on the city itself with hostile intent; and that Humphrey, moreover, was provoking a major rebellion in Gloucestershire. Since the news at first lacked confirmation, the king was not much disturbed, but when he learnt from the despatches of his own servants that what had at first been rumoured was indeed true, he was struck by great fear; for he had neither an army nor arms ready for his supporters, and did not know whence he could gather a reliable force at that time in a town so little devoted to his interests, which hitherto had cherished the name of Richard. But since it was essential to act quickly in order not to give his enemies the opportunity of increasing their numbers, he despatched against the enemy his whole retinue, including his bodyguard, to the total of 3,000 men, even although they were ill equipped: for the greater part had made armour for themselves from leather. Meanwhile the king assembled soldiers from every possible source. The extemporised forces which had been sent forward advanced hurriedly until they approached the enemy camp, where they immediately announced the royal terms: that the king would voluntarily extend his pardon to those who laid down their arms. This step proved to be the salvation of the king. For Francis, whether because as a result of this offer he had less faith in his troops, or because the irresolute fellow was seized by groundless fear, fled secretly by night from his men. When the flight of their leader was known, they all submitted themselves without delay to the king's authority. . . .

Henry reigned twenty-three years and seven months. He lived for fifty-two years. By his wife Elizabeth he was the father of eight children, four boys and as many girls. He left three surviving children, an only son Henry prince of Wales,[1] and two daughters, Margaret married to James king of Scotland, and Mary betrothed to Charles prince of Castile. His

[1] Henry VIII. — T. G. B.

body was slender but well built and strong; his height above the average.
His appearance was remarkably attractive and his face was cheerful,
especially when speaking; his eyes were small and blue, his teeth few,
poor and blackish; his hair was thin and white; his complexion sallow.
His spirit was distinguished, wise and prudent; his mind was brave and
resolute and never, even at moments of the greatest danger, deserted him.
He had a most pertinacious memory. Withal he was not devoid of scholarship. In government he was shrewd and prudent, so that no one dared
to get the better of him through deceit or guile. He was gracious and
kind and was as attentive to his visitors as he was easy of access. His
hospitality was splendidly generous; he was fond of having foreigners at
his court and he freely conferred favours on them. But those of his subjects who were indebted to him and who did not pay him due honour or
who were generous only with promises, he treated with harsh severity. He
well knew how to maintain his royal majesty and all which appertains to
kingship at every time and in every place. He was most fortunate in war,
although he was constitutionally more inclined to peace than to war. He
cherished justice above all things; as a result he vigorously punished violence, manslaughter and every other kind of wickedness whatsoever. Consequently he was greatly regretted on that account by all his subjects,
who had been able to conduct their lives peaceably, far removed from the
assaults and evil doing of scoundrels. He was the most ardent supporter
of our faith, and daily participated with great piety in religious services.
To those whom he considered to be worthy priests, he often secretly gave
alms so that they should pray for his salvation. He was particularly fond
of those Franciscan friars whom they call Observants, for whom he
founded many convents, so that with his help their rule should continually flourish in his kingdom. But all these virtues were obscured latterly
only by avarice, from which (as we showed above) he suffered. This
avarice is surely a bad enough vice in a private individual, whom it forever torments; in a monarch indeed it may be considered the worst vice,
since it is harmful to everyone, and distorts those qualities of trustful-
ness, justice and integrity by which the state must be governed.

Blessed be our Lord God Jesus Christ
Mary mother of God
Pray for us all
Amen.

REFORMATIONS,
PROTESTANT AND CATHOLIC
Chapter 5

"On this I stand, I can do no other. God help me. Amen." Thus Martin Luther concluded the defense of his theological position before the German states in the Imperial Diet at Worms in 1521. Was his defense the cry of conscience of a tortured soul or the bold striking of a confrontational posture by an unyielding ideologue? It was both, and therefore it was the characteristic stance of the Reformation era. Protestantism was not just another heresy for several reasons, not the least of which was that it succeeded as had no other heresy in a thousand years in splitting the Christian Church asunder in both dogma and constitution. Yet the fundamental distinction between Protestantism and all previous challenges to the faith was that it was an attack on the entire structure of the faith from an ideological position that could not be reconciled with established theology, authority, or practice in the Church.

That ideological position was nothing less than the denial of the efficacy of the Church as the intermediary between man and God. This is not to say that the reformers had no use for and intended to dismantle the organized Church. They held that salvation does not depend upon the good works of the Christian done in a state of grace that has been imparted through the sacraments of the Church. ("Grace" is best defined as "divine regeneration" of the soul, the receiving of God's favor.) Luther said that a man is saved by his faith alone ("justification by faith"), that God imparts grace to the faithful to assure them of their salvation and to comfort them, and that the sacraments serve to strengthen faith and sustain grace. Calvin said that a man is saved by God's sole decision, made before time began, that the individual would be saved, that by faith God calls that individual to repent his sins and so to be righteous in God's eyes, that God imparts grace as a sign (though not the assurance) of his salvation, and that the sacraments are the external means of uniting all those saved in the fellowship of Christ, the Church. The traditional teaching of the Church, that Christ would redeem all men from death if they would turn away from sin and lead new lives that made them righteous and deserving of salvation, was repudiated by the reformers, who argued that no man could deserve salvation, but could only hope that God would or had saved him by His merciful will. Therefore, the paraphernalia of acts and observances ordained by the Church by which men were justified and made deserving of salvation were irrelevant at best, a vehicle for extortion at worst. In the reformers' scheme, the Church would continue to exist, but its role would be secondary, for no longer would it have the Keys to Heaven, no longer could it "bind" or "loose" the individual Christian from the consequences of his sin.

Neither would the Church be a source of authority in the reformers' scheme. By "authority" they meant the foundation of the faith, and for the reformers there was only one foundation for Christian belief — the Scriptures. Peter's successor (the Pope) and the great councils of all the bishops of the Church could at best be interpreters of authority, the Scriptures, not authorities themselves sharing with the Scriptures God's mandate to reveal God's truth.

If the efficacy of the Church's agency was denied in theology and as authority, the practices traditional to the Western Church would have to be altered beyond recognition. Not only indulgences, but the structure of penance (including oral confession to the priest and absolution for the sins confessed with assignment and fulfillment of penitential acts), the system of canon law, and much of the distinctive role of the bishops and priests would disappear. The liturgy of the Church would be altered, particularly the great sacrament of the Eucharist or Mass. All the reformers repudiated the doctrine that the sacrifice of Christ on the cross was reenacted in the Eucharist to enable each communicant to partake of the body and blood of the Savior and so to receive saving grace. Luther's position was less radical than that of the other reformers, but even for him the body and blood of Christ "under" the bread and wine of the Eucharist was a sign signifying the blessing of the sacrament, which is forgiveness of sins and life everlasting. The Swiss reformer Zwingli went much further, holding that the Eucharist was nothing more than a memorial of Christ's sacrifice, with nothing of Christ in it, nothing from Christ received with it, and nothing to Christ given by it. Calvin largely accepted Zwingli's teaching on this point.

Everywhere the first round of the ideological struggle was won by the reformers. The Catholic Church reacted hesitantly, politically, and disparately to the challenge. Each new reformed church tended to be more radical than its predecessors. In the Council of Trent (1545–1563) the Catholic Church reaffirmed its traditional theology, authority, and practice, clearly drawing the issue with the reformers. But almost as a corollary to each traditional position reaffirmed there was a new and vigorous dynamic of action undertaken. The new dynamic was the Catholic Reformation or Counter-Reformation. Hesitancy and disparateness vanished with the centering of total responsibility for the counterattack in the hands of the Pope. The overly political — hence secular — reaction to Protestantism gave way to a spiritual rebirth. In no institution was that clearer than in the Society of Jesus. In no man was it more patent than in the Jesuits' founder, Ignatius Loyola. The "new Catholic" was almost a "convert" to his faith, through a conversion bought by an awesome discipline to submerge the self in God by contemplating Christ's sacrifice. Thus the traditional practices of the faith were given renewed meaning and were made the tools to recapture whole areas of Europe for Rome.

From the beginning, Protestantism depended upon the assistance or sanction of secular powers to survive and to succeed. Even after it broadened its response beyond political action the Catholic Church did not cease to seek success (and often find it) in regaining or retaining the allegiance of secular powers. However, the Reformation cannot be understood principally in terms of politics. It was a civil war within the European world fought over the first potent ideology of the culture, its faith.

Luther on the Mass as the New Testament

The three best known and most influential works of Martin Luther (1483–1546) were published in 1520. They were defiant, somewhat intemperate pamphlets that together formed Luther's reply to Pope Leo X's admonition to him to recant his heresy. Address to the Christian Nobility of the German Nation, The Babylonian Captivity of the Church, *and* On Christian Liberty *stated the reformer's program and his views on the polity of a reformed church. All three were peculiarly subject to misinterpretation — the first especially so, for it advanced the idea of "the priesthood of all believers" in conjunction with a call to the secular powers to reform the Church, an invitation to a resurgence of the quasi-priestly role of kingship.*

In 1519, under cooler circumstances and in a more reflective and avowedly theological mood, Luther had written his tract A Treatise on the New Testament, That Is the Holy Mass. *Almost his least-known work, it conveys with unusual clarity, compactness, and comprehensive-*

ness Luther's developed theological position: Justification by faith
(section 6), emphasis on the value of "primitive" or early Church practice (section 4), distrust of the value of law in matters of faith (sections
1 and 3), the "unworthiness" of man to be saved (section 15), the Eucharist as a compression into one act of the entire promise of the New
Testament, not a sacrifice (sections 10, 24, and 25), and the role of laity
in the Eucharist (sections 27 and 28), which is a more precise and per-
suasive rendering of Luther's notion of the "priesthood of all believers." What happens in the Eucharist — whether Christ is present in body
and blood (as according to accepted theology) or spiritually present
commingled with the bread and wine (as according to Luther's consubstantiation) — was not yet so well defined as it would be later, but
this tract at least hinted at consubstantiation.

A Treatise on the New Testament
That Is the Holy Mass

Jesus

1. Experience, all chronicles, and the Holy Scriptures besides, teach
us this truth: the less law, the more justice; the fewer commandments,
the more good works. No well-regulated community ever existed long, if
at all, where there were many laws. Therefore, before the ancient law of
Moses, the Patriarchs of old had no prescribed law and order for the service of God other than the sacrifices; as we read of Adam, Abel, Noah
and others. Afterward, circumcision was enjoined upon Abraham and his
household, until the time of Moses, through whom God gave the people
of Israel divers laws, forms, and practices, for the sole purpose of teaching human nature how utterly useless many laws are to make people
pious. For although the law leads and drives away from evil to good
works, it is still impossible for man to do them willingly and gladly; but
he has at all times an aversion for the law and would rather be free. Now
where there is unwillingness, there can never be a good work. For what
is not done willingly is not good, and only seems to be good. Consequently, all the laws cannot make one really pious without the grace of
God, for they can produce only dissemblers, hypocrites, pretenders, and
proud saints, such as have their reward here, and never please God. Thus
He says to the Jews, Malachi i: "I have no pleasure in you; for who is
there among you that would even as much as shut a door for me, willingly and out of love?" . . .

3. Christ, in order that He might prepare for Himself an acceptable
and beloved people, which should be bound together in unity through

From *Works of Martin Luther*, vol. 1 (Philadelphia, 1915), pp. 294–98, 300–01, 304–05,
312–13, 315–17. Reprinted by permission of Fortress Press.

love, abolished the whole law of Moses. And that He might not give further occasion for divisions, He did not again appoint more than one law or order for His entire people, and that the holy mass. For, although baptism is also an external ordinance, yet it takes place but once, and is not a practice of the entire life, like the mass. Therefore, after baptism there is to be no other external order for the service of God except the mass. And where the mass is used, there is a true service, even though there be no other form, with singing, playing, bell-ringing, vestments, ornaments and postures; for everything of this sort is an addition invented by men. When Christ Himself first instituted this sacrament and held the first mass, there were no patens, no chasuble, no singing, no pageantry, but only thanksgiving to God, and the use of the sacrament. After this same simplicity the Apostles and all Christians long time held mass, until the divers forms and additions arose, by which the Romans held mass one way, the Greeks another; and now it has finally come to this, that the chief thing in the mass has become unknown, and nothing is remembered except the additions of men.

4. The nearer, now, our masses are to the first mass of Christ, the better, without doubt, they are; and the farther from Christ's mass, the more perilous. For that reason we may not boast of ourselves, against the Russians or Greeks, that we alone have a right to hold mass; as little as a priest who wears a red chasuble may boast against him who wears one of white or black. For such external additions and differences may by their dissimilarity make sects and dissensions, but they can never make the mass better. Although I neither wish nor am able to displace or discard all such additions, still, because such pompous forms are perilous, we must never permit ourselves to be led away by them from the simple institution by Christ and from the right use of the mass. . . .

6. If man is to deal with God and receive anything from Him, it must happen in this wise, not that man begin and lay the first stone, but that God alone, without any entreaty or desire of man, must first come and give him a promise. This word of God is the beginning, the foundation, the rock, upon which afterward all works, words and thoughts of man must build.[1] This word man must gratefully accept, and faithfully believe the divine promise, and by no means doubt that it is and comes to pass just as He promises. This trust and faith is the beginning, middle, and end of all works and righteousness. For, because man does God the honor of regarding and confessing Him as true, He becomes to him a gracious God, Who in turn honors him and regards and confesses him as true. Thus it is not possible that man, of his own reason and strength, should by works ascend to heaven and anticipate God, moving Him to be gracious; but God must anticipate all works and thoughts, and make a promise clearly expressed in words, which man then takes and keeps with

---

[1] This is a play on the "Petrine" idea, in that Christ said to Peter, "Upon this rock I build my Church." See *Unam Sanctam.* — T. G. B.

a good, firm faith. Then follows the Holy Spirit, Who is given him because of this same faith. . . .

10. What then is this testament, and what is bequeathed us therein by Christ? Forsooth, a great, eternal and unspeakable treasure, namely, the forgiveness of all sins, as the words plainly state, "This is the cup of a new eternal testament in My blood, that is shed for you and for many for the remission of sin." As though He said: "Behold, man, in these words I promise and bequeath thee forgiveness of all thy sin and eternal life. And in order that thou mayest be certain and know that such promise remains irrevocably thine, I will die for it, and will give My body and blood for it, and will leave them both to thee as sign and seal, that by them thou mayest remember Me." So He says: "As oft as ye do this, remember Me." Even as a man who bequeathes something includes therein what shall be done for him afterward, as is the custom at present in the requiems and masses for the dead, so also Christ has ordained a requiem for Himself in his testament; not that He needs it, but because it is necessary and profitable for us to remember Him; whereby we are strengthened in faith, confirmed in hope and made ardent in love. For as long as we live on earth our lot is such that the evil spirit and all the world assail us with joy and sorrow, to extinguish our love for Christ, to blot out our faith, and to weaken our hope. Wherefore we sorely need this sacrament, in which we may gain new strength when we have grown weak, and may daily exercise ourselves unto the strengthening and uplifting of the spirit. . . .

15. Now there are two temptations which never cease to assail you; the first, that you are entirely unworthy of so rich a testament, the second, that even were you worthy, the blessing is so great that human nature is terrified by the greatness of it; for what do not forgiveness of all sin and eternal life bring with them? If either of these temptations comes to you, you must, as I have said, esteem the words of Christ more than such thoughts. It will not be He that lies to you, your thoughts will be deceiving you.

Just as though a poor beggar, yea, a very knave, were bequeathed a thousand gulden: he would not demand them because of his merit or worthiness, nor fail to claim them because of the greatness of the sum; and if anyone should cast up to him his unworthiness and the greatness of the sum, he would certainly not allow anything of that sort to frighten him, but would say: "What is that to you? I know full well that I am unworthy of the inheritance; I do not demand it on my merits, as though it had been due me, but on the favor and grace of the testator. If he did not think it too much to bequeath to me, why should I so despise myself and not claim and take it?" So also must a timid, dejected conscience insist, against its own thoughts, upon the testament of Christ, and be stubborn in firm faith, despite its own unworthiness and the greatness of the blessing. For this very reason that which brings to such unworthy ones so great a blessing is a divine testament, by which God desires above all things to awaken love to Him. So Christ comforted those dejected ones who thought the blessing too great and said: "Faint-hearted little flock, fear not; it hath pleased your Father to give you the eternal Kingdom."

24. Now if you ask what is left in the mass to give it the name of a sacrifice, since so much is said in the Office about the sacrifice, I answer: Nothing is left. For, to be brief and to the point, we must let the mass be a sacrament and testament, and this is not and cannot be a sacrifice any more than the other sacraments — baptism, confirmation, penance, extreme unction, etc. — are sacrifices. Otherwise we should lose the Gospel, Christ, the comfort of the sacrament and every grace of God. Therefore we must separate the mass clearly and distinctly from the prayers and ceremonies which have been added by the holy fathers, and keep the two as far apart as heaven and earth, that the mass may remain nothing else than the testament and sacrament comprehended in the words of Christ. . . .

25. We should, therefore, give careful heed to this word "sacrifice," that we do not presume to give God something in the sacrament, when it is He who therein gives us all things. We should bring spiritual sacrifices, since the external sacrifices have ceased and have been changed into the gifts to churches, monastic houses and charitable institutions. What sacrifices then are we to offer? Ourselves, and all that we have, with constant prayer, as we say: "Thy will be done on earth as in heaven." Whereby we are to yield ourselves to the will of God, that He may do with us what He will, according to His own pleasure; in addition, we are to offer Him praise and thanksgiving with our whole heart, for His unspeakable, sweet grace and mercy, which He has promised and given us in this sacrament. And although such a sacrifice occurs apart from the mass, and should so occur, for it does not necessarily and essentially belong to the mass, as has been said, yet it is more precious, more seemly, more mighty and also more acceptable when it takes place with the multitude and in the assembly where men provoke, move and inflame one another to press close to God, and thereby attain without all doubt what they desire. . . .

27. Few, however, understand the mass in this way. For they suppose that only the priest offers the mass as a sacrifice before God, although this is done and should be done by everyone who receives the sacrament, yea, also by those who are present at the mass and do not receive the sacrament. Furthermore, such offering of sacrifice every Christian may make, wherever he is and at all times, as St. Paul says: "Let us offer the sacrifice of praise continually through Him," and Psalm cx: "Thou art a priest forever." If He is a priest forever, then He is at all times a priest and is offering sacrifices without ceasing before God. But we cannot be continually the same, and therefore the mass has been instituted that we may there come together and offer such sacrifice in common. . . . Thus it

becomes clear that it is not the priest alone who offers the sacrifice of the mass, but every one's faith, which is the true priestly office, through which Christ is offered as a sacrifice to God. This office the priest, with the outward ceremonies of the mass, simply represents. Each and all are, therefore equally spiritual priests before God.

28. From this you can see for yourself that there are many who rightly observe mass and make this sacrifice, who themselves know nothing about it, nay, who do not realize that they are priests and can observe mass. Again, there are many who take great pains and apply themselves with all diligence, thinking that they are keeping the mass properly and offering a right sacrifice, and yet there is nothing right about it. For all those who have the faith that Christ is a priest for them in heaven before God, and who lay on Him their prayers and praise, their need and their whole selves, and present them through Him, not doubting that He does this very thing, and offers Himself for them, these take the sacrament and testament, outwardly or spiritually, as a sign of all this, and do not doubt that all sin is thereby forgiven, that God has become their gracious Father and that everlasting life is prepared for them.

All such, then, wherever they may be, are true priests, observe the mass aright and also obtain by it what they desire. For faith must do everything. It alone is the true priestly office and permits no one else to take its place. Therefore all Christians are priests; the men, priests, the women, priestesses, be they young or old, masters or servants, mistresses or maids, learned or unlearned. Here there is no difference, unless faith be unequal. Again, all who do not have such faith, but presume to make much of the mass as a sacrifice, and perform this office before God, are figure-heads. They observe mass outwardly and do not themselves know what they are doing, and cannot be well pleasing to God. For without true faith it is impossible to please Him, as St. Paul says in Hebrews xi. Now there are many who, hidden in their hearts, have such true faith, and themselves know not of it; many there are who do not have it, and of this, too, they are unaware.

Zwingli on the Mass as Memorial

The significance of the redoubtable German-Swiss reformer of Zurich, Ulrich Zwingli (1484–1531), both in his own day and since, has paled in comparison with that of Luther, his contemporary, and Calvin, his successor. This is unfortunate, for Zwingli was one of the boldest and most creative of the reformers, far in advance of Luther in his emphasis on the "primitive" Church as the criterion for practice, and his work as the real founder of the Reformation in Alpine Europe was the basis upon which Calvin built his reformation. Zwingli's principal theological contribution (virtually accepted entire by Calvin and later reformers) was the toppling of the sacraments, particularly the Eucharist, as an essential in receiving and sustaining grace. According to Zwingli, the sacraments were merely signs *of a sacred thing, of grace already given, and were not a vehicle for grace in any form. Zwingli was killed in battle as the militant chaplain of Protestant forces fighting Catholic troops in a religious war among the Swiss cantons. Had he lived longer, he might have continued to be a major influence in the Reformation.*

Reckoning of the Faith to the Roman Emperor Charles V, from Zurich, July 3, 1530

Seventhly. I believe, yea, I know, that all the sacraments are so far from conferring grace that they do not even convey or distribute it. In this matter, most powerful Caesar, I may seem to thee perhaps too bold. But my opinion is fixed. For as grace is produced or given by the Divine Spirit (for when I use the term "grace" I am speaking the Latin for pardon, *i.e.,* indulgence and gratuitous kindness), so this gift pertains to the Spirit alone.

Moreover, a channel or vehicle is not necessary to the Spirit, for He Himself is the virtue and energy whereby all things are borne, and has no need of being borne; neither do we read in the Holy Scriptures that perceptible things, as are the sacraments, bear certainly with them the Spirit, but if perceptible things have ever been borne with the Spirit, it has been the Spirit, and not perceptible things, that has borne them. . . .

Briefly, the Spirit breathes wherever He wishes; *i.e.,* just as the wind bloweth where it listeth, and thou hearest the sound thereof, and canst not tell whence it cometh or whither it goeth, so is everyone that is born of the Spirit; *i.e.,* invisibly and imperceptibly illumined and drawn. This the truth spake. Therefore, the Spirit of grace is conveyed not by this mersion, not by this draught, not by this anointing; for if it were thus it would be known how, where, whence, and wither the Spirit is given.

For if the presence and efficacy of grace are bound to the sacraments, they work where these are conveyed; and where these are not applied, all things languish. Neither is it the case that theologians allege this as material or subject, because the disposition for this is first required; *i.e.,* because the grace of baptism or the Eucharist (for thus they speak) is conferred on one who is first prepared for this. For he who through the sacraments

From S. M. Jackson, *Huldreich Zwingli* (New York, 1900), pp. 466–71, 478.

receives according to them this grace, either prepares himself for this or is prepared by the Spirit. If he prepares himself, we can do something of ourselves, and prevenient grace is nothing. If he be prepared by the Spirit for the reception of grace, I ask whether this be done through the sacrament as a channel or without the sacrament? If the sacrament intervene, man is prepared by the sacrament for the sacrament, and thus there will be a process *ad infinitum;* for a sacrament will always be required as a preparation for a sacrament. But if we be prepared without the sacrament for the reception of sacramental grace, the Spirit is present in His kindness before the sacrament, and hence grace is both rendered and is present before the sacrament is administered. From this it is inferred (as I willingly and gladly admit in regard to the subject of the sacraments) that the sacraments are given as a public testimony of that grace which is previously present to every individual. This baptism is administered in the presence of the Church to one who before receiving it either confessed the religion of Christ, or has the word of promise whereby he is known to belong to the Church. Hence it is that when we baptise an adult we ask him whether he believes. If he answer, Yea, then at length he receives baptism. Faith, therefore, has been present before he receives baptism. Faith, then, is not given in baptism. But when an infant is offered the question is asked whether its parents offer it for baptism. When they reply through witnesses that they wish it baptised, the infant is baptised. Here also God's promise precedes, that He regards our infants as belonging to the Church no less than those of the Hebrews. For when they who are of the Church offer it, the infant is baptised under the law that since it has been born of Christians it is regarded by the divine promise among the members of the Church. By baptism, therefore, the Church publicly receives one who had previously been received through grace. Baptism, therefore, does not bring grace, but testifies to the Church that grace has been given for him to whom it is administered.

I believe, therefore, O Emperor, that a sacrament is a sign of a sacred thing — *i.e.,* of grace that has been given. I believe that it is a visible figure or form of invisible grace — viz., which has been provided and given by God's bounty; *i.e.,* a visible example which presents an analogy to something done by the Spirit. I believe that it is a public testimony. As when we are baptised the body is washed with the purest element, but by this it is signified that by the grace of divine goodness we have been drawn into the assembly of the Church and God's people, wherein we ought to live pure and guiltless. Thus Paul explains the mystery in Romans vi. He testifies, therefore, that he who receives baptism is of the Church of God, which worships its Lord in integrity of faith and purity of life. For this reason the sacraments, which are holy ceremonies (for the Word is added to the element, and it becomes a sacrament),[1] should be

---

1 Compare to Luther's emphasis on the Word in the Eucharist, in the preceding selection. — T. G. B.

religiously cherished, *i.e.*, highly valued, and should be treated with respect; for while they are unable to give grace they nevertheless associate visibly with the Church, us who have previously been received into it invisibly; and this should be esteemed with the highest devotion when declared and published in their administration, together with the words of the divine institution. For if we think otherwise of the sacraments, as that when externally used they cleanse internally, Judaism is restored, which believed that crimes were expiated, and grace, as it were, purchased and obtained, by various anointings, ointments, offerings, victims, and banquets. Nevertheless, the prophets, especially Isaiah and Jeremiah, always most steadfastly urged in their teaching that the promises and benefits of God are given by God's liberality, and not with respect to merits or external ceremonies. I believe also that the Anabaptists,[2] in denying baptism to the infants of believers are entirely wrong; and not here only, but also in many other things, of which there is no opportunity to speak. To avoid their folly or malice, relying upon God's aid, and not without danger, I have been the first to teach and write against them, so that now, by God's goodness, this pestilence among us has greatly abated; so far am I from receiving, teaching, or defending anything of this seditious faction.

Eighthly. I believe that in the holy Eucharist — *i.e.*, the supper of thanksgiving — the true body of Christ is present by the contemplation of faith; *i.e.*, that they who thank the Lord for the kindness conferred on us in His Son acknowledge that He assumed true flesh, in it truly suffered, truly washed away our sins in His own blood; and thus everything done by Christ becomes present to them by the contemplation of faith. But that the body of Christ in essence and really — *i.e.*, the natural body itself — is either present in the supper or masticated with our mouth or teeth, as the Papists and some who long for the flesh-pots of Egypt assert, we not only deny, but firmly maintain is an error opposed to God's Word. This, with the divine assistance, I will in a few words, O Emperor, make as clear as the sun. First, by citing the divine oracles; secondly, by attacking the adversaries with arguments derived therefrom, as with military engines; lastly, by showing that the ancient theologians held our opinion. Thou, meanwhile, Creator Spirit, be present, enlighten the minds of Thy people, and fill with grace and light the hearts that Thou hast created!

Christ Himself, the mouth and the wisdom of God, has said: "The poor always ye have with you, but me ye have not always." Here the presence of the body alone is denied, for according to His divinity he is always present, because He is always everywhere, according to His word: "Lo, I am with you alway, even unto the end of the world"; viz., according to divinity, truth, and goodness. Augustine agrees with us. Neither is there any foundation for the assertion of the adversaries that the hu-

---

2 The Anabaptists were the most radical Protestants. — T. G. B.

manity of Christ is wherever the divinity is, and that otherwise the person is divided; for this would destroy Christ's true humanity.

For nothing but God can be everywhere. And that humanity is in one place, but divinity everywhere, does not thus divide the person; just as the Son's assumption of humanity does not divide the unity of essence. Yea, it would be more effectual for separating unity of essence if one person assumes to itself a creature which the rest do not at all assume, than it is for separating the person, that humanity is in one place, but divinity everywhere, since we see even in creatures that bodies are confined to one place, but their power and virtue are most widely diffused. The sun is an example, whose body is in one place, while his virtue pervades all things. The human soul also surmounts the stars and penetrates hell, but the body is nevertheless in one place. . . .

Ninthly. I believe that ceremonies which are neither, through superstition, contrary to faith or God's Word (although I do not know whether such be found), can be tolerated by charity until the Day-star arise. But at the same time I believe that by the same charity as mistress the ceremonies mentioned should be abolished when it can be done without great offence, however much they who are of a faithless mind may clamour. For Christ did not prohibit Magdalene from pouring out the ointment, although the avarice and dishonesty of Judas made a disturbance. Images, moreover, that are prostituted for worship, I do not reckon among ceremonies, but among the number of those things that conflict diametrically with God's Word. But I am so far from condemning those that are not offered for worship that I acknowledge both painting and statuary as God's gifts.

Calvin on Election and Damnation

Jean Calvin (1509–1546) was a generation younger than Luther and Zwingli, and profited considerably from their theological innovations. Lucid, systematic, and intellectually fearless, Calvin managed first to synthesize and then to carry to a higher, and novel, stage of development the theological structure of Protestantism. The following selection deals with his greatest contribution to Protestant theology, the doctrine of predestination. This doctrine was at least plausibly implicit in St. Paul, suggested in St. Augustine, and accepted without receiving much emphasis by Luther. Calvin founded "Reformed Protestantism" on the doctrine, and it became the theological banner of that large and growing legion of true believers who bore the name Calvinists.

The statement of Calvin's doctrines and his polity was made in his

Institutes of the Christian Religion, first published in 1536 but enlarged and elaborated during his lifetime. Geneva became the base of his power, the model for his polity, and the great missionary center for the spread of Calvinism throughout Europe. Yet Calvin's masterfulness as an organizer and disciplinarian does not account for the growth of Calvinism as the most powerful and dynamic branch of Protestantism from the 1540's onward. The grim doctrine of predestination — the awful working of the will of God to elect some to everlasting life and condemn others to everlasting damnation — gave purpose and meaning to the lives of those who felt God within them, detected signs of their election, and undertook to do God's work against sin as members of the great company of visible saints. It was a purpose distinctly different from the purposes to which other reformers called their devout. Predestination to election proved the most attractive force produced in the Reformation era.

Institutes of the Christian Religion

CHAPTER 21. ETERNAL ELECTION, OR GOD'S
PREDESTINATION OF SOME TO SALVATION,
AND OF OTHERS TO DESTRUCTION

The covenant of life not being equally preached to all, and among those to whom it is preached not always finding the same reception, this diversity discovers the wonderful depth of the Divine judgment. Nor is it to be doubted that this variety also follows, subject to the decision of God's eternal election. If it be evidently the result of the Divine will, that salvation is freely offered to some, and others are prevented from attaining it, — this immediately gives rise to important and difficult questions, which are incapable of any other explication, than by the establishment of pious minds in what ought to be received concerning election and predestination — a question, in the opinion of many, full of perplexity; for they consider nothing more unreasonable, than that, of the common mass of mankind, some should be predestinated to salvation, and others to destruction. But how unreasonably they perplex themselves will afterwards appear from the sequel of our discourse. Besides, the very obscurity which excites such dread, not only displays the utility of this doctrine, but shows it to be productive of the most delightful benefit. We shall never be clearly convinced as we ought to be, that our salvation flows from the fountain of God's free mercy, till we are acquainted with his eternal election, which illustrates the grace of God by this comparison,

From Jean Calvin, *Institutes of the Christian Religion*, vol. 2, ed. Benjamin B. Warfield, trans. John Allen, 6th American ed. (Philadelphia, 1936), pp. 140–41, 144–45, 148–50, 178.

that he adopts not all promiscuously to the hope of salvation, but gives to some what he refuses to others. Ignorance of this principle evidently detracts from the Divine glory, and diminishes real humility. But according to Paul, what is so necessary to be known, never can be known, unless God, without any regard to works, chooses those whom he has decreed. "At this present time also, there is a remnant according to the election of grace. And if by grace, then it is no more of works; otherwise, grace is no more grace. But if it be of works, then it is no more grace; otherwise, work is no more work." [1] If we need to be recalled to the origin of election, to prove that we obtain salvation from no other source than the mere goodness of God, they who desire to extinguish this principle, do all they can to obscure what ought to be magnificently and loudly celebrated, and to pluck up humility by the roots. In ascribing the salvation of the remnant of the people to the election of grace, Paul clearly testifies, that it is then only known that God saves whom he will of his mere good pleasure, and does not dispense a reward to which there can be no claim. They who shut the gates to prevent any one from presuming to approach and taste this doctrine, do no less injury to man than to God; for nothing else will be sufficient to produce in us suitable humility, or to impress us with a due sense of our great obligations to God. Nor is there any other basis for solid confidence, even according to the authority of Christ, who, to deliver us from all fear, and render us invincible amidst so many dangers, snares, and deadly conflicts, promises to preserve in safety all whom the Father has committed to his care. Whence we infer, that they who know not themselves to be God's peculiar people will be tortured with continual anxiety; and therefore, that the interest of all believers, as well as their own, is very badly consulted by those who, blind to the three advantages we have remarked, would wholly remove the foundation of our salvation. And hence the Church rises to our view, which otherwise, as Bernard justly observes, could neither be discovered nor recognized among creatures, being in two respects wonderfully concealed in the bosom of a blessed predestination, and in the mass of a miserable damnation. . . .

V. Predestination, by which God adopts some to the hope of life, and adjudges others to eternal death, no one, desirous of the credit of piety, dares absolutely to deny. But it is involved in many cavils, especially by those who make foreknowledge the cause of it. We maintain, that both belong to God; but it is preposterous to represent one as dependent on the other. When we attribute foreknowledge to God, we mean that all things have ever been, and perpetually remain, before his eyes, so that to his knowledge nothing is future or past, but all things are present; and present in such a manner, that he does not merely conceive of them from ideas formed in his mind, as things remembered by us appear present to our minds, but really beholds and sees them as if actually placed be-

[1] Romans XI : 5, 6.

fore him. And this foreknowledge extends to the whole world, and to all the creatures. Predestination we call the eternal decree of God, by which he has determined in himself, what he would have to become of every individual of mankind. For they are not all created with a similar destiny; but eternal life is foreordained for some, and eternal damnation for others. Every man, therefore, being created for one or the other of these ends, we say, he is predestinated either to life or to death. . . .

VII. Though it is sufficiently clear, that God, in his secret counsel, freely chooses whom he will, and rejects others, his gratuitous election is but half displayed till we come to particular individuals, to whom God not only offers salvation, but assigns it in such a manner, that the certainty of the effect is liable to no suspense or doubt. These are included in that one seed mentioned by Paul; for though the adoption was deposited in the hand of Abraham, yet many of his posterity being cut off as putrid members, in order to maintain the efficacy and stability of election, it is necessary to ascend to the head, in whom their heavenly Father has bound his elect to each other, and united them to himself by an indissoluble bond. Thus the adoption of the family of Abraham displayed the favour of God, which he denied to others; but in the members of Christ there is a conspicuous exhibition of the superior efficacy of grace; because, being united to their head, they never fail of salvation. Paul, therefore, justly reasons from the passage of Malachi which I have just quoted [2] that where God, introducing the covenant of eternal life, invites any people to himself, there is a peculiar kind of election as to part of them, so that he does not efficaciously choose all with indiscriminate grace. The declaration, "Jacob have I loved," respects the whole posterity of the patriarch, whom the prophet there opposes to the descendants of Esau. Yet this is no objection to our having in the person of one individual a specimen of the election, which can never fail of attaining its full effect. These, who truly belong to Christ, Paul correctly observes, are called "a remnant"; for experience proves, that of a great multitude the most part fall away and disappear, so that often only a small portion remains. That the general election of a people is not always effectual and permanent, a reason readily presents itself, because, when God covenants with them, he does not also give them the spirit of regeneration to enable them to persevere in the covenant to the end; but the external call, without the internal efficacy of grace, which would be sufficient for their preservation, is a kind of medium between the rejection of all mankind and the election of the small number of believers. The whole nation of Israel was called "God's inheritance," though many of them were strangers; but God, having firmly convenanted to be their Father and Redeemer, regards that gratuitous favour rather than the defection of multitudes; by whom his truth was not violated, because

[2] "Was not Esau Jacob's brother? saith the Lord: yet I loved Jacob, and I hated Esau." — Malachi I : 2, 3.

his preservation of a certain remnant to himself, made it evident that his calling was without repentance. For God's collection of a Church for himself, from time to time, from the children of Abraham, rather than from the profane nations, was in consideration of his covenant, which, being violated by the multitude, he restricted to a few, to prevent its total failure. Lastly, the general adoption of the seed of Abraham was a visible representation of a greater blessing, which God conferred on a few out of the multitude. This is the reason that Paul so carefully distinguishes the descendants of Abraham according to the flesh, from his spiritual children called after the example of Isaac. Not that the mere descent from Abraham was a vain and unprofitable thing, which could not be asserted without depreciating the covenant; but because to the latter alone the immutable counsel of God, in which he predestinated whom he would, was of itself effectual to salvation. But I advise my readers to adopt no prejudice on either side, till it shall appear from adduced passages of Scripture what sentiments ought to be entertained. In conformity, therefore, to the clear doctrine of the Scripture, we assert, that by an eternal and immutable counsel, God has once for all determined, both whom he would admit to salvation, and whom he would condemn to destruction. We affirm that this counsel, as far as concerns the elect, is founded on his gratuitous mercy, totally irrespective of human merit; but that to those whom he devotes to condemnation, the gate of life is closed by a just and irreprehensible, but incomprehensible, judgment. In the elect, we consider calling as an evidence of election, and justification as another token of its manifestation till they arrive in glory, which constitutes its completion. As God seals his elect by vocation and justification, so by excluding the reprobate from the knowledge of his name and the sanctification of his Spirit, he affords an indication of the judgment that awaits them. Here I shall pass over many fictions fabricated by foolish men to overthrow predestination. It is unnecessary to refute things which, as soon as they are advanced, sufficiently prove their own falsehood. I shall dwell only on those things which are subjects of controversy among the learned, or which may occasion difficulty to simple minds, or which impiety speciously pleads in order to stigmatize the Divine justice.

CHAPTER 24. ELECTION CONFIRMED BY THE DIVINE CALL.
THE DESTINED DESTRUCTION OF THE REPROBATE
PROCURED BY THEMSELVES

But, in order to a further elucidation of the subject, it is necessary to treat of the calling of the elect, and of the blinding and hardening of the impious. On the former I have already made a few observations, with a view to refute the error of those who suppose the generality of the promises to put all mankind on an equality. But the discriminating election of God, which is otherwise concealed within himself, he manifests only by his calling, which may therefore with propriety be termed the testification or evidence of it. "For whom he did foreknow, he also did predestinate to be conformed to the image of his Son. Moreover, whom he did predestinate, them he also called; and whom he called, them he also justified," in order to their eventual glorification.[3] Though by choosing his people, the Lord has adopted them as his children, yet we see that they enter not on the possession of so great a blessing till they are called; on the other hand, as soon as they are called, they immediately enjoy some communication of his election. On this account Paul calls the Spirit received by them, both "the Spirit of adoption, and the seal and earnest of the future inheritance"; [4] because, by his testimony, he confirms and seals to their hearts the certainty of their future adoption. . . .

The First Jesuit Girds for Battle
by Contemplating Death

Ignatius Loyola (1491–1556) had a short, lively career as a soldier until wounds forced him to a long convalescence and considerable soul-searching. In 1522 he spent a rigorous year of self-examination in isolation in the small Spanish town of Manresa. From this experience came the disciplined exercise of mind and soul by prayer, meditation, and the examination of conscience by which he would "prepare and dispose the soul to rid itself of all inordinate attachments . . . and to seek and find the will of God." In normal times, entrance into a monastery would have been the outlet for a young man of Loyola's new-found commitment. In the first challenging days of the Reformation the outlet was a profound sense of mission to rescue the Church from the torments of its divisions by serving it as a spiritual soldier. Loyola and the small group of intimates he recruited at the University of Paris in the later 1520's finally received papal approbation as the Company (later Society) of Jesus and launched the remarkable career of the Jesuits. Loyola and his followers became the front-line troops of the reformed Catholic counterattack against Protestantism. Their field manual was Loyola's Spiritual Exercises, *the product of his Manresa year. It was not a theological document; it was a detailed, compelling handbook for the practice of self-denial and self-denigration in order*

3 Romans VIII : 29, 30.
4 Romans VIII : 15, 16; Ephesians I : 13, 14.

to find the self in God as an instrument of God's will. Its object was entirely practical: to create for the Lord a soldier astute in combat and faithful unto death. A long line of Jesuit martyrs proved to be both.

Loyola's *Spiritual Exercises*

Soul of Christ, sanctify me.
Body of Christ, save me.
Blood of Christ, inebriate me.
Water out of the side of Christ, wash me
Passion of Christ, strengthen me.
O good Jesus, hear me;
Hide me within thy wounds;
Suffer me not to be separated from Thee;
Defend me from the malignant enemy;
Call me at the hour of my death,
And bid me come unto Thee,
That with Thy Saints I may praise Thee
For all eternity. Amen.[1]

ADDITIONAL RECOMMENDATIONS

IN THE FORM OF RESOLUTIONS, WHICH WILL ASSIST US IN MAKING THE EXERCISES WELL, AND OBTAINING FROM GOD WHAT WE ASK OF HIM

1. On lying down, before going to sleep, during the short time which will suffice for repeating the "Hail Mary," I will fix the hour of my rising, and review in my mind the points of my meditation.

2. On awaking, immediately excluding all other thoughts, I will apply my mind to the truth on which I am going to meditate; at the same time I will excite in my heart suitable sentiments. For example, before the Exercise on the "triple sin," I will say to myself while I dress, "And I, loaded with so many graces, the object of predilection to my Lord and King, I stand convicted of ingratitude, of treason, of rebellion, before His eyes and those of His whole court." Before the Exercises on personal sins, "Behold me, a criminal deserving death, led before my Judge loaded with chains." These sentiments must accompany the act of rising, and will vary according to the subject of meditation.

3. Standing a few paces from the spot where I am going to make my meditation, I must recollect myself, raise my mind above earthly things, and consider our Lord Jesus Christ, as present and attentive to what I

From *Manresa: Or the Spiritual Exercises of St. Ignatius*, new ed. (London, 1881), pp. xxxi, 12–13, 278–83.

1 The medieval prayer "Anima Christi," used often in the Spiritual Exercises. — T. G. B.

am about to do. Having given to this preparation the time required to say the "Our Father," I will offer the homage of my soul and body to our Saviour, assuming an attitude full of veneration and humble respect.

4. I will then begin my meditation, if I am alone in my chamber, or elsewhere without witnesses, in the posture most suitable to the end I propose to myself, sometimes with my face bowed to the earth, sometimes standing, sometimes sitting; only observing that if I obtain what I seek kneeling, or in any other attitude, I ought to remain so without seeking anything better. In the same way, if any particular point causes me to experience the grace which I am seeking, I must remain there calmly until my devotion is satisfied, without caring for anything more.

5. After having finished the Exercise, I will either walk about or sit still, and examine how it has succeeded. If it has not, I will ascertain the cause, sincerely repent, and make firm resolutions for the future. If the success has been satisfactory, I will make acts of thanksgiving, and resolve to follow the same method for the future.

6. I will lay aside during the first week all joyful thoughts, such, for instance, as the glorious resurrection of Jesus Christ. This thought would dry up the tears which I ought at this period to shed over my sins. I must rather call up thoughts of death and judgment, in order to assist my sorrow.

7. For the same purpose, I will shut out the daylight, only allowing sufficient light to enter my room to enable me to read and take my meals.

8. I will carefully avoid all laughter, or anything which can lead to it.

9. I will not look at anyone, unless obliged to salute them or say adieu. . . .

FIRST EXERCISE ON DEATH

Preparatory Prayer

First prelude. Transport yourself in thought to the bedside of a dying person, or beside a grave ready to receive a coffin, or into the middle of a cemetery.

Second prelude. Ask of our Lord a salutary fear of death, and the grace to be prepared for it every day.

1. *What is it to die?* It is to bid adieu to every thing in this world — to fortune, pleasures, friends, family; a sad adieu, heart-rending, irrevocable. It is to leave my house, to be thrown into a deep narrow pit, without any garment but a shroud, without any society but reptiles and worms. It is to pass to the most humiliating state, the nearest to nothingness, where I shall become the prey of corruption, where I shall fall to pieces, where I shall decompose into an infectious putrefaction. It is for

my soul to enter in the twinkling of an eye into an unknown region called eternity, where I shall go to hear from the mouth of God in what place I am to make that great retreat which will last for ever, whether it be in heaven or in the depths of hell.

2. *Must I die?* Most certainly. And what assures me of it? Reason, faith, experience. Yes; notwithstanding all precautions, all cares, all the efforts of physicians, I shall die. Where are those who preceded me in life? In the grave, in eternity. And from this grave, from this eternity, they cry to me, "Yesterday for me, and to-day for thee" (Ecclus xxxviii. 23).

3. *Shall I die soon?* Yes. Why? Because ever since my birth I have been only dying. An action continued without interruption is soon accomplished. All other actions have some cessation; business, study, pleasure, sleep, — all these have intervals; death is the only action never interrupted. How can I be long dying when I have been dying ever since I was born, and every moment of the day and night? Where is now that portion of my life that death has already taken from me? As death has taken the past from me, so it will take the future; with the same rapidity, with the rapidity of lightning.

4. *When shall I die?* At what age? In old age? In mature age? Will it be after a long illness? will it be from a fall from a fire, beneath the knife of an assassin? In what place? In my own house, or in a strange house? at table, at play, at the theatre, at church, in my bed, on a scaffold? What day shall I die? Will it be this year? this week? to-morrow? to-day? In what state shall I die? Will it be in a state of grace, or in that of sin? To all these questions, Jesus Christ answers me, "Watch; for ye know not the day nor the hour" (Matt. xxv. 13).

5. *How often shall I die?* Once only; therefore, any error in this great action is irreparable. The misfortune of a bad death is an eternal misfortune. And on what does this bad death depend? On a single instant. It only requires a moment to offend the Lord mortally. It, then, only requires a moment to decide my eternity. If I had died this year, on such a day, such an hour of my life, when I was the enemy of God, where should I be now?

AFFECTIONS

Fear; desire; resolution.

COLLOQUY

Represent to yourself our Lord dying on the cross and recommend the hour of your death to him.

Pater [*Noster*]. *Ave* [*Maria*].[2]

2 The Lord's Prayer and the Hail Mary conclude this exercise and the one following. — T. G. B.

SECOND EXERCISE ON DEATH

FIRST CONTEMPLATION

Your agony

Preparatory Prayer

First and second preludes. The same as in the preceding.

APPLICATION OF THE SENSES

1. *Application of the sight.* Contemplate (1) Your apartment dimly lighted by the feeble gleam of a lamp; all the objects that surround you and seem to say: "You are leaving us, and for ever." (2) The persons who surround you, — your servants, your family, the minister of Jesus Christ. (3) Yourself laid on a bed of pain, and violently struggling against death. (4) At your side devils and holy angels, who dispute for your soul.

2. *Application of the hearing.* Listen to the noise of your painfully interrupted breathing, to the stifled sobs of the assistants, to the prayers of the Church recited in the midst of tears: "From an evil death, from the pains of hell, from the snares of the devil, deliver him, O Lord." "Depart, Christian soul, in the name of God the Father Almighty, who created thee; of Jesus Christ, who suffered for thee; of the Holy Ghost, who sanctified thee." The holy words that the priest suggests to you: "Lord Jesus, receive my soul; Mary, mother of grace, mother of mercy," &c.

3. *Application of the taste.* Represent to yourself all the bitterness of the agony of a dying man. For the present; — what bitterness in this separation from your possessions, your family, your body; in the weariness, the fears that precede the last sigh! For the past; — what bitterness in the memory of your infidelities, of your resistance to grace! For the future; — what bitterness in the thought of the judgment you are about to undergo!

4. *Application of the touch.* Imagine yourself holding between your hands the crucifix which the priest presents to you. Touch your own body on the point of dissolution; those icy feet, those rigid arms, that chest labouring painfully with interrupted respiration, that heart beating with an almost imperceptible movement. It is in this state that your relations and friends will see you before very long. Make now on yourself the reflections that your agony will soon inspire to those who witness it.

End by a colloquy with our dying Lord: "Into Thy hands, O Lord, I commend my spirit."

SECOND CONTEMPLATION

Your state after death

Preparatory Prayer

Preludes. The same.

1. *Application of the sight.* Consider (1) Some moments after your death; your corpse wrapped in a shroud; at your side the crucifix, the holy water, relations and friends; a priest praying for you; the public officer writing in a registry of deaths the day, the hour of your decease; the servants occupied with the preparations for your funeral. (2) The day after your death: your inanimate body in the coffin, taken from your apartment, laid at the foot of the altar; then taken to its last home, the grave. (3) Some time after your death: contemplate that stone already blackened by time, and under this stone the sad state of your body; the putrefied flesh, the separated limbs, the bones consumed by the corruption of the grave.

2. *Application of the hearing.* Again go over the different scenes where you yourself are the spectacle: the dismal sound of the bells asking prayers for you, the prayers recited at the foot of your death-bed, "De profundis clamavi"; the discourse of the servants, who speak freely of you; the friends and relations, who communicate to each other their reflections on your loss; the attendants called in to arrange your funeral; the chants of the Church during the funeral ceremony: "Deliver me, O Lord, from eternal death in that dreadful day, when the heavens and the earth shall tremble; when Thou shalt come to judgment — a day of wrath, calamity, and misery, — that great and bitter day"; the conversation of the persons attending your funeral; what is said of you in society after your death.

3. *Application of the smell and the touch.* Imagine that you respire the odour that your body exhales after your soul has abandoned it, — the infection it would spread if taken from the coffin a few months after your death. Imagine that you touch the damp earth where you have been laid, the shroud in rags, the bare skull, the separated limbs, the mass of corruption enclosed in a grave, after a few months the sight alone of which is horrible.

In presence of this sad scene, ask yourself what the world is, and what is life? "Vanity of vanities, and all is vanity" (Eccl. i. 2). End by a colloquy with our Lord dying: "Into Thy hands, O Lord, I commend my spirit."

Pater [Noster]. Ave [Maria].

THE POLITICS
OF THE REFORMATION
Chapter 6

With his election as Holy Roman Emperor in 1519, Charles V crowned a huge inheritance comprising Spain (with its Italian possessions and American colonies), Burgundy (with the Netherlands and Franche-Comté), and Austria. Since 1438, the imperial dignity had been vested at each election in his family, the Hapsburg, and although it brought little power, it conferred influence and involvement in all the affairs of central Europe and the fragmented German states. Charles had a vision of not merely advancing the Hapsburg dynasty but of uniting all Europe under one scepter, a truly Holy and Roman Empire.

At best the vision was anachronistic; at worst it was destructive of what little unity remained in the sensibilities of Europeans. Charles was a staunch Catholic whose imperial dignity and ambitions arrived at the same moment as Martin Luther challenged the Church and summoned the state to join him in reforming it. Lutheranism's success in winning the active support of numerous German princes — moved by conviction in some very few instances, by lust for the property of the Church in many, and by opposition to the emperor in all — sealed the fate of Charles's grandiose vision. His initial mistake of not devoting enough attention to Lutheranism in the 1520's was compounded in the 1530's by his failure to deal decisively with the religio-political challenge raised by Lutheranism. Ironically, a belated attempt at repression beginning in 1546 brought the Hapsburg dynastic foe, Catholic France, into the struggle on the side of the Lutheran princes. The Religious Peace of Augsburg of 1555 was the emperor's admission that Hapsburg hegemony fashioned on common adherence to the Catholic faith could not be. The imperial ideal was dead, and the German states were deeply divided over religion. The truce of 1555 could not be permanent.

The Peace of Augsburg ignored Calvinism, the most dynamic force in the political spectrum of the Reformation. The spread of Calvinism was a constant provocation to the Catholic Church, which recognized Calvin's disciples as the prime enemy and thus directed its resurgence to combating Calvinism. Calvinism was also a provocation to other Protestant adherents — Lutheran in Germany, Anglican in England — because it was always corrosive of the civil, secular authority. Unlike Lutheranism and Anglicanism, Calvinism was not prepared to "tarry for the magistrate" in reforming the Church. Calvinists were sincerely respectful of the civil power, but in religion they arrogated to themselves the responsibility for the administration of the Church, including the spiritual discipline of its members.

The common misconception that Calvinism sought to establish a "theocracy" is a grievous error. Geneva was operated as a theocratic city-state by force of Calvin's personality, but Calvinists elsewhere were seldom so ambitious. A "godly" ruler, one who did not impede the "elect" of the Church in fulfilling God's ordinances as understood by the Church, was enough. To a great extent political circumstances dictated this forbearance. Calvinism was strongest and most effective at the level of the congregation. At the level of the synod, or collection of lay and clerical representatives of the congregations, it was still workable but had reached the real limits of its organizational construct and abilities. In short, Calvinism was most vital in a fairly compact and geographically limited political entity — ideally, a city. This alone goes far toward explaining why Calvinism was primarily an urban phenomenon. The rest of the explanation lies in a kind of reverse "Weber thesis:" The burgeoning capitalist townsfolk of Europe found the Calvinist virtues of sobriety, hard work, and thrift highly congenial. Where the state was a city or a territory heavily dependent and centered upon a city, such as in Geneva itself, the Rhineland states of Germany, or the cities of the Netherlands, Calvinism established itself easily and without much political dislocation. Where the state was a larger entity, such as in Scotland, France, some of the larger German states, Poland, Hungary, and later England, Calvinism inevitably came into conflict with the civil authority supported by the rural hinterland, regardless of the ruler's religious inclination. No doctrine of the separation of Church and state existed in sixteenth-century Europe, and the organizational thrust of the Calvinists, their vision of a "new Jerusalem" raised by the "elect," their willingness to turn the Calvinist community (such as a city) into a state-within-the-state threatened the authority and the control of the ruler. Nowhere was this more evident than in the growth of the French Huguenot communities, which became the power base for the Calvinists after the Massacre of St. Bartholomew's Day in 1572 shut off the possibility that a national Calvinist state might be established under the auspices of a French nobility converted to Calvinism. The Wars of Religion in France became increasingly dynastic after 1572, and even the Calvinist champion, Henry of Navarre, could consolidate his tenuous military and political victory only by his conversion to Catholicism. The Edict of Nantes in 1598, extending state recognition to the Calvinist power base in numerous French cities, was not a consolation prize for Henry's former coreligionists; it was as much a political necessity as had been his conversion to Catholicism five years before.

The potentially most significant development of Reformation politics was the emergence of England as a major European power under Queen Elizabeth (1558–1603). England challenged Spain in its New World colonies by piracy and incursions on its trade; it challenged Spanish control of the Netherlands with aid to the Dutch rebels; and it challenged Spanish influence on the French dynastic struggle with assistance to Henry of Navarre. For a season, the cockpit of early modern European dynastic warfare and its religio-ideological accompaniment shifted from central Europe to the Atlantic. Spain's massive knockout blow, the Armada of 1588, failed woefully. But the jubilation of anti-Hapsburgs and Protestants everywhere was short-lived, for Spain was not finished as a great power and England had not yet become an oceanic one. Yet the stage was set for a European rivalry more far-ranging than any during the age of the Renaissance and Reformation — between England and the new France under its Bourbon dynasty, which emerged from the Wars of Religion. The next act, however, belonged to the Hapsburgs and the Thirty Years' War, which followed the breakdown of the Peace of Augsburg in 1618.

Tenuous Peace Between Catholic and Lutheran Rulers in Germany, 1555

Between the Imperial Diet at Worms in 1521, when the Reformation became a principal element in the relations of the German states with each other and with the emperor, and the Diet at Augsburg in 1555, which approved the following compromise after hard negotiations, individual German rulers had gained in strength at the expense of the emperor and in wealth at the expense of the church (both Catholic and

*Lutheran). The Peace of Augsburg recognized the new-found power of
the individual prince, and the operative formula of the compromise
stated that his religious adherence determined the religion of the state,
albeit with toleration of the other faith, if it was Catholic or Lutheran,
for clause 5 excepted Calvinism and the other Protestant sects.*

Constitution of the Peace Between Their Imperial and Royal Majesties, on the One Hand, and the Electors and Estates of the Realm, on the Other

We, Ferdinand, by God's grace king of the Romans and at all times
widener of the empire, king of Germany, Hungary, Bohemia, Dalmatia,
Croatia, and Slavonia, infanta of Spain, archduke of Austria, etc., etc., —
Whereas, at all the diets held during the last thirty years and more, and
at several special sessions besides, there have often been negotiations and
consultations to establish between the estates of the Holy Empire a general, continuous, and enduring peace in regard to the contending religions; and several times terms of peace were drawn up, which, however,
were never sufficient for the maintenance of peace, but in spite of them
the estates of the Empire remained continually in bitterness and distrust
toward each other, from which not a little evil has had its origin; . . . to
secure again peace and confidence, in the minds of the estates and subjects toward each other, and to save the German nation, our beloved
fatherland, from final dissolution and ruin; we, on the one hand, have
united and agreed with the electors, the princes and estates present, and
with the deputies and embassies of those absent, as they, on the other
hand, with us.

1. We therefore establish, will, and command that from henceforth no
one, whatsoever his rank or character, for any cause, or upon any pre-
tense whatsoever, shall engage in feuds, or make war upon, rob, seize, in-
vest, or besiege another. Nor shall he, in person or through any agent,
descend upon any castle, town, manor, fortification, villages, estates,
hamlets, or against the will of that other seize them wickedly with violence, or damage them by fire or in other ways. Nor shall any one give
such offenders counsel or help, or render them aid and assistance in any
other way. Nor shall one knowingly or willingly show them hospitality,
house them, give them to eat or drink, keep or suffer them. But every

From *Readings in European History*, vol. 2, ed. J. H. Robinson (New York, 1906), pp.
113–16. Reprinted by permission of Ginn and Company.

one shall love the other with true friendship and Christian love. It is provided also that no estate or member of the Holy Empire shall deprive or cut off any other estate from free access to provisions and food, or interfere with its trade, rents, money, or income; for justice should be administered not irregularly but in suitable and fixed places. In every way shall his Imperial Majesty, and we, and all the estates, mutually adhere to all the contents of this present religious and general constitution for securing the peace of the land.

2. And in order that such peace, which is especially necessary in view of the divided religions, as is seen from the causes before mentioned, and is demanded by the sad necessity of the Holy Roman Empire of the German nation, may be the better established and made secure and enduring between his Roman Imperial Majesty and us, on the one hand, and the electors, princes, and estates of the Holy Empire of the German nation on the other, therefore his Imperial Majesty, and we, and the electors, princes, and estates of the Holy Empire will not make war upon any estate of the empire on account of the Augsburg Confession [1] and the doctrine, religion, and faith of the same, nor injure nor do violence to those estates that hold it, nor force them, against their conscience, knowledge, and will, to abandon the religion, faith, church usages, ordinances, and ceremonies of the Augsburg Confession, where these have been established, or may hereafter be established, in their principalities, lands, and dominions. Nor shall we, through mandate or in any other way, trouble or disparage them, but shall let them quietly and peacefully enjoy their religion, faith, church usages, ordinances, and ceremonies, as well as their possessions, real and personal property, lands, people, dominions, governments, honors, and rights. . . .

3. On the other hand, the estates that have accepted the Augsburg Confession shall suffer his Imperial Majesty, us, and the electors, princes, and other estates of the Holy Empire, adhering to the old religion, to abide in like manner by their religion, faith, church usages, ordinances, and ceremonies. They shall also leave undisturbed their possessions, real and personal property, lands, people, dominions, government, honors, and rights, rents, interest, and tithes. . . .

5. But all others who are not adherents of either of the above-mentioned religions are not included in this peace, but shall be altogether excluded.

6. And since, in the negotiation of this peace, there has been disagreement about what should be done when one or more of the spiritual estates should abandon the old religion, on account of the archbishoprics, bishoprics, prelacies, and benefices that were held by them, about which

---

[1] The Augsburg Confession of 1530 was the credo of the Lutherans. — T. G. B.

the adherents of both religions could not come to an agreement; therefore, by the authority of the revered Roman Imperial Majesty, fully delegated to us, we have established and do hereby make known, that where an archbishop, bishop, prelate, or other spiritual incumbent shall depart from our old religion, he shall immediately abandon, without any opposition or delay, his archbishopric, bishopric, prelacy, and other benefices, with the fruits and incomes that he may have had from it, — nevertheless without prejudice to his honor.

7. But since certain estates or their predecessors have confiscated certain foundations, monasteries, and other spiritual possessions, and have applied the income of these to churches, schools, charitable institutions, and other purposes, such confiscated property, which does not belong to them, shall (if the holders are immediately subject to the empire and are estates of the empire, and if the clergy did not have possession of the said property at the time of the convention of Passau [2] or since that time) be included in this agreement of peace, shall be considered as confiscated, and shall be regulated by the rules governing each estate in dealing with confiscated properties. . . .

10. No estate shall urge another estate, or the subjects of the same, to embrace its religion.

11. But when our subjects and those of the electors, princes, and estates, adhering to the old religion or to the Augsburg Confession, wish, for the sake of their religion, to go with wife and children to another place in the lands, principalities, and cities of the electors, princes, and estates of the Holy Empire, and settle there, such going and coming, and the sale of property and goods, in return for reasonable compensation for serfdom and arrears of taxes, . . . shall be everywhere unhindered, permitted, and granted. . . .

13. And in such peace the free knights who are immediately subject to his Imperial Majesty and us, shall also be included; and it is further provided that they shall not be interfered with, persecuted, or troubled by any one on account of either of the aforesaid religions.

14. But since in many free and imperial cities both religions — namely, our old religion and that of the Augsburg Confession — have hitherto come into existence and practice, the same shall remain hereafter and be held in the same cities; and citizens and inhabitants of the said free and imperial cities, whether spiritual or secular in rank, shall peacefully and quietly dwell with one another; and no party shall venture to abolish the religion, church customs, or ceremonies of the other, or persecute them therefor. . . .

[2] A preliminary peace concluded in 1552 at the close of Charles V's last and unsuccessful war with the Protestant princes.

Geneva's Seed on the Rocky Soil of Scotland: Civil Authority and Ecclesiastical Discipline

Calvin's most vigorous and successful disciple was the formidable Scot, John Knox (1505–1572). An early advocate of Protestantism in Scotland, he found Edward VI's Protestant England a haven until Catholic Mary Tudor came to the throne in 1553 and forced him and other Protestants to flee to the Continent. He settled in Geneva to imbibe the doctrines of the master. In 1559, he returned to Scotland and organized a Scottish reformed church, gaining the adherence of important Scottish noblemen who were politically opposed to Queen Mary Stuart and her French alliance.

The following selections are taken from the two foundation documents of the Scottish Calvinist Church, both largely the work of Knox himself. They are "pure" Calvinism in doctrine, but they reflect in their explicitness and detail the very infirm political situation of the reformers in 1560–1561. Mary was still very much in control of the state, and Edinburgh was not Geneva (even though Knox wished he could act like Calvin). The selection on the "civil magistrate" — that is, the civil ruler — is clear enough if we recognize that the magistrate is to maintain "true Religion" but not determine what it is. The Calvinist discipline, essentially congregational in form, was to be thorough and purgative, and it would govern "as well the rulers as they that are ruled."

In 1567 the Scottish nobility forced Mary's abdication in favor of her infant son James VI, the future James I of England, who was raised under a Calvinist regency. Mary herself was forced to escape to England the next year, where her involvement with Catholic plots against Queen Elizabeth brought her to the block in 1587. With her abdication, Knox's reformation was successfully accomplished: "I have fought against spiritual wickedness in heavenly things and have prevailed!"

Knox: The Confession of Faith Professed and Believed by the Protestants Within the Realm of Scotland, 1560

CHAPTER 24. OF THE CIVIL MAGISTRATE

We Confess and acknowledge empires, kingdoms, dominions, and cities to be distincted and ordained by God: the powers and authorities in the same (be it of Emperors in their empires, of Kings in their realms, Dukes and Princes in their dominions, or of other Magistrates in free cities), to be God's holy ordinance, ordained for manifestation of his own glory, and for the singular profit and commodity of mankind. So that whosoever goes about to take away or to confound the whole state of civil policies, now long established, we affirm the same men not only to be enemies to mankind, but also wickedly to fight against God's expressed will. We further Confess and acknowledge, that such persons as are placed in authority are to be loved, honoured, feared, and held in most reverent estimation; because [that] they are the lieutenants of God, in whose session God himself doth sit and judge (yea even the Judges and Princes themselves), to whom by God is given the sword, to the praise and defence of good men, and to revenge and punish all open malefactors. Moreover, to Kings, Princes, Rulers, and Magistrates, we affirm that chiefly and most principally the conservation and purgation of the Religion appertains; so that not only they are appointed for civil policy, but also for maintenance of the true Religion, and for suppressing of idolatry and superstition whatsomever, as in David, Jehoshaphat, Hezekiah, Josiah, and others, highly commended for their zeal in that case, may be espied. And therefore we confess and avow, that such as resist the supreme power (doing that thing which appertains to his charge), do resist God's ordinance, and therefore cannot be guiltless. And further, we affirm, that whosoever deny unto them their aid, counsel, and comfort, while the Princes and Rulers vigilantly travail in the executing of their office, that the same men deny their help, support, and counsel to God, who by the presence of his lieutenant craveth it of them.

From John Knox, *History of the Reformation in Scotland,* vol. 2, ed. William Croft Dickinson (London, 1949), p. 271. Reprinted by permission of Thomas Nelson & Sons Ltd.

Knox: The Book of Discipline of the Scottish Reformed Church, 1561

THE SEVENTH HEAD, OF ECCLESIASTICAL DISCIPLINE

As that no Commonwealth can flourish or long endure without good laws, and sharp execution of the same, so neither can the Church of God be brought to purity, neither yet be retained in the same, without the order of Ecclesiastical Discipline, which stands in reproving and correcting of those faults which the civil sword doth either neglect, either may not punish. Blasphemy, adultery, murder, perjury, and other crimes capital, worthy of death, ought not properly to fall under censure of the Church; because all such open transgressors of God's laws ought to be taken away by the civil sword. But drunkenness, excess (be it in apparel, or be it in eating and drinking), fornication, oppression of the poor by exactions, deceiving of them in buying or selling by wrong mete or measure, wanton words and licencious living tending to slander, do properly appertain to the Church of God, to punish the same as God's word commandeth.

But because this accursed Papistry hath brought in such confusion in the world, that neither was virtue rightly praised, neither vice severely punished, the Church of God is compelled to draw the sword, which of God she hath received, against such open and manifest offenders, cursing and excommunicating all such, as well those whom the civil sword ought to punish as the others, from all participation with her in prayers and sacraments, till open repentance manifestly appear in them. As the order of Excommunication and proceeding to the same ought to be grave and slow, so, being once pronounced against any person, of what estate and condition that ever they be, it must be kept with all severity. For laws made and not kept engendereth contempt of virtue and brings in confusion and liberty to sin. And therefore this order we think expedient to be observed before and after excommunication.

First, if the offence be secret and known to few, and rather stands in suspicion than in manifest probation, the offender ought to be privately admonished to abstain from all appearance of evil; which, if he promises to do, and to declare himself sober, honest, and one that feareth God, and feareth to offend his brethren, then may the secret admonition suffice for his correction. But if he either contemn the admonition, or, after promise made, do show himself no more circumspect than he was before, then must the Minister admonish him; to whom if he be found inobedi-

From John Knox, *History of the Reformation in Scotland*, vol. 2, ed. William Croft Dickinson (London, 1949), pp. 306–09. Reprinted by permission of Thomas Nelson & Sons Ltd.

ent, they must proceed according to the rule of Christ, as after shall be declared.

If the crime be public, and such as is heinous, as fornication, drunkenness, fighting, common swearing, or execration, then ought the offender to be called in the presence of the Minister, Elders, and Deacons, where his sin and offence ought to be declared and agredged,[1] so that his conscience may feel how far he hath offended God, and what slander he hath raised in the Church. If signs of unfeigned repentance appear into him, and if he require to be admitted to public repentance, the Ministry may appoint unto him a day when the whole Church conveneth together, that in presence of all he may testify the repentance which before them he professed. Which, if he accept, and with reverence do, confessing his sin, and damning the same, and earnestly desiring the Congregation to pray to God with him for mercy, and to accept him in their society, notwithstanding his former offence, then the Church may, and ought [to] receive him as a penitent. For the Church ought to be no more severe than God declareth himself to be, who witnesseth, that "In whatsoever hour a sinner unfeignedly repenteth, and turns from his wicked way, that he will not remember one of his iniquities." And therefore the Church ought diligently to advert that it excommunicate not those whom God absolveth. . . .

[Provisions for those who do not repent, ultimately coming under sentence of excommunication, follow.]

After which sentence may no person (his wife and family only excepted) have any kind of conversation with him, be it in eating and drinking, buying or selling, yea, in saluting or talking with him, except that it be at the commandment or licence of the Ministry for his conversion; that he by such means confounded, seeing himself abhorred of the faithful and godly, may have occasion to repent and be so saved. The sentence of his Excommunication must be published universally throughout the Realm, lest that any man should pretend ignorance.

His children begotten or born after that sentence and before his repentance, may not be admitted to baptism, till either they be of age to require the same, or else that the mother, or some of his especial friends, members of the Church, offer and present the child, abhorring and damning the iniquity and obstinate contempt of the impenitent. If any think it severe that the child should be punished for the iniquity of the father, let them understand that the sacraments appertain only to the faithful and to their seed: But such as stubbornly contemn all godly admonition, and obstinately remain in their iniquity, cannot be accounted amongst the faithful.

---

1 "Shown to be grave." [The Elders and Deacons were laymen, who with the Ministers composed the presbyterian system of church government, on the Geneva model. — T. G. B.]

PERSONS SUBJECT TO DISCIPLINE

To Discipline must all Estates within this Realm be subject if they offend, as well the rulers as they that are ruled; yea and the Preachers themselves, as well as the poorest within the Church. And because the eye and mouth of the Church ought to be most single and irreprehensible, the life and conversation of the Ministers ought most diligently to be tried. Whereof we shall speak, after that we have spoken of the election of Elders and Deacons, who must assist the Ministers in all public affairs of the Church, &c.

St. Bartholomew's Day Massacre, 1572

This account of the St. Bartholomew's Day Massacre of 1572, in which the Catholic dynastic faction in France, headed by the dowager Queen Catherine de' Medici, murdered the Huguenot leadership and thousands of its followers, is particularly interesting because it is written, retrospectively, by Henry IV's great minister, Maximilien de Béthune, Duc de Sully (1560–1641). In 1572, the future minister was already attached to young Henry, king of Navarre, who was seven years his senior. The terror of that night comes through the dry words written two-thirds of a century later. There is a fine touch of irony in that the king, who is reputed to have remarked after his conversion to Catholicism in 1593 that "Paris is worth a Mass," had found in 1572 that his life was worth a Mass.

Henry of Navarre and His Page
Escape the Long Knives of August 24

They flattered themselves at the court of Charles IX, that the disasters which befel the Protestants during the preceding reigns would at last oblige them either to submit to the king's will, or to leave the kingdom. The loss of two great battles, in one of which the Prince of Condé, their leader, fell; the utter dispersion of their troops, and the little probability of their being able to reanimate the feeble remains of their army, discouraged by a long series of misfortunes, all contributed to persuade the court that the moment of their ruin approached; but a courage superior

From *Memoirs of the Duke of Sully*, vol. 1, new ed. (London, 1877), pp. 57–59, 63–67, 85–89.

to all reverses supported them in circumstances so distressful: they recalled their soldiers, who were scattered throughout the provinces, and
now began to draw together from Burgundy, Bourbon, and Berry. La
Charité was named for the place of their general rendezvous; Vezelai, and
some other towns, still holding out for them in that neighbourhood.
They had even the boldness to talk of approaching the Seine and Paris,
as soon as they should be reinforced by some considerable supplies of
horse and foot from Germany, which had been raised there for the assistance of the Huguenots. This news gave great uneasiness to the queen-
mother, Catherine de Medicis; but she flattered herself that it would not
be difficult to prevent their junction, and afterwards to disperse the
troops, which she supposed would be by that means thrown into a con-
sternation. For this purpose she ordered a powerful army to march, in
which Strozzi, La Chatre, Tavannes, La Valette, and all the general officers
in France, were desirous of serving; and the Marshal de Cossé, who was
to have the supreme command, suffered himself to be intoxicated with
the glory he should acquire, by extirpating even the last Huguenot soldier, and bringing the chiefs of the party, bound hand and foot, to the
queen-mother, but he was soon undeceived: the Protestant army received
him with great intrepidity; they were always the first to offer battle; in
the skirmishes, which were frequent, the advantage was wholly on their
side, and they even obtained a kind of victory at the encounter of Arnai-
le-Duc. So much obstinacy convinced the queen-mother that to ruin the
Protestant party it would be necessary to have recourse to other measures
than open hostilities: treachery seemed to her the securest; and in order
to gain time to prepare for it, she listened so favourably to proposals for
an accommodation, that a peace was concluded when it was least expected, and upon conditions very advantageous for the Huguenots. This
was the peace of 1570. After which, during the space of two years, each
party tasted the sweets of a repose that had been equally desired by
both. . . .

   As for what relates to me personally: at the time of which I have been
speaking, I entered into my eleventh year, being born on the 13th of
December, 1560. Although I was but the second of four sons, yet the
natural imperfections of my eldest brother made my father look upon me
as the future head of his family; all the indications of a strong and vigorous constitution recommending me still more to his favour. My parents
bred me in the opinions and doctrine of the Reformed religion, and I
have continued constant in the profession of it; neither threats, promises,
vicissitude of fortune, nor the change even of the king, my protector,
joined to his most tender solicitations, have ever been able to make me
renounce it.

   Henry, King of Navarre, who will have the principal share in these
Memoirs, was seven years older than me, and when the peace of 1570 was

concluded, entered into his eighteenth year.[1] A noble, open, and insinuating countenance, free, easy, and lively manners, with an uncommon
dexterity in performing all the exercises suitable to his age, drew the
esteem and admiration of all who knew him. He began early to discover
those great talents for war which have so highly distinguished him among
other princes. Vigorous and indefatigable by the education of his in-
fancy, he breathed nothing but labour, and seemed to wait with impatience for occasions of acquiring glory. The crown of France not being
yet the object of his aspiring wishes, he indulged himself in forming
schemes for recovering that of Navarre, which Spain had unjustly usurped
from his family; and this he thought he might be enabled to perform, by
maintaining a secret intelligence with the Moors in Spain. The enmity
he bore to this Power was open and declared; it was born with him, and
he never condescended to conceal it. He felt his courage inflamed at the
relation of the battle of Lepanta,[2] which was fought at that time; and a
like opportunity of distinguishing himself against the Infidels became one
of his most ardent wishes. The vast and flattering expectations which the
astrologers agreed in making him conceive were almost always present to
his mind. He saw the foundation of them in that affection which Charles
IX early entertained for him, and which considerably increased a short
time before his death: but animated as he was with these happy presages,
he laboured to second them only in secret, and never disclosed his
thoughts to any person but a small number of his most intimate con-
fidants. . . .

If I were inclined to increase the general horror inspired by an action
so barbarous as that perpetrated on the 24th of August, 1572, and too
well known by the name of the *massacre of St. Bartholomew*, I should in
this place enlarge upon the number, the rank, the virtues, and great talents of those who were inhumanly murdered on that horrible day, as
well in Paris as in every other part of the kingdom; I should mention at
least the ignominious treatment, the fiend-like cruelty, and savage insults
these miserable victims suffered from their butchers, whose conduct was a
thousand times more terrible than death itself. I have writings still in my
hands which would confirm the report, of the court of France having
made the most pressing solicitations to the courts of England and Germany, to the Swiss and the Genoese, to refuse an asylum to those Huguenots who might fly from France; but I prefer the honour of the nation
to the satisfying a malignant pleasure, which many persons would take,
in lengthening out a recital wherein might be found the names of those
who were so lost to humanity as to dip their hands in the blood of their
fellow-citizens, and even of their own relations. I would, were it in my

[1] At the Peace of August, 1570, Henry was sixteen, in his "seventeenth year." —
T. G. B.
[2] Against the Turks in 1571. — T. G. B.

power, for ever obliterate the memory of a day that Divine vengeance made France groan for, by a continual succession of miseries, blood, and horror, during six-and-twenty years; for it is impossible to judge otherwise, when one reflects on all that happened from that fatal moment till the peace of 1598.[3] It is even with regret that I cannot omit what happened upon this occasion to the prince who is the subject of these Memoirs, and to myself.

Intending on that day to wait upon the king my master,[4] I went to bed early on the preceding evening; about three in the morning I was awakened by the cries of people, and the alarm-bells, which were everywhere ringing. M. de Saint Julian, my tutor, and my valet, who had also been roused by the noise, ran out of my apartments to learn the cause of it, but never returned, nor did I ever after hear what became of them. Being thus left alone in my room, my landlord, who was a Protestant, urged me to accompany him to mass in order to save his life, and his house from being pillaged; but I determined to endeavour to escape to the College de Bourgogne, and to effect this I put on my scholar's gown, and taking a book under my arm, I set out. In the streets I met three parties of the Life-guards; the first of these, after handling me very roughly, seized my book, and, most fortunately for me, seeing it was a Roman Catholic prayer-book, suffered me to proceed, and this served me as a passport with the two other parties. As I went along I saw the houses broken open and plundered, and men, women, and children butchered, while a constant cry was kept up of, "Kill! Kill! O you Huguenots! O you Huguenots!" This made me very impatient to gain the college, where, through God's assistance, I at length arrived, without suffering any other injury than a most dreadful fright. The porter twice refused me entrance, but at last, by means of a few pieces of money, I prevailed on him to inform M. La Faye, the principal of the college and my particular friend, that I was at the gate, who, moved with pity, brought me in, though he was at a loss where to put me, on account of two priests who were in his room, and who said it was determined to put all the Huguenots to death, even the infants at the breast, as was done in the Sicilian vespers. However, my friend conveyed me to a secret apartment, where no one entered except his valet, who brought me food during three successive days, at the end of which the king's proclamation prohibiting any further plunder or slaughter, was issued; at the same time also, two soldiers of the guard, named Ferrières and Viéville, dependants of my father, came armed to the college to inquire after me on the part of my father, who was under great apprehensions for my safety, and from whom, three days after, I received a letter ordering me to remain in Paris, and there pursue my studies; and the better to do this, he advised me to

[3] The Edict of Nantes. See the next selection. — T. G. B.
[4] Henry of Navarre. — T. G. B.

go to mass, as the king my master had agreed to do, and above all things to follow that prince's fortune, even to death, that no one might reproach me with having left him in his distress.

With respect to the King of Navarre, he and the Prince of Condé, his brother, were awakened about two o'clock in the morning of St. Bartholomew by a great number of soldiers, who rushed boldly into a chamber of the Louvre, where they lay, and insolently commanded them to dress themselves, and attend the king. They would not suffer the two princes to take their swords with them; and as they passed along they beheld several of their gentlemen massacred before their eyes. The king waited for them, and received them with a countenance and eyes in which fury was visibly painted: he ordered them with oaths and blasphemies, which were familiar with him, to quit their *fine* religion, which they had only taken up, he said, to serve for a cloak to their rebellion. On the princes making some refusal to abjure their religion, the king, transported with anger, told them, in a fierce and haughty tone, "That he would no longer be contradicted in his opinions by his subjects; that they, by their example, should teach others to revere him as the image of God, and cease to be enemies to the images of his mother"; and concluded by declaring, that if they did not go to mass he would treat them as criminals guilty of treason, divine and human. The manner in which these words were pronounced, not suffering the princes to doubt of their sincerity, they yielded to necessity, and acceded to what was required of them. Henry was even obliged to send an edict into his dominions, by which the exercise of any other religion but the Romish was forbid. Though this submission preserved his life, yet in other things he was not better treated, and he suffered a thousand capricious insults from the court; free by intervals, but more often closely confined and treated as a criminal; his domestics, of which I was always one, sometimes permitted to attend him, then all on a sudden not suffered to come near him.

The French State Divided

The compromise conceded by Henry IV in the Edict of Nantes ran counter to the long struggle of the French royal house — the Valois until 1589, Bourbon now — to repress local particularism and to increase the power of the monarchy. The traditional struggle had been against the feudatories — the Bourbons of Navarre not least among them — and that struggle continued through the reign of the pinnacle of French absolutism, Louis XIV, and even beyond. The Huguenot threat of particularism was distinct from that of the feudatories, but its ideological complexion made it more difficult to cope with in a state that still viewed religious unity as the handmaiden of monarchical centralism. The Edict of Nantes has been hailed as a triumph of toleration. It proved to be anything but that, because the threat raised by the power afforded the Huguenot cities invited royal pressure to reduce the terms of the Edict, even to attack the cities, and ultimately, in 1685, to revoke the Edict. In this sense, the Edict built civil strife into the French state.

Edict of Nantes, 1598

I. First, that the memory of all past transactions, both on the one part and the other, since the beginning of the month of March, 1585, up to our accession to the crown, and during the preceding troubles, and on account of them, shall remain extinct and dormant as though they had never happened. And it shall not be allowed or permitted to our procureurs-general, or any other person whatever, public or private, at any time, or on any occasion whatever, to make mention thereof, or institute a suit or prosecution in any courts or jurisdictions whatever.

II. We forbid all our subjects, of whatever state or quality, from perpetuating the memory [of those past transactions], attacking, resenting, injuring, or provoking the one the other by reproaches for what has passed, under any cause and pretext whatever, from disputing, contesting, quarrelling, or outraging or offending by word or deed: but to restrain themselves and to live peaceably together like brothers, friends, and citizens, under pain of being punished as breakers of the peace and disturbers of public order.

III. We command that the Catholic religion, Apostolic and Roman, shall be reinstated and re-established in all places and parts of this our kingdom, and within the bounds of our authority, where its exercise has been intermitted, that it may be peaceably and freely exercised without any disturbance or impediment. Expressly forbidding any person of any state, quality, or condition whatever, under the above-mentioned penalties, from troubling, disturbing, or molesting the ecclesiastics in the celebration of divine service, from the enjoyment and receipt of the tithes, fruits, and revenues of their benefices, and all other rights and duties appertaining thereto: and that all those who during the troubles have taken possession of churches, houses, properties, and revenues belonging to said ecclesiastics, and who still hold and occupy them, shall yield to

From *Tercentenary Celebration of the Promulgation of the Edict of Nantes, April 13, 1598,* by the *Huguenot Society of America* (New York, 1900), pp. 62–69, 81.

them their entire possession and peaceful enjoyment, with such rights, liberties, and sureties as they had before they were seized. Forbidding very expressly those of the said so-called Reformed religion from preaching or any exercise of their religion in the churches, houses, and habitations of the said ecclesiastics. . . .

VI. And that all occasion of troubles and differences among our subjects may be taken away, we have and do permit persons of the so-called Reformed religion to live and remain in all the cities and places of this our kingdom, and countries under our authority, without being questioned, vexed, molested, or constrained to do anything with regard to religion contrary to their consciences, nor on account of it shall they be searched in their houses and places where they desire to dwell, provided they comport themselves in accordance with the provisions of our present Edict.

VII. We have also given permission to all seigneurs, gentlemen, and other persons, denizens or otherwise, making a profession of the so-called Reformed religion, holding within our kingdom and country under our authority, high judicial office, or a full fief of knighthood (as in Normandy) whether as property or usufruct, in whole or in half, or even in third part, to have, in such of the houses of the said high justices, or said knights, as they shall hold themselves ready to name to our bailiffs or seneschals, each in his own right, as his chief place of residence, the exercise of the said religion, as long as they reside therein; and in their absence, their wives, their family, or a part of it; and if the title of either justice or knight shall be questioned, still the exercise of said religion shall be allowed, provided the above-mentioned persons have actual possession of said offices, although the procureur-general be a party in the case. We also permit the said worship to be held in other houses belonging to those high functionaries, or knights, as long as they are present and not otherwise, with all who belong to them, their families, and subjects, as well as such others as may wish to attend.

VIII. In the houses of tenants, or persons of the said religion who are not high functionaries or knights, the said worship can be for their families alone. However, this is not to be understood as allowing a search in cases where other persons, to the number of thirty, chance to arrive, or friends come to visit them: provided, also, said houses are not within cities, towns, or villages belonging to high Catholic lords, other than ourselves, in which said Catholic lords have houses; in which case, those of the said religion cannot, in said cities, towns, or villages, have religious services, unless by permission and consent of the said Catholic lords, and not otherwise.

IX. We also permit members of the said religion to do and continue the exercise of it in all villages and places under our authority where it has been established by them, and publicly performed at several and divers times in the year 1596, and in the year 1597, until the end of the month of August, all decrees and judgments to the contrary notwithstanding.

X. Likewise the said worship may be established and re-established in all villages and places where it has been introduced, or should have been, by the Edict of Pacification, made in the year 1577, by the private articles and conferences of Nerac [1578] and Felix [1580], without the possibility of the said establishment being prevented in the places and situations granted by the said edict, articles, and conferences, as places for bailiwicks, or which will be henceforth, though they have been alienated to Catholic persons, or will be thereafter. It is not to be understood, however, that the said worship may be re-established in places and situations of the said domain, which have been heretofore possessed by persons of the so-called Reformed religion, to whom it might have been granted for personal considerations, or on account of feudal privileges, if the said fiefs are at present in the possession of persons of the Catholic, Apostolic, and Roman religion.

XI. Besides in each of the ancient bailiwicks, seneschalships, and governments holding the place of bailiwicks, being plainly under the jurisdiction of the courts of parliament, we order that in the suburbs of a city, excepting those which have been granted by the said Edict to them, as also by special articles and conferences, and where there are no cities, in a burgh or a village, the exercise of the so-called Reformed religion may be made publicly by all those who wish to go there, although in the said bailiwicks, seneschalships, and governments there may be several places in which the said exercise may be at present established, [save and excepting for the said places of bailiwicks newly granted, by the present Edict, the cities in which there is an archbishop or bishop, although the members of the so-called Reformed religion have the power to ask for and name, for the said place of their worship, the boroughs and villages in the neighborhood of those cities; excepting also the places and seigneurships belonging to ecclesiastics, in the which we must not be understood as allowing the establishment of the said second place of the bailiwick, these being excepted and reserved by special favor.] We mean and understand by the name ancient bailiwicks those which in the time of the late King Henry, our very honored lord and father-in-law, were held for bailiwicks, seneschalships, and governments, being clearly under the jurisdiction of our courts. . . .

XIII. All persons of the said religion are very expressly forbidden from making any exercise of it, either of ministry, regulation, discipline, or public instruction of children, and other matters in this our kingdom, and in countries under our authority, in what concerns religion, except in those places permitted and allowed in the present edict.

XIV. Also from performing any exercise of said religion in our court and suite, and also in our lands and countries which are beyond the mountains, and also in our city of Paris, or within five leagues of said city. . . .

XVI. In accordance with the second article of the Conference of Nerac, permission is hereby given to those holding said religion to build places for the exercise of it in such villages and places as are granted to them, and those shall be restored to them that they have hitherto built, or the site of them, in such state as they may be in at present, even in those places where the exercise of their worship is not allowed, except they have been changed into other kinds of edifices; in which case there shall be given to them, by the possessors of said edifices, places and situations of the same value and price which they had before they were built on, or the proper value of them, to be determined by experts: but the said proprietors and possessors may have recourse against whom of right they may. . . .

XVIII. We forbid all our subjects, of whatever quality or condition soever, from bearing away by force or stratagem, against the consent of their parents, children of the said religion, in order to have them baptized or confirmed in the Church Catholic, Apostolic, and Roman. The members of the said so-called Reformed religion are under the same prohibition, under pain of being severely punished. . . .

XXI. Books concerning the said so-called Reformed religion shall be printed and sold publicly only in the cities and places where the public exercise of said religion is permitted; and in regard to the other books, which shall be printed in other cities, they shall be seen and visited, as well by our officers as by theologians, as it is commanded by our ordinances. We very expressly forbid the printing, publication, and sale of all books, libels, and defamatory writings, under the penalties contained in our ordinances, enjoining all our judges and officers to see their execution.

XXII. We order that there shall be no difference or distinction made with regard to said religion, in receiving scholars to be instructed in the universities, colleges, and schools, as well as the sick and poor in the hospitals, lazarettos, and charitable institutions.

XXIII. Those belonging to the so-called Reformed religion shall be bound to respect the laws of the Catholic Church, Apostolic and Roman, which are received in this our kingdom, in regard to marriages contracted, and to be contracted, within the degrees of consanguinity and affinity.

XXIV. In like manner the members of the said religion shall pay the entrance fees, as is the custom, for the employments and offices with which they are provided, without being constrained to be present at any ceremonies contrary to their religion; and when about to be sworn shall be bound only to raise the hand, swear, and promise to God to tell the truth; and may also dispense with the oath by them to be taken in passing contracts and obligations. . . .

XXVI. No one of our subjects shall be disinherited or deprived of his property, either in the past or future, by will or otherwise, made only from hatred, or on account of religion. . . .

XXVIII. We order, in regard to the interment of the dead of persons of the said religion, for all the cities and places of this kingdom, that there be promptly provided in each place, by our officers and magistrates, and by the commissioners we shall appoint for the execution of the present edict, a place as commodious as possible; and the cemeteries hitherto held by them, and of which they have been deprived by the troubles, shall be returned to them; but if they should be found to be occupied at the present time, by edifices and buildings of whatever sort, they shall be provided with others gratuitously in their place. . . .

XXX. To the end that justice may be rendered and administered to our subjects, without any suspicion, hatred, or favor, as being one of the principal means of preserving them in peace and concord, we have ordered and do order, that in our court of parliament of Paris shall be established a chamber, composed of a president and sixteen councillors of said parliament, which shall be called and entitled the Chamber of the *Edict,* and shall have cognizance not only of causes and suits of persons of the so-called Reformed religion, who shall be within the jurisdiction of said court, but also of suits of our parliaments of Normandy and Brittany, according to the jurisdiction which shall be given to it by this Edict, until such time as in each of the said parliaments there shall have been established a chamber to render justice in those places. We order, also, that of the four offices of councillors in our said parliament, remaining from the last appointments made by us, there shall be chosen and received into this parliament four of this so-called Reformed religion, competent and capable men, who shall be distributed thus: the first to the Chamber of the Edict, and the other three, as they shall be selected, to three of the Chambers of Inquiry. And beside, the first two offices of lay councillors of said court, which shall become vacant by death, shall be filled by two persons of the said religion; and these shall be distributed among the other two Chambers of Inquiry. . . .

LXXIII. If there be any prisoners who are still held by authority of justice, or otherwise, even in the galleys, on account of the troubles, or of said religion, they shall be freed and set at full liberty.

LXXIV. Persons of the said religion shall not hereafter be overtaxed and burdened with any ordinary or extraordinary charges, more than the Catholics, and in proportion to their possessions and privileges; and the parties who claim to be overtaxed can bring the matter before judges to whom the jurisdiction belongs: and all our subjects, whether of one religion or the other, shall be indifferently discharged from all charges, which have been imposed by the one party on the other during the troubles, against their consent; with debts contracted but not paid, expenses made without their consent, without, however, suffering the moneys employed in the payment of said charges to be reclaimed.

The Miraculous Victory of 1588

It is fitting that this account of the defeat and dispersion of the Spanish Armada was written by a Dutch patriot-publicist, Emanuel van Meteran. The defeat of the Spanish Armada was as significant for the survival of Dutch independence from Spain as it was for English independence. The account is a particularly fine early example of "poopdeck history," that is, history written from the vantage point of the primacy of seapower in English history. In this instance, the primacy is real enough. This selection is taken from the collections of the English maritime propagandist Richard Hakluyt, whose volumes recounting English exploration and maritime feats, published in the last years of the sixteenth and first years of the seventeenth centuries, spurred English oceanic commerce and colonialism.

Meteran: The Defeat of the Spanish Armada

Upon Tuesday which was the three and twentie of July, the navie being come over against Portland, the wind began to turne Northerly, insomuch that the Spaniards had a fortunate and fit gale to invade the English. But the Englishmen having lesser and nimbler Ships, recovered againe the vantage of the winde from the Spaniards, whereat the Spaniards seemed to bee more incensed to fight then before. But when the English Fleete had continually and without intermission from morning to night, beaten and battered them with all their shot both great and small: the Spaniardes uniting themselves, gathered their whole Fleete close together into a roundell, so that it was apparant that they ment not as yet to invade others, but onely to defend themselves and to make hast unto the place prescribed unto them, which was neere unto Dunkerk, that they might joine forces with the duke of Parma, who was determined to have proceeded secretly with his small shippes under the shadow and protec-

From *The Principal Navigations . . . of the English Nation,* ed. Richard Hakluyt (London, 1598), pp. 598–99, 601–04, 608–09.

tion of the great ones, and so had intended circumspectly to performe the whole expedition.

This was the most furious and bloodie skirmish of all, in which the lord Admirall of England continued fighting amidst his enimies Fleete, and seeing one of his Captaines afarre off, hee spake unto him in these wordes: Oh George what doest thou? Wilt thou nowe frustrate my hope and opinion conceived of thee? Wilt thou forsake mee nowe? With which wordes hee being enflamed, approched foorthwith, encountered the enemie, and did the part of a most valiant Captaine. His name was George Fenner, a man that had bene conversant in many Seafights.

In this conflict there was a certaine great Venetian ship with other small ships surprised and taken by the English.

The English navie in the meane while increased, whereunto out of all Havens of the Realme resorted ships and men: for they all with one accord came flocking thither as unto a set field, where immortall fame and glory was to be attained, and faithfull service to bee performed unto their prince and countrey. . . .

But it seemeth that the Duke of Parma and the Spaniards grounded upon a vaine and presumptuous expectation, that all the ships of England and of the Low countreys would at the first sight of the Spanish and Dunkerk Navie have betaken themselves to flight, yeelding them sea roome, and endevouring onely to defend themselves, their havens, and sea coasts from invasion. Wherefore their intent and purpose was, that the Duke of Parma in his small and flat-bottomed shippes, should as it were under the shadow and wings of the Spanish fleet, convey over all his troupes, armour, and warlike provision, and with their forces so united, should invade England; or while the English fleet were busied in fight against the Spanish, should enter upon any part of the coast, which he thought to be most convenient. Which invasion (as the captives afterward confessed) the Duke of Parma thought first to have attempted by the river of Thames; upon the bankes whereof having at his first arrivall landed twenty or thirty thousand of his principall souldiers, he supposed that he might easily have woonne the Citie of London; both because his small shippes should have followed and assisted his land-forces, and also for that the Citie it-selfe was but meanely fortified and easie to overcome, by reason of the Citizens delicacie and discontinuance from the warres, who with continuall and constant labour might be vanquished, if they yeelded not at the first assault. They were in good hope also to have mette with some rebels against her Majestie, and such as were discontented with the present state, as Papists, and others. Likewise they looked for ayde from the favourers of the Scottish Queene, who was not long before put to death; all which they thought would have stirred up seditions and factions.

Whenas therefore the Spanish fleet rode at anker before Caleis, to the end they might consult with the Duke of Parma what was best to be done according to the Kings commandement, and the present estate of their affaires, and had now (as we will afterward declare) purposed upon the second of August being Friday, with one power and consent to have put their intended businesse in practise; the L. Admirall of England being admonished by her Majesties letters from the Court, thought it most expedient either to drive the Spanish fleet from that place, or at leastwise to give them the encounter: and for that cause (according to her Majesties prescription) he tooke forthwith eight of his woorst & basest ships which came next to hand, & disburthening them of all things which seemed to be of any value, filled them with gun-powder, pitch, brimstone, and with other combustible and firy matter; and charging all their ordinance with powder, bullets, and stones, he sent the sayd ships upon the 28 of July being Sunday, about two of the clocke after midnight, with the winde and tide against the Spanish fleet: which when they had proceeded a good space, being forsaken of the Pilots, and set on fire, were directly carried upon the King of Spaines Navie: which fire in the dead of the night put the Spaniards into such a perplexity and horrour (for they feared lest they were like unto those terrible ships, which Frederic Jenebelli three yeeres before, at the siege of Antwerpe, had furnished with gun-powder, stones, and dreadfull engines, for the dissolution of the Duke of Parma his bridge, built upon the river of Scheld) that cutting their cables whereon their ankers were fastened, and hoising up their sailes, they betooke themselves very confusedly into the maine sea.

In this sudden confusion, the principall and greatest of the foure galliasses falling fowle of another ship, lost her rudder: for which cause when she could not be guided any longer, she was by the force of the tide cast into a certaine showld upon the shore of Caleis, where she was immediately assaulted by divers English pinasses, hoyes, and drumblers. . . .

Upon the 29 of July in the morning, the Spanish Fleet after the foresayd tumult, having arranged themselves againe into order, were, within sight of Greveling, most bravely and furiously encountered by the English; where they once againe got the winde of the Spaniards: who suffered themselves to be deprived of the commodity of the place in Caleis rode, and of the advantage of the winde neere unto Dunkerk, rather then they would change their array or separate their forces now conjoyned and united together, standing onely upon their defence.

And albeit there were many excellent and warlike ships in the English fleet, yet scarse were there 22 or 23 among them all which matched 90 of the Spanish ships in bignesse, or could conveniently assault them. Wherefore the English shippes using their prerogative of nimble stirrage, whereby they could turne and wield themselves with the winde which way they listed, came often times very neere upon the Spaniards, and charged them so sore, that now and then they were but a pikes length asunder: & so continually giving them one broad side after another, they discharged all their shot both great and small upon them, spending one whole day from morning till night in that violent kinde of conflict, untill such time as powder and bullets failed them. In regard of which want they thought it convenient not to pursue the Spaniards any longer, because they had many great vantages of the English, namely for the extraordinary bignesse of their ships, and also for that they were so neerely conjoyned, and kept together in so good array, that they could by no meanes be fought withall one to one. The English thought therefore, that they had right well acquited themselves, in chasing the Spaniards first from Caleis, and then from Dunkerk, and by that meanes to have hindered them from joyning with the Duke of Parma his forces, and getting the winde of them, to have driven them from their owne coasts.

The Spaniards that day sustained great losse and damage having many of their shippes shot thorow and thorow, and they discharged likewise great store of ordinance against the English; who indeed sustained some hinderance, but not comparable to the Spaniards losse: for they lost not any one shippe or person of account. . . .

[July 29.] The Spaniards seeing now that they wanted foure or five thousand of their people and having divers maimed and sicke persons, and likewise having lost 10 or 12 of their principall ships, they consulted among themselves, what they were best to doe, being now escaped out of the hands of the English, because their victuals failed them in like sort, and they began also to want cables, cordage, ankers, masts, sailes, and other naval furniture, and utterly despaired of the Duke of Parma his assistance (who verily hoping and undoubtedly expecting the returne of the Spanish Fleet, was continually occupied about his great preparation, commanding abundance of ankers to be made, & other necessary furniture for a Navy to be provided) they thought it good at length, so soone as the winde should serve them, to fetch a compasse about Scotland and Ireland, and so returne for Spaine.

For they well understood, that commandement was given thorowout all Scotland, that they should not have any succour or assistance there. Neither yet could they in Norway supply their wants. Wherefore, having taken certaine Scotish and other fisherboats, they brought the men on boord their owne ships, to the end they might be their guides and Pilots. Fearing also lest their fresh water should faile them, they cast all their horses and mules overboord: and so touching no where upon the coast of Scotland, but being carried with a fresh gale betweene the Orcades and Faar-Isles, they proceeded farre North, even unto 61 degrees of latitude, being distant from any land at the least 40 leagues. Heere the Duke of Medina generall of the Fleet commanded all his followers to shape their course for Biscay: and he himselfe with twenty or five and twenty of his ships which were best provided of fresh water and other necessaries, holding on his course over the maine Ocean, returned safely home. The residue of his ships being about forty in number, and committed unto his Viceadmirall, fell neerer with the coast of Ireland, intending their course for Cape Clare, because they hoped there to get fresh water, and to refresh themselves on land. But after they were driven with many contrary windes, at length, upon the second of September, they were cast by a tempest arising from the Southwest upon divers parts of Ireland, where many of their ships perished. And amongst others, the shippe of Michael de Oquendo, which was one of the great Galliasses: and two great ships of Venice also, namely, la Ratta and Belanzara, with other 36 or 38 ships more, which perished in sundry tempests, together with most of the persons contained in them. . . .

Also a while after the Spanish Fleet was departed, there was in England, by the commandement of her Majestie, and in the united Provinces,[1] by the direction of the States, a solemne festivall day publikely appointed, wherein all persons were enjoyned to resort unto the Church, and there to render thanks and praises unto God: and the Preachers were commanded to exhort the people thereunto. The foresayd solemnity was observed upon the 29 of November; which day was wholly spent in fasting, prayer, and giving of thanks.

Likewise, the Queenes Majestie herselfe,[2] imitating the ancient Romans, rode into London in triumph, in regard of her owne and her subjects glorious deliverance. For being attended upon very solemnly by all the principall estates and officers of her Realme, she was carried thorow her sayd City of London in a tryumphant chariot, and in robes of triumph, from her Palace unto the Cathedrall Church of Saint Paul, out of the which the ensignes and colours of the vanquished Spaniards hung displayed. And all the Citizens of London in their Liveries stood on either side the street, by their severall Companies, with their ensignes and banners: and the streets were hanged on both sides with Blew cloth, which, together with the foresayd banners, yeelded a very stately and gallant prospect. Her Majestie being entered into the Church, together with her Clergie and Nobles gave thanks unto God, and caused a publike Sermon to be preached before her at Pauls crosse; wherein none other argument was handled, but that praise, honour, and glory might be rendered unto God, and that Gods name might be extolled by thanksgiving. And with her owne princely voice she most Christianly exhorted the people to doe the same: whereupon the people with a loud acclamation wished her a most long and happy life, to the confusion of her foes.

Thus the magnificent, huge, and mighty fleet of the Spaniards (which themselves termed in all places invincible) such as sayled not upon the Ocean sea many hundreth yeeres before, in the yeere 1588 vanished into smoake, to the great confusion and discouragement of the authours thereof. . . .

---

[1] Of the Netherlands. — T. G. B.
[2] Elizabeth. — T. G. B.

THE BORDERLANDS OF EUROPE
Chapter 7

"Borderlands of Europe" is nothing more than a tag to identify the geographical areas of the Eurasian land mass inhabited by nations other than Germany, Italy, France, the Netherlands, Spain-Portugal, and Britain. A bit more positively, the borderlands include Scandinavia to the north, the land of the Slavic peoples (including Russia to the Urals) to the east, and the land of the south Slavic peoples of the Balkans and western Black Sea regions and Greece to the southeast. The situation of the last region was complicated by the hegemony of the Ottoman Turks, whose empire by 1500 included all the Balkans, Greece, and the western Black Sea area except northern Rumania, as well as Turkey proper, other parts of the Middle East, and parts of North Africa.

At its height in the sixteenth century under Sultan Suleiman the Magnificent (1520–1566), the Ottoman Empire included 50,000,000 people of many nationalities, languages, and religions, a sizable minority of whom were European Christians. Turkish rule was regarded with horror by Europeans, who quite unjustly considered the Moslem Turks uncultured barbarians. Conscription of Christian youths into slave service under the sultan was a grievance, but it afforded the conscript an opportunity to acquire wealth and power otherwise unattainable and was more rewarding and less onerous than the serfdom under which the majority of European peasants still labored in 1500. The Janissaries, the elite soldiers of the Sultan with large police responsibilities as well as military duties, were recruited by conscription. The Turks were remarkably tolerant of religious diversity, including Christianity, and their subject peoples enjoyed considerable autonomy in matters of civil law. The vitality of Turkish society, the incredible military prowess of the Turks that carried them to the gates of Vienna, and the prodigious commercial activity of Turkish cities both impressed and repelled European visitors.

The European subjects of the Ottomans and the Slavic peoples of eastern Europe and Russia were preponderantly Orthodox Christians, with religious allegiance not to the Pope in Rome but to the Patriarch of Constantinople. The Byzantine emperor in Constantinople exercised a control over the Orthodox patriarchate that did not permit the rivalry between the religious and the secular authorities that was so much a feature of Western, Roman Christianity. The Orthodox Church evangelized Slavic Europe. The conversion of the Russians to Orthodox Christianity in the late tenth century proved a major determinant in Russian history because the division between the two branches of the Christian faith tended to insulate Russia from the intellectual and social currents of Western lands for centuries. Significantly, after the Turks took Constantinople in 1453, the grand duke of Moscow took the title "tsar (caesar) of all the Russias" and assumed Byzantine-like control over the Russian Church, claiming to be the successor of the Byzantine imperial ideal.

Although it has been fashionable recently to point out that Russia never experienced the Renaissance or the Reformation, in one area its development did parallel the Western European experience in the fifteenth and sixteenth centuries. The tsars of that epoch set out to build a centralized state under a powerful monarchy as effectually as their regal counterparts in the west. The intended victims were the same, the nobility whose territories were absorbed into the new state. The tsars were ruthless in dealing with them. Exile and execution of the nobility were commonplace, and the curbing of their power and privilege was routine policy. During the youth of Ivan IV, from 1533 to 1547, the nobility enjoyed a respite from effective tsarist control and fought among themselves for the spoils of office. In 1547 Ivan, nicknamed "the Terrible," took command and, moving from a position of power, within twenty years reduced the nobility to a servitude more rigorous than any of the western feudatories suffered under absolutist monarchs. The resulting anger of the Russian nobility seldom attained such articulateness as in Prince Kurbsky's indictment of the tsar. The advancement of the enserfment of the originally free Russian peasantry was one demand of the nobility with which the tsars of the period concurred, and they furthered it by legislation. The process of enserfment stands in stark contrast to the increasing liberation of the serfs in most of Western Europe during the same era. Europe — and the world beyond — has paid dearly for Russia's "peculiar institution" of serfdom and its contribution to the Revolution of 1917.

Other areas of the borderlands also experienced the trend toward the creation of a centralized state, notably Scandinavia, where monarchs with a thirst for absolutism attempted to curb the feudatories. The elective nature of Scandinavian kingship impeded monarchical absolutism, however. One borderland state, Poland-Lithuania, had a potential for greatness that was never realized. After 1386, Poland and

Lithuania existed as separate entities under the same ruler. In 1569, by the Union of Lublin, they were merged in an imperfect confederation in which each retained its own administration and laws but had a common representative assembly (diet), currency, and system of land tenure. The joint territory was vast, including all modern Poland and parts of Russia and Germany from the Baltic to the Black seas. But the proud nobility of this kingdom with an elective kingship used the diet as an instrument not only to contain kingly power but even to reduce it. The result was a leaderless "republic of noblemen" increasingly unable to meet the great external pressures from east and west that ultimately obliterated it.

The Ottoman Turks
Through Hostile Eyes

Though European accounts of the Ottoman Turks were invariably biased, that bias itself was an important historical fact. From even the most hostile accounts we can derive a good deal of information, not untinged by respect for the qualities that made the Turks so fearsome to Christendom. Fynes Moryson was a peripatetic Scots gentleman who spent a decade wandering around Europe and the Near East principally for curiosity's sake. Keen of eye, lively, and with a proper but not overpowering sense of disdain, his account of Constantinople in 1597 is valuable. Father Vincenzo da Siena, an Italian missionary of the Carmelite Order, traveled to India in 1655. His observations on the Turkish fleet, which had been badly beaten three-quarters of a century before at Lepanto, indicate how Western technological superiority was advancing in comparison with that of other cultures.

Fynes Moryson: Constantinople in 1597

Having cast anchor (as I said) in the Port of Constantinople, behold, as soone 'as day began to breake, many companies of Turkes rushing into our Barke, who like so many starved flies fell to sucke the sweete Wines,

From Fynes Moryson, *An Itinerary Containing His Ten Years Travell Through the Twelve Dominions of Germany, Bohmerland, Switzerland, Netherland, Denmarke, Poland, Italy, Turky, France, England, Scotland and Ireland*, vol. 2, pp. 90–91, 94–95, 98–102. Reprinted by permission of Macmillan London and Basingstoke.

each rascall among them beating with cudgels and ropes the best of our Marriners, if he durst but repine against it, till within short space the Candian Merchant having advertised the Venetian Ambassadour of their arrivall, he sent a Janizare to protect the Barke, and the goods; and assoone as he came, it seemed to me no lesse strange, that this one man should beate all those Turkes, and drive them out of the Barke like so many dogs, the common Turkes daring no more resist a souldier, or especially a Janizare, then Christians dare resist them. And the Serjant of the Magistrate having taken some of our Greeke Marriners (though subject to the State of Venice) to worke for their Ottoman in gathering stones, and like base imployments, this Janizary caused them presently to be released, and to be sent againe into their Barke, such is the tyranny of the Turkes against all Christians aswel their subjects as others, so as no man sayleth into these parts, but under the Banner of England, France, or Venice, who being in league with the great Turke, have their Ambassadours in this Citie, and their Consuls in other Havens, to protect those that come under their Banner, in his sort sending them a Janizare to keepe them from wrongs, so soone as they are advertised of their arrivall.

. . . Here is the Church of Saint Sophia,[1] opposite to the Court Gate, of old built by the Christians after the forme of Salomons Temple, and indowed with the annuall rent of three hundred thousand Zechines, now made a Mosche or Mahometan Church. And howsoever the Turks cannot indure that unwashed Christians (so called by them, because they use not Baths so continually as they doe) should enter their Mosches, or passe over their Sepulchers, yet my self entered this Church with the Janizare my guid, trusting to his power to defend me, yet he willed me first to put of my shooes, and according to the Turkes custome to leave them in the porch, where they were safe till we returned. The Church is of a round forme, and built of bricke, and supported with faire pillars, and paved with marble (over which the Turks layed Mats to kneele, and prostrate themselves more commodiously upon them.) The roofe is beautified with pictures of that rich painting, which the Italians call alla Mosaica, shining like enameled work, which now by antiquity were much decaied, and in some parts defaced. . . . And when a Chaus (or Pensioner) being on horseback did see mee close by the Emperours side, hee rushed upon me to strike me with his mace, saying, What does this Christian dog so neere the person of our great Lord? But the Janizare, whom our Ambassadour had given me for a Guide and Protector, repelled him from doing mee any wrong, and many Janizares (according to their manner) comming to helpe him, the Chaus was glad to let mee alone, and they

1 Until the fall of Constantinople in 1453, the great cathedral church of the patriarch, spiritual leader of Orthodox Christianity. — T. G. B.

bade me be bold to stand still, though I were the second or third person
from the Emperour.

. . . Between the fifth and the sixth hill, is the old Pallace of the Great
Turke, (which the Italians call Seraglio vecchio), where the Concubines
of the deceased Emperour, and the present Emperours sisters and a great
number of his concubines, (for the fairest and dearest to him are taken to
live in his Court), are kept by Eunuches within this old Seraglio, which
is of great circuit, containing many houses and gardens compassed within
one wall. Upon the sixth hill stands the foresaid wonderfull Mosche and
Sepulcher of Solyman [the Magnificent]. . . .

The tops of the Sepulchers and Mosches, being of a round forme and
covered with brasse, and the spacious gardens of Cypresse and Firre trees,
make shew of more beauty and magnificence to the beholder from any
high place, or without the wals, then in deed the City hath. The Sepulchers are no doubt very stately built, having upon the top one two or
more round globes covered with leade or brasse. On the inside they seeme
like lightsome Chappels with many windowes, and they being built in a
round forme, the dead Emperour is laied in the middest or center of the
Sepulcher, in a chest or coffin raised some three foot from the ground,
having the Tulbent which hee wore upon his head in his life time laied
upon his Tombe, being set forth with the Jewels he most esteemed,
(which Tulbent is made of some twenty or more yards of pure and fine
white linnen, foulded in many foulds, in the forme of a halfe globe).
Next the Emperour lies the Sultana or Empresse, in her Coffin, (so they
call his Concubine, Mother of his Heire and Successour), provided
alwaies that shee have had a letter of dowry by which shee is made his
wife; for otherwise shee is not buried with him. And round about the
Emperour and Empresse in Coffins lower than theirs, lie the bodies of his
male children, which (according to their manner) are strangled by his
Successour assoone as he was dead, and upon their Coffins likewise their
Tulbents are laied severally. These children are laied in little Coffins of
Cypresse, and this middle part wherein the dead bodies lie, is compassed
with a grate, so as betweene the bodies and the windowes there is a gal-
lery round about, which is spred with Turkey carpets, and upon them the
Priests that keepe the Sepulcher, doe lie by night, and sit crosse legged by
day, neither is the roome at any time without some of these Keepers, so
as the Emperours are attended even after death.

The buildings of the City have no magnificence, being partly of a matter like bricke, but white, and (as it seemes) unhardned by fire, partly of
timber and clay, excepting some few pallaces which are of free stone, but
nothing so stately built as might be expected from the pride and riches
of the great Turkes chiefe servants. . . . In many places of the streetes
lye carcases, yea sometimes the bodies of dead men, even till they be

putrified, and I thinke this uncleanlinesse of the Turks (who otherwise place Religion in washing their bodies, and keeping their apparrell, especially their Tulbent pure and cleane) is the chiefe cause that this Citie, though most pleasantly seated, yet above all the Cities of the world is continually more or lesse infected with the plague. They say, that Job, famous for his pietie and patience, is buried in this Citie: but I did not see his monument, and thinke it probable, that the same and all like Christian monuments, were defaced by the Turkes when they tooke the Citie.

And by the way as we passed by land, an old woman meeting us, and taking me for a Captive to be sold, demaunded my price of the Janizare; who for mirth entertained her offer to buy me and another Gentleman, servant to the Ambassadour, whom hee had sent to beare me company: but because I was very slender and leane after my long sicknes, he could not induce her to give more then one hundred aspers for me, though she offered foure hundred aspers for the other Gentleman in my company, as the Janizare told me in the Italian tongue. . . .

Father Vincenzo da Siena:
The Turkish Navy in 1655

The naval forces of this Empire are in my belief greatly unequal to the land forces, not for any want of manpower, lumber, or any other thing needful for the formation of such powerful fleets as it may desire, but rather for the lack of talent, ability and inclination for such pursuits among the natives. The abundance of lumber, which they possess on the shores or the Black Sea, in Greece, and in Asia, makes it possible to assemble galliots, men-of-war and every other sort of sea-going vessel with such ease that one surely could not wish it greater. The forests are exceedingly vast, and close to the water, being thus more convenient. Adjacent to these are certain large villages exempt from the usual obligations and bound instead to prepare the material or to transport the same to the place where need requires it; so that one need but command, and in a few days as much wood as is wanted will be found in the appointed places, arranged and prepared for any undertaking, however grand. There are many places on the Black Sea where they build galleys and men-of-war continually. In addition, the Empire possesses three great shipyards, the first in Constantinople, another in Gallipoli, a third in Suez, the first having 144 covered vaults and the others fewer, in each of

From Carlo M. Cipolla, *Guns and Sails in the Early Phase of European Expansion, 1400–1700* (London, 1965), pp. 160–62. Reprinted by permission of Collins Publishers, Walker and Company, and Carlo M. Cipolla.

which, excepting the last, the Sultan maintains more than a thousand salaried carpenters, augmenting their number according to the occasion; and these men apply themselves to nothing else but the construction of ships of every kind for his service.

The iron which they require comes from Samacho, a place in Greece not far from Salonica, where it is extracted from the mines. The ropes are made in Constantinople. The cost of labour is minimal (I heard of this from very well-informed persons): for the outfitting of a galley a chief craftsman will get no more than 14 to 15 *sequins* it being within the power of the officers to demand that the work be done at whatever price they wish to pay. From all the preceding one can understand why it is that whenever the Turk's armada has gone down in ruins, it very soon appears restored, for neither expense nor inaccessibility of materials, nor lack of workmen hinders him. A fact of great importance, however, is this: all the ships are badly made, and last but a very short while; in three or four years they are old and no longer seaworthy because the wood is always cut in the wrong season, i.e. in the early summer, when the moisture is diffused throughout the trunk, so that it tends to decay and be eaten by worms. Moreover, they put the wood to use straightaway after cutting it, while it is still drying, and thus the hulls of the ships expand so much that sometimes before ever being launched they lie on the shore full of gaps and cracks and totally useless. And it must be added that the workmen, being paid so poorly by the Sultan, spare on the iron, whence the ships turn out so badly made, and so unseaworthy, that they are often lost before ever reaching Constantinople.

The Sultan mans his galleys with four men to the oar; first with his own slaves, who in winter are kept in custody in camps constructed for this purpose; secondarily with convicts; and lastly, with men brought from Asia, which region provides him with as great a quantity of them as he wants for this purpose, for he has imposed this duty on a great many villages, and indeed might appoint many more yet; and for every ten persons in these villages, one is chosen, who must report for service without question, or else redeem himself by sending another at his own expense. The Sultan pays to each slave, and to each of these men from Asia, 25 *sultanins*, with which they must make do until such time as they return to port, nothing further being given them save only victuals; this payment is called the *Avarische* and is raised through a tax on those lands from which children are not taken as a tribute. For the outfitting of 200 galleys, three *sultanins* are collected from each hearth, the hearth being composed of four houses. However, these Asiatics are so ill suited to the sea, that many succumb to nausea, and others perish from hardship, so that very often the armada is afflicted with sickness; and were it not for the aid of the slaves who are accustomed to the sea, it would surely be very weak and almost useless. In order to provide the fleet with sailors and soldiers, the Sultan keeps in his pay many thousands of men, whose job it is to perform whatever service is imposed on them by the Captain of the Navy; and though these people are no less spirited than bold, they are nonetheless wanting in experience, and not well suited to action on the water; whence it is, that if the Captain happens upon some vexing storm, it becomes difficult to control them, and make them do what is necessary; indeed, they are in dire peril of their lives.

Each galley carries 70 soldiers or more, up to 100, provisions being furnished by the Islands of Lesbos (*Meteline*), Euboea (*Negroponte*), and others nearby; 3,000 feud-holders (*Timari*) are bound to this service, in addition to the great number of Janissaries who volunteer to the service. . . .

. . . The Turks make little use of artillery, and indeed seem not to care for it, nor value its use except for siege operations. In naval battles they rely heavily on the sail and on boarding, so that in an encounter they seek to ram the enemy as quickly as possible, hoping to exploit their advantage in numbers; the very few guns which they do use on their ships are loaded with stone shot more often than with iron, for they believe that stone, in splintering, hits more surely and does more harm. They store the naval artillery in the *Pera,* where it is also manufactured, and the land artillery in Constantinople; both are under the command of the Captain General. The copper for its manufacture is taken from the mines which they possess in Alexandria, from whence comes also such a quantity of powder as is sufficient to their need. But a great advantage on the side of the Christians, it seems to me, is in having more guns, and greater skill in handling them. . . .

Ivan the Terrible

Prince Andrey Kurbsky was a leading general of Ivan IV (1533–1584) until his defection to the Polish-Lithuanian enemy during the Livonian War in 1564, the year in which Ivan moved to crush the power of the nobility. His vituperation, spilled out in five letters to Ivan, was cast in the heavily religious rhetoric that was both an accepted literary convention in Orthodox Russia and a shaft directed at the most vulnerable attribute of the tsar, who was the guardian of the Orthodox faith and invested with almost priestly honor. The charges are hardly exaggerated. Letters in reply to Kurbsky, ostensibly from Ivan, are suspect.

Answer of the Lowly Andrey Kurbsky, Prince of Kowel, to the Second Epistle of the Tsar of Moscow

Remaining abroad and in lowliness because of your persecution, I have omitted your grandiose and lengthy title (for from the lowly, you, the great tsar, have no need of this; but rather [in letters] from tsar to tsar is it befitting to read out such titles with [such] excessive verbosity); and as for your recounting to me (as to a priest) your confession — I am unworthy, being a simple man in military service, to listen to this even out of the corner of my ear, all the more so [as I am] weighed down with many and countless sins. But nevertheless it would indeed be meet — not only for me, who was once your true servant, but also for all tsars and Christian peoples — to rejoice and be right glad, if your repentance were true, as was that of Manasseh in the Old [Testament]; for it is said that he repented after much blood-drinking and unrighteousness, and lived in the covenant of the Lord, gentle and just even unto death, and did not offend [anyone] any more either in a large or a small way; and as, in the New [Testament], Zacchaeus' most praiseworthy repentance and his fourfold restoration to those offended by him.

If only your repentance corresponded with those sacred examples which I have taken from the Holy Scriptures and brought forward both from the New and from the Old [Testaments]! But what follows afterwards in your epistle appears not only not corresponding [to the examples I have produced], but astonishing and worthy of amazement and limping strongly on both hips and betraying the unseemly movements of the inner man — all the more so in the lands of your adversaries where there are many men, not only skilled in secular philosophy, but also strong in the sacred writings. Now you humiliate yourself exceedingly, now you raise yourself up without limit and beyond measure! The Lord says unto his apostles: "when ye shall have done all those things which are commanded you, say: we are unprofitable servants"; but the devil urges us sinners to repent only with our mouth[s], but in our heart[s] to hold an exceedingly high [opinion] of ourselves and to rate ourselves on a level with the holy and most glorious of men. The Lord commands not to judge anybody before the day of judgment and first to cast out the beam out of one's own eye and then to pull out the mote from one's brother's eye; but the devil urges [us] only to bleat with words, as though that were repentance, but not [to repent] in deed, but only to raise oneself up and to boast of countless transgressions and bloodshed; but you learn not

From *The Correspondence Between Prince A. M. Kurbsky and Tsar Ivan IV of Russia, 1564–1579*, ed. and trans. J. L. I. Fennell (Cambridge, 1955), pp. 199, 201, 203, 205, 207, 209. Reprinted by permission of Cambridge University Press and J. L. I. Fennell.

only to curse distinguished holy men, but to call them devils, just as of old the Jews [called] Christ at one time a deceiver and possessed, at another time a caster out of devils by Beelzebub, the prince of devils; as can be seen in the epistle of Your Majesty — you call Orthodox and holy men devils, and are not ashamed in devilish spirit to slander those who are guided by the Divine Spirit, as it were renouncing the great apostle: "for no man," he said, "can say that Jesus is the Lord, but by the Holy Ghost." And whoever slanders an Orthodox Christian slanders not him, but the very Holy Ghost, who abides in him, and himself brings upon his head incurable sin, as the Lord said: "whosoever slandereth against the Holy Ghost, it shall not be forgiven him, neither in this world nor in the world to come."

And furthermore, what is more abhorrent and filthy than to slander your confessor and to conceive false accusations against him who led your royal soul to repentance and bore your sins upon his neck, and, having lifted you from the most blatant impurity, placed you, as one pure, before the purest King, Christ our God, having purified you with repentance! Is it thus that you recompense him even after death? O wonder! that envy, conceived by your evil and cunning maniacs against holy and venerable men, does not fade even after [their] death! Are you not frightened, O Tsar, by the story of Ham, who laughed at his father's nakedness? [Remember] how a curse was laid upon his descendants for that! And if such a story happened on account of fleshly fathers, how much the more, when spiritual [fathers] are concerned, must we cover up [any nakedness], should anything happen through human weakness, as your flatterers slandered that priest, [saying] that he frightened you, not with true, but with false apparitions. And in truth even I say: he was a flatterer, a cunning man and [yet] an intriguer for the good, for he took you, having torn you from the nets of the devil and from the jaws of the lion of the soul and led you to Christ our God. The same thing in truth do the wise physicians do; they cut the raw flesh and the incurable gangrene with knives even as far as the living flesh and then draw [the flesh] together little by little and cure the sick. Thus did the priest act, the blessed Sylvester, seeing the sickness of your soul, which had become hardened with many years and difficult to heal. As certain wise men say: "when evil customs in men's souls have become hardened with age, they become innate and become incurable." So did he, the venerable one, because of your incurable sickness, apply plasters — now attacking you and abusing you with biting words, cutting as it were with a razor your unholy habits by means of harsh punishments — perhaps he remembered that word of the prophet: "may you rather suffer the wounds of a friend than the tender kisses of an enemy"; but you did not remember that or you forgot it, being blinded by the charms of your most evil and cunning [friends], [and] you drove him from yourself, and with him our Christ — now, as with a firm bridle and reins, holding back your lack of restraint and your excessive lust and your wrath. In him the word of Solomon was not fulfilled: "teach a wise man and he will increase in learning with gratitude," and "rebuke a wise man and he will love thee." I will be silent on the other verses which follow, laying them on your royal conscience, knowing you to be skilled in the Holy Scriptures. And furthermore, so as not to give [too] much offence with biting words to your Royal Highness, let me, the lowly one, who am able to contain myself, refrain from bickering; for it is exceedingly unbefitting for us warriors to bicker like servants.

You might also have remembered how, thanks to the Grace of God, in the time of your days of piety, things prospered for you according to your will, owing to the prayers of the Saints and the chosen counsel of your eminent advisers; and how, afterwards, when the most wicked and cunning adulators seduced you, the destroyers of you and of their fatherland, events turned out and what plagues [were] sent by God; hunger, I say, and the arrows of pestilence, and afterwards the sword of the barbarian, the avenger of the law of God, and the sudden burning of the most renowned city of Moscow, and the laying waste of all the land of Russia! And — what is bitterest and most shameful — the collapse of the tsar's soul and the turning of the tsar's shoulders (which formerly were brave) to flight, as certain people here inform us, so that, hiding at that time from the Tatars in the woods, you might not shortly perish of hunger together with your children of darkness! Yet that same Ishmaelite dog formerly, when you lived in a manner pleasing to God, found no place [of rest] in his flight over the wild field before us, [even] the most insignificant of your servants, and instead of your present vast and heavy tribute, with which you ransom Christian blood, payment was made in Muslim heads with the sabres of us your warriors, and thus was tribute given to him.

But as for what you write, calling us traitors because we were forced by you to kiss the Cross against our will — for there it is the custom with you, that should anyone not swear allegiance, he would die the bitterest death — my answer to you on this [is]: all wise men are agreed on this, [that] should anyone swear allegiance or vow against his will, no sin is [imputable] to him who kisses the Cross, but rather to him who forces [him to], even if there is no persecution; for if anyone, because of most fierce persecution, does not flee — then he is as it were a murderer of himself, acting against the word of the Lord: "if they persecute you in [this] city, flee ye into another." And of this our Lord God showed an example to his faithful, fleeing not only from death but from the ill-will of the God-destroying Jews.

And as for what you have said, that I, as it were, "having fallen into wrath against man have given offence to God," that is to say that I destroyed and fired the churches of God — to this I answer (you): either do not slander us for no reason or consider, O Tsar, the Scriptures, how even

David was compelled because of Saul's persecution to wage war on the land of Israel together with a pagan king; but I was fulfilling order[s] [given] not by pagan tsars but by Christian tsars; by their order did I take the field. But I confess my sin — namely that I was forced by your command to burn down the great place of Vitebsk and in it twenty-four Christian churches; likewise by King Sigismund Augustus too was I forced to wage war on the district of [Velikie] Luki. And there together with Prince Koretsky we took great care that the faithless burned not and destroyed not the churches of God; and in truth I was not able, owing to the multitude of the soldiers, to guard them, for at that time we had with us fifteen thousand troops, amongst whom there was no small number both of Ishmaelite barbarians and of other heretics, revivers of ancient heresies, the enemies of the Cross of Christ; and without our knowledge, after our departure, the impious ones stole in and burned one church together with a monastery. May the monks who were freed by us from captivity bear witness of this! And then after one year your main enemy, the Tsar of Perikop,[1] sent [messengers], both entreating the king and asking us that we [*lit.* he] might go with him against that part of the Russian land which is beneath your power; but I, even though the king ordered me, refused: I did not wish even to consider this folly — of marching beneath a Muslim banner against a Christian land with a foreign tsar, an unbeliever. Then was the king himself amazed at this and he praised me, that I had not likened myself to the fools who had ventured on such a course before me. . . .

The Legislative Culmination
of the Enserfment of
the Russian Peasantry, 1649

Tsarist legislation to further enserfment at the behest of the nobility was directed at immobilizing the peasants by forcing them to remain on the lands of their lords in debt-servitude, preventing migration by which they might escape the burden of debt. The device used was to make any peasant who escaped recoverable by his lord. The legislation culminated in the provisions of the Ulozhenie *(code) of 1649, which removed any time limit for the recovery of the escapee and even his wife and children under certain conditions.*

1 The Crimea. — T. G. B.

The Law on the Peasants,
Containing Thirty-Four Items

1. Any peasants of the Sovereign and labourers of the crown villages and black volosts who have fled from the Sovereign's crown villages and from the black volosts [1] and live on the land of the Patriarch, metropolitans, archbishops, bishops or the monasteries or the boyars,[2] chamberlains and the men of the Council or the chamber and the sewers, bearers of insignia and the Moscow gentlemen and the clerks and the attendants, town gentlemen and the junior boyars and the foreigners and any lords holding an estate by inheritance or service and [those peasants and labourers] are in the inquisition registers which the officers in the Service Tenure Department submitted to other Departments after the Moscow fire of the past year, 134,[3] those fugitive peasants, or their fathers, who are recorded as the Sovereign's, and those fugitive peasants and labourers of the Sovereign, being sought out, are to be brought to the crown villages of the Sovereign and to the black volosts to their old lots according to the registers of inquisition with wives and children and with all their peasant property without term of years.

2. Also should there be any lords holding an estate by inheritance or service who start to petition the Sovereign about their fugitive peasants and labourers and say that their peasants and labourers who have fled from them live in the crown villages of the Sovereign and in black volosts or among the artisans in the artisan quarters of towns or among the musketeers, cossacks or among the gunners, or among any other serving men in the towns beyond Moscow or in the Ukraine or on the land of the Patriarch, metropolitans, archbishops and bishops or the monasteries or the boyars, chamberlains and the men of the Council and the chamber and the sewers, bearers of insignia, the Moscow gentlemen and the clerks and the attendants, town gentlemen and the junior boyars and the foreigners and any lords holding an estate by inheritance or service, then those peasants and labourers in accordance with law and the [right of] search are to be handed over according to the inquisition registers which the officers handed in to the Service Tenure Department after the Moscow fire of the past year, 134, if those, their fugitive peasants, are entered under them in those registers, or if after these inquisitions these same peasants or their children were entered in accordance with new grants to anyone in registers of allotment or withdrawal. And fugitive peasants and

From *The Enserfment of the Russian Peasantry*, ch. 11, ed. R. E. F. Smith (Cambridge, 1968), pp. 141–45, 147–48. Reprinted by permission of Cambridge University Press and R. E. F. Smith.

1 Administrative areas. — T. G. B.

2 Great nobles. — T. G. B.

3 The fire of 1626 destroyed many documents in the archives of the Departments in Moscow.

labourers are to be handed over from flight according to the registers to men of every rank without term of years.

3. But if anyone is required to hand over runaway peasants and labourers in accordance with justice and the search, they are to hand over those peasants with their wives and children and with all their property and with their grain, standing and threshed. And the holdings of those peasants for former years prior to the present Law Code are not dealt with; but if any runaway peasants, while runaways, married off their daughters, sisters or nieces to peasants of those holding by inheritance or service under whom they lived, or on the side into some other village or hamlet, that [peasant] is not to be held guilty and the husbands of those girls are not to be handed over to their [i.e. the runaways'] former lords holding by inheritance or service, because there was no Sovereign's prohibition as regards this until the present Sovereign's decree that no one was to accept peasants, but terms of years were decreed for runaway peasants because after the officers [of the inquisition had done their work] in many years the estates held by inheritance and service had changed for many tenants.

4. And if runaway peasants and labourers are handed over to anyone: the Department people of the Sovereign's crown villages and black volosts and lords holding estates by inheritance or service are to have from those people, for the peasants and labourers and their property, lists in their hand to be held in case of argument. And the lists are ordered to be written at Moscow and in the towns by the public junior clerks, and in villages and hamlets, where there are no public junior clerks, such lists are ordered to be written by the area or church reader of other villages and they are to give such lists in their own hand. But if any people are illiterate, they are ordered that in their place their father confessors should put their hand to those lists, or anyone else they trust of people on the side, but it is not ordered that a priest or reader or any [such unauthorised] person should write such lists, so that in future no one should have an argument with anyone about such lists. . . .

9. But if any peasants and labourers recorded [as living] under anyone in the enumeration registers of the past years, 154 and 155,[4] after those enumerations ran away, or henceforward begin to run away, from those people under whom they were recorded in the registers, those runaway peasants and labourers and their brethren and children and nephews and grandchildren with their wives and children and with all their property, with their grain, standing and threshed, are to be handed over from flight to those people from whom they ran away, according to the enumeration registers, without term of years, and henceforward no one is by any means to accept the peasants of others or to hold them. . . .

19. But if any lord holding by service or inheritance begins to let go

4 1645/6 and 1646/7. — T. G. B.

from his service or heritable estate unmarried or widowed daughters of peasants to marry anyone's people or peasants, or anyone's bailiffs or reeves [do so], they are to give those unmarried or widowed daughters of peasants charters of manumission in their own hand or that of their father confessors against any future argument. And the payment is to be had for those daughters of peasants in accordance with the contract. And as to who takes the payment, that is to be written by name in the charters of manumission.

20. But if any people come to anyone in an estate held by inheritance or service and say that they are free and those people want to live under them as peasants or as labourers, then those people to whom they come are to question them: who are those free people, and where is their birthplace and under whom did they live and where have they come from, and are they not somebody's runaway people, peasants and labourers, and whether they have charters of manumission. And if any say they do not have charters of manumission on them, those holding estates by service and inheritance are to get to know genuinely about such people, are they really free people; and after genuinely getting to know, to take them the same year to be registered, to Moscow in the Service Tenure Department; and the Kazan' and Kazan' suburb people to Kazan'; and the Novgorod and Novgorod suburb people to Novgorod; and the Pskov and Pskov suburb people to Pskov; and in the Service Tenure Department and in the towns the military commanders are to question such free people about that and to record their speech correctly. And if those people who are brought to be recorded are liable, according to their speeches on being questioned, to be handed over as peasants to those people who bring them to be recorded, those people to whom they are handed over as peasants are ordered to append their signature to the speeches at questioning when they take them. . . .

22. And if any peasants' children deny their fathers and mothers they are to be tortured.

The Less Perfect Union:
Poland and Lithuania

The Union of Lublin, in 1569, created a potentially great power in Eastern Europe. The new kingdom, composed of Poland and Lithuania, retained its integrity if not its independence for a little over two centuries but never fulfilled its potential for greatness. In part this failure — and Poland's ultimate failure, its disappearance in the three partitions of the late eighteenth century — grew from the increasing power of Poland's near neighbors, Austria, Prussia, and especially Russia. In part it grew from the imperfectness of the union itself, particularly the unwillingness of the noble feudatories of the two countries to provide explicitly for a strong monarchy.

The Union is a fascinating constitutional instrument. In the sixteenth century it was rare for changes in state constructs to be memorialized and given effect in documentary form. As such, the Union of Lublin bears comparison with the Union of Utrecht, 1579, which created the United Netherlands in revolt against Spain and was a less explicitly constitutional document because it was dictated by the exigencies of revolution. The Union of Lublin is most readily compared with the great series of constitutional instruments that began with the American Articles of Confederation of 1777 and the American Constitution of 1789. The Union of Lublin provided for a stronger union than the Articles of Confederation, but a less strong union and less definition of governmental powers than the Constitution of 1789. Yet, as in the case of all written constitutions, the Union of Lublin's ultimate success or failure depended more upon the subsequent development or lack of development of the nation's institutions than upon the text itself.

The Union of Lublin, 1569

In the Lord's name, Amen. To the eternal memory of the matter described below. We, prelates and Council of Lords, both clergy and laity, and elected representatives of the provinces of the Polish Crown, together with the Council of Lords and elected representatives and other estates of the Grand Duchy of Lithuania, at this general Diet of Lublin . . . [followed by names with titles].

1. Declare by this document, to everyone now and all future generations who might learn about this document that we, having continuously before our eyes our duty towards our Fatherland, the renowned Polish Crown, to which we are obliged to provide all loyalty, pride, common good and above all security from danger, both internal and external, and also bearing in mind and having before our eyes a praiseworthy union and commonalty which is indeed due both nations, which by our forefathers at one time with the citizens of that time of the Grand Duchy of Lithuania for eternal times, on the basis of common written consent given by both nations and by documents, seals, oaths, and honor was

From Polska Akademja Umiejetnosci I Towarzystwo Naukowe Warszawskie, *Akta Unji Polski z Litwa, 1385–1791*, ed. Stanislaw Kutrzeba and Wladyslaw Semkowicz (Krakow, 1932), pp. 90–91, 94–95. Translated from Polish by Malgorzata I. Winkler.

strengthened by both parties and maintained for quite a long time due to the friendliness and steadfastness of both parties, but later was jeopardized somewhat during bad and jealous times. Nonetheless, so we as our forebears always deliberated about this and constantly reminded our lords of glorious memory about this, Polish King Zygmunt as well as the Polish King Zygmunt August, presently reigning over both nations, Poland and Lithuania, and turned to them with our request, . . . for the execution and conclusion of a common written agreement as well as other laws and privileges, . . . [to] condescend to help by bringing us together with the Council of Lords and other estates of the Grand Duchy of Lithuania into one place to execute this praiseworthy matter useful to both nations . . . [followed by reference to various agreements which preceded this document]. Therefore, we made these treaties described below and this agreement which, by the grace of God we brought to an end and to this conclusion with the agreeable and unified consent of both parties and together put in a written form, not derogating anything of the Warsaw Act or other privileges. Because of this, praise be to God, one in the Trinity, and eternal thanks to His Majesty, Lord Zygmunt August, the King by the grace of God, and glory and praise for eternal times to the Polish Crown and the Grand Duchy of Lithuania.

2. First of all, however, there were in existence agreements of friendship and alliance which had in purpose the growth and better order of the commonwealth, both the Polish Crown and the Grand Duchy of Lithuania, but which were not always compatible with honest and sincere brotherly trust; therefore . . . we renew these old alliances and amend all as described below.

3. That the Polish Kingdom and the Grand Duchy of Lithuania is one inseparable and not unlike body and also one, not unlike, united Commonwealth, which came about out of two states and nations integrated into one.

4. That this twofold nation for eternal times is to be governed by one head, one lord and one common king, elected by common votes of the Poles and Lithuanians, the place of election being in Poland, and who will later be anointed and crowned in Krakow for the Polish Kingdom. . . .

5. That the election and inauguration of the Grand Duke of Lithuania, which previously took place separately in Lithuania, will now be abolished . . . and that the title and offices of the Grand Duchy of Lithuania are to remain; therefore during the election and coronation he [the Grand Duke of Lithuania] must be proclaimed King of Poland as well as Grand Duke of Lithuania, Ruthenia, Prussia, Mazovia, Samogitia, Kiev, Volynia, Podlasia, and Inflanty.

6. That if the natural succession or right to inheritance would serve in the interest of His Majesty or whomever in the Grand Duchy of Lithuania for whatever cause, it should not interfere for time eternal with this

alliance and union of both nations and the election of one common lord, and this, which His Majesty has renounced to the [Polish] Crown, is on the understanding and condition that we neither dispossess His Majesty personally nor his descendants, if God may grant them to Him, but that, in case they are not called to kingship, they may have, from the Commonwealth, honorable material conditions according to their status, [although] by this not dismembering the Crown in any way, about which there is sufficient description and guarantee in the declaration of His Majesty and in the Act of the general Diet of Warsaw.

7. That at the coronation of the new King, the laws, privileges and liberties of all subjects of both nations and states, thus united, are to be sworn to by the crowned King and at once confirmed by one document and in one language for eternal times.

8. That this twofold nation, under a Polish King, its Lord, is always to have common Diets and Councils, and that lords [of one nation] among lords [of the other nation] as well as elected representatives among elected representatives are to be present and counsel each other about common needs, both at the Diet as well as outside the Diet, in Poland and Lithuania.

9. That also in order that one party serve as counsel and aid to the other and in order that His Majesty firmly and permanently preserve for all lands and nations, both of the Polish Crown as well as the Grand Duchy of Lithuania and lands belonging to them, the privileges and laws granted them with whatever document by all of His Majesty's predecessors and by His Majesty himself, from long ago and the beginning of the Union by whatever means granted for everybody, both commonly and individually, all liberties and nominations for high offices, prerogatives and offices of the twofold nations, then all laws, courts, tribunals, titles and privileges of the princes and nobility of these two nations, decrees of the court, from long ago to the present time are to be preserved wholly and permanently for every estate.

10. [Deals with the procedure of oaths.]

11. That in all adversities we, prelates, councils, barons and all estates, are to help one another, with all our effort and ability, when the common Council deems it in our interest and need, considering our successes and misfortunes as common, and assisting each other loyally. *Foedera aut pacta* [1] or agreements and covenants with foreign nations should not, according to the Act of Warsaw, be planned nor concluded, nor should any ambassadors be sent to foreign countries for important matters, otherwise than with the knowledge and common counsel of both nations; and alliances or decisions made previously with whatever nation which are harmful to either party should not be maintained.

---

[1] Treaties or pacts. — T. G. B.

12. That the currency will be common both in Poland and Lithuania. . . .

13. [Deals with duties and tolls.]

14. That all statutes and acts, whichever ones and for whatever reason, against the Polish nation and Lithuania, which are drafted and resolved regarding the acquisition and possession of property in Lithuania by a Pole, by whatever means he may have received it, either through marriage or by merit or by purchase or through deed of gift or by exchange or by whatever method of acquisition according to customs and common law, that all these statutes are not to have any power as they are contrary to law and justice as well as brotherhood, union and common fusion, so that a Pole in Lithuania as well as a Lithuanian in Poland might always, on the basis of every just mean, acquire property and possess it according to the law by which the property is governed.

15. [Deals with the name of the Grand Duchy of Lithuania and its offices.]

16. That from the present time onwards His Majesty will not call any separate Diets of the Crown or of Lithuania, but will always call common Diets for this twofold nation, which is as one body, wherever in Poland His Majesty and the Councils of the Crown and Lithuania will deem it most fitting.

17. That His Majesty will not place anyone in any high offices or other offices which are now vacant or will be vacant in the future until the given person makes an oath to His Majesty and His successors, crowned Polish Kings, and to this inseparable body, the Polish Crown.

18. [Deals with the regulations concerning possessions.]

19. [Deals with the obligations and pledges to maintain the union.]

20. And that all these matters here resolved and guaranteed are never to be shaken or changed through the ages, neither by His Majesty, nor by the Lords of the Council, nor by any other estates or elected representatives of the lands of both nations, neither by joint, collective nor individual consent, but are to be preserved eternally, wholly and strongly.

And for better testimony of the matters above described and for its eternal memorial, we, sworn prelates, Lords of the Council, both clergy and laity, of the Crown and elected representatives of the provinces, put our seals on this document at this general and common Diet of Lublin. Written and issued at this common Diet of Lublin on the first of July in the Lord's year 1569.

SOCIAL, INTELLECTUAL, AND CULTURAL DYNAMISM, 1500–1660

Chapter 8

The Reformation was a powerful solvent of accepted verities, not only in faith and the politics of church and state, but in the whole range of human endeavor. Its influence was often indirect and largely imperceptible to contemporaries. Yet as the universal authority of the See of St. Peter retreated, other authorities that had seemed universal and immutable shrank and changed also. A new dynamism moved the European world.

This new dynamism had begun before the Reformation. In fact, it was rooted in the origins of European civilization and had gathered impetus during the Renaissance, despite the geographic and social limits of the Renaissance. The Reformation, unlike the Renaissance, touched virtually every European and all European society. It demanded that each Catholic and Protestant examine his relationship to God, and therefore it bid him examine his relationship to his fellow men. European man began to accept the dissolution of the static ordering of social hierarchy into a dynamic disorder of social movement that blurred the distinguishing characteristics of societal groupings. In disputing the traditional authority of the Church, the Reformation challenged both the form and the substance of the hierarchy of medieval knowledge fashioned in the clerical universities of the Middle Ages. From that challenge developed a new intellectual direction that remains dominant to our day: the search for proximate causes of the dynamic process of change, unencumbered by the necessity to search for first causes or to establish the immutable.

Behind the social dynamism were the demographic and economic facts of sixteenth-century European life: increasing population, quickening internal migration, rapid urbanization, expanding manufacturing, mounting trade, rising prices, agrarian change, the beginnings of colonization. European society was an "opportunity society." Unrest traceable to social and economic, as distinct from political and religious, causes (the distinction is often hard to make) was the unrest of rising expectations and its corollary, unrest from the frustration of individual relative decline in social status. Unrest of rising expectations resulted in sporadic outbursts of violence principally by craftsmen, both urban and rural, for whom recurrences of trade depression and all too frequent crop failures resulting in scarcity, which frequently accompanied depression, spelled temporary but maddening hardship. Unrest stemming from the frustration of individuals who found their social status reduced in relation to that of others ran the length of society. At the bottom, peasants who once had been individual small farmers increasingly found themselves forced by economic circumstances to work for day-wages as laborers on estates. Apprentices in crafts were always depressed and volatile, as were an increasing number of laborers in the expanding industries of northern Europe especially. The status of clergy generally declined, more in Protestant than in Catholic countries, and the Church and universities everywhere offered fewer opportunities for clerical advancement than they had previously. At the top of the social hierarchy, the old nobility found its preeminence diluted by the new nobility created by monarchs recruiting talent from among the lawyers and urban bourgeoisie, its privileges restricted by absolutism's repression and its wealth eroded by the price rise. In periods of political instability the upper ranks who suffered from relative decline in status became particularly dangerous, sometimes furnishing leadership to the lower ranks in disorder and even insurrection. Francis Bacon (1561–1626) enunciates the era's continuous fear of social turbulence in his essay on sedition and troubles.

Bacon's essay demonstrates how rudimentary social theory was in explaining the causes and the nature of social unrest. When we move from Bacon's microcosm to Copernicus' macrocosm, diffuseness gives way to focus; in short, theory sharpens, and explanation edges out description. From the beginning, the physical sciences have enjoyed a significant lead over the social and political sciences in explaining phenomena. The many reasons for this are hotly debated by the historians of science, but one fairly clear contributor to the lead was the physical scientist's primary tool for analysis and explanation — mathematics. This tool was not the creation of the scientific revolution that began with Copernicus (1473–1543), for the Ptolemaic conception of the universe that Copernicus overturned had been cast in mathematical (geometric) terms, and the increasing expression of physical phenomena in mathematical terms from the later Middle Ages had pointed toward the kinds of questions that could be answered by mathematical theory.

By 1500 the Ptolemaic model was generally admitted to be in need of rationalization and reconciliation of the discrepancies between it and the increasing body of astronomical observations. A new mathematical formula that would explain the observations and salvage the model appeared necessary. Copernicus concluded that the physical system described by the model did not fit the mathematics of observation. He dismantled the components of Ptolemy's model and constructed a new model with the sun at the center as the static entity, the earth revolving around it as the other planets do, and the moon revolving around the earth. The new model made at least as much sense as the old — but not more sense, for Copernicus had only rearranged the Ptolemaic universe of spheres rolling in perfect circles.

New observations were bound to raise questions about the circular motion of the celestial bodies. Tycho Brahe (1546–1601) made those observations with the intention of disproving Copernicus' heliocentric theory. His assistant, Johannes Kepler (1571–1630), used those observations to rationalize Copernicus' model and, by postulating elliptical rather than circular motion, brought the universe to as high a degree of descriptive sophistication as was possible without new technical devices. He sought and found universal physical laws to explain the motions of the universe in quantitative terms. But he could not explain the cause of the motions. That explanation would depend upon the discovery of the laws governing the mechanics of motion, the work of Galileo Galilei (1564–1642).

Galileo, by virtue of what he did and of how he did it, was the pivotal figure between the old, basically metaphysical, science and the modern science of physical realism. Kepler's commentary on Galileo's astronomical observations with a telescope is the salute of the scientific past to the scientific future in the year 1610. The work of Kepler and his predecessors among sixteenth-century scientists did not produce a restatement of scientific method. The Greek method, derived principally from Aristotle — the deduction of explanation of phenomena from previously established universal truths — remained the theory of scientific methodology even if it was repeatedly breached in practice. Galileo, however, did produce a new scientific method, albeit implicitly, in his own work. As practiced by Galileo, scientific knowledge is derived from study of the phenomena, theories generalized from the phenomena by abstraction (especially mathematical abstraction), and the testing of the theories by experimentation. Scientific knowledge so derived is a framework of mental constructs giving order to experience and representing the reality of nature, and, therefore, it is an adequate understanding of nature. This is very close to the scientific method of today.

Galilean methodology did not win a universal victory. A brilliant French philosopher a generation younger than Galileo, René Descartes (1596–1650), shared with him the ideal of applying mathematics to the study of science. But Descartes sought certainty of reality, not merely a representation of reality. The only certainty that he could assume was his own existence because, although his skepticism required that he think nothing existed, his act of thinking could only lead him to the conclusion that he must exist. Upon the assurance afforded him by his self-awareness, Descartes inched, by the use of reason, out toward reality beyond himself. He recognized his own imperfectness, and this recognition led him to conclude by reasoning that he must hold the idea of his imperfectness from "some Nature which in reality" is more perfect than himself. His triumphant conclusion was that this "Nature" was God. From the first-cause, God, perceived to be real by the use of reason, Descartes established self-evident principles from which (again by the use of reason) he deduced universal and all-embracing truths or laws of nature. Descartes came to be a new Aristotle, deducing reality from first principles. His approach was diametrically opposed to Galileo's more modest and essentially inductive and empirical methodology. Cartesianism proved sterile in science proper but productive in philosophy by virtue of its emphasis on rationalism. Even in science, Descartes provided the theoretical point of departure for the giant of the next age, Isaac Newton.

Bacon on Seditions and Troubles

Sir Francis Bacon (1561–1626) was the most luminous ornament of learning in his age. Prolific, his range of interests was wide — law (his profession), letters, political theory, history, metaphysics, ethics, epistemology, science — as was his capacity, which ranged from the profound to the shallow. Despite an active and successful career in law and politics, which came to an abrupt close with his conviction for corruption by a politically motivated Parliament in 1621, he sought to compose an encyclopedia of all knowledge.

Bacon's reputation for importance in the scientific development of his age is only partially deserved, for his scientific methodology, while emphasizing empiricism, made empiricism the seedbed of theorization rather than its testing ground. Bacon was best at sharp, brilliant insights, not sustained analysis and argumentation. Cynical, observant, and witty, he displayed a shrewd grasp of men, motives, and movements in his essays written in the 1590's and the first two decades of the seventeenth century. "Of Seditions and Troubles" is extraordinarily perceptive. Bacon's analysis of the immediate causes of social disorder has been little improved upon and has become so much a part of conventional wisdom that today it is echoed in reams of testimony before commissions on urban and campus violence.

Essay 15

Shepherds of people had need know the calendars of tempests in state, which are commonly greatest when things grow to equality; as natural tempests are greatest about the equinoctia, and as there are certain hollow blasts of wind and secret swellings of seas before a tempest, so are there in states: "He often warns, too, that secret revolt is impending, that treachery and open warfare are ready to burst forth." Libels and licentious discourses against the state, when they are frequent and open; and in like sort false news, often running up and down, to the disadvantage of the state, and hastily embraced, are amongst the signs of troubles. Virgil, giving the pedigree of Fame, saith she was sister to the giants: "Mother earth, exasperated at the wrath of the Deities, produced her, as they tell, a last birth, a sister to the Giants Coeus and Enceladus."

As if fames were the relics of seditions past; but they are no less indeed the preludes of seditions to come. Howsoever he noteth it right, that seditious tumults and seditious fames differ no more but as brother and sister, masculine and feminine; especially if it come to that, that the best actions of a state, and the most plausible, and which ought to give greatest contentment, are taken in ill sense, and traduced: for that shows the envy great, as Tacitus saith, "Great public odium once excited, his deeds whether good or whether bad, cause his downfall." Neither doth it follow, that because these fames are a sign of troubles, that the suppressing of them with too much severity should be a remedy of troubles; for the despising of them many times checks them best, and the going about to stop them doth but make a wonder long-lived. Also that kind of obedience, which Tacitus speaketh of, is to be held suspected: "They attended to their duties, but still, as preferring rather to discuss the commands of their rulers, than to obey them"; disputing, excusing, cavilling upon mandates and directions, is a kind of shaking off the yoke, and assay of disobedience; especially if in those disputings they which are for the direction speak fearfully and tenderly, and those that are against it audaciously.

Also, as Machiavel noteth well, when princes, that ought to be common parents, make themselves as a party, and lean to a side; it is, as a boat that is overthrown by uneven weight on the one side; as was well seen in the time of Henry the Third of France; [1] for first himself entered league for the extirpation of the Protestants, and presently after the same league was turned upon himself: for when the authority of princes is made but an accessary to a cause, and that there be other bands that tie faster than the band of sovereignty, kings begin to be put almost out of possession.

From *The Moral and Historical Works of Lord Bacon*, ed. Joseph Devey (London, 1852), pp. 38–45.
[1] 1574–1589. — T. G. B.

Also, when discords, and quarrels, and factions, are carried openly and audaciously, it is a sign the reverence of government is lost; for the motions of the greatest persons in a government ought to be as the motions of the planets under "primum mobile," [2] according to the old opinion, which is, that every of them is carried swiftly by the highest motion, and softly in their own motion; and therefore, when great ones in their own particular motion move violently, and as Tacitus expresseth it well, "Too freely to remember their own rulers," it is a sign the orbs are out of frame: for reverence is that wherewith princes are girt from God, who threateneth the dissolving thereof; "I will unloose the girdles of kings."

So when any of the four pillars of government are mainly shaken or weakened (which are religion, justice, counsel, and treasure), men had need to pray for fair weather. But let us pass from this part of predictions (concerning which, nevertheless, more light may be taken from that which followeth), and let us speak first of the materials of seditions; then of the motives of them; and thirdly of the remedies.

Concerning the materials of seditions, it is a thing well to be considered; for the surest way to prevent seditions (if the times do bear it) is to take away the matter of them; for if there be fuel prepared, it is hard to tell whence the spark shall come that shall set it on fire. The matter of seditions is of two kinds; much poverty and much discontentment. It is certain, so many overthrown estates, so many votes for troubles. Lucan noteth well the state of Rome before the civil war: "Hence devouring usury, and interest accumulating in lapse of time — hence shaken credit, and warfare, profitable to many."

It is likewise to be remembered, that, forasmuch as the increase of any estate must be upon the foreigner (for whatsoever is somewhere gotten is somewhere lost), there be but three things which one nation selleth unto another; the commodity, as nature yieldeth it; the manufacture; and the vecture, or carriage; so that, if these three wheels go, wealth will flow as in a spring tide. And it cometh many times to pass, . . . that the work and carriage is more worth than the material, and enricheth a state more: as is notably seen in the Low Countrymen, who have the best mines above ground in the world.

Above all things, good policy is to be used, that the treasure and monies in a state be not gathered into few hands; for, otherwise, a state may have a great stock, and yet starve: and money is like muck,[3] not good except it can be spread. This is done chiefly by suppressing, or, at least, keeping a strait hand upon the devouring trades of usury, engrossing great pasturages, and the like.

For removing discontentments, or, at least, the danger of them, there is in every state (as we know) two portions of subjects, the nobles and the commonalty. When one of these is discontent, the danger is not great;

---

2 Prime mover. — T. G. B.
3 Manure. — T. G. B.

for common people are of slow motion, if they be not excited by the greater sort; and the greater sort are of small strength, except the multitude be apt and ready to move of themselves: then is the danger, when the greater sort do but wait for the troubling of the waters amongst the meaner, that then they may declare themselves. The poets feign that the rest of the gods would have bound Jupiter; which he hearing of, by the counsel of Pallas, sent for Briareus, with his hundred hands, to come in to his aid: an emblem, no doubt, to show how safe it is for monarchs to make sure of the goodwill of common people.

To give moderate liberty for griefs and discontentments to evaporate (so it be without too great insolency or bravery), is a safe way: for he that turneth the humours back, and maketh the wound bleed inwards, endangereth malign ulcers and pernicious imposthumations.

The part of Epimetheus [4] might well become Prometheus, in the case of discontentments, for there is not a better provision against them. Epimetheus, when griefs and evils flew abroad, at last shut the lid, and kept Hope in the bottom of the vessel. Certainly, the politic and artificial nourishing and entertaining of hopes, and carrying men from hopes to hopes, is one of the best antidotes against the poison of discontentments: and it is a certain sign of a wise government and proceeding, when it can hold men's hearts by hopes, when it cannot by satisfaction; and when it can handle things in such manner as no evil shall appear so peremptory but that it hath some outlet of hope; which is the less hard to do, because both particular persons and factions are apt enough to flatter themselves, or at least to brave that which they believe not.

This same "warfare profitable to man" is an assured and infallible sign of a state disposed to seditions and troubles; and if this poverty and broken estate in the better sort be joined with a want and necessity in the mean people, the danger is imminent and great; for the rebellions of the belly are the worst. As for discontentments, they are in the politic body like to humours in the natural, which are apt to gather a preternatural heat and to inflame; and let no prince measure the danger of them by this, whether they be just or unjust: for that were to imagine people to be too reasonable, who do often spurn at their own good; nor yet by this, whether the griefs whereupon they rise be in fact great or small; for they are the most dangerous discontentments where the fear is greater than the feeling: "To grief there is a limit, not so to fear"; besides, in great oppressions, the same things that provoke the patience, do withal mate [5] the courage; but in fears it is not so; neither let any prince or state be secure concerning discontentments, because they have been often, or have been long, and yet no peril hath ensued: for as it is true

---

[4] The myth of Pandora's box, which is here referred to, is related in the "Works and Days" of Hesiod. Epimetheus was the personification of "Afterthought," while his brother Prometheus represented "Forethought," or prudence. It was not Epimetheus that opened the box, but Pandora.

[5] Daunt. — T. G. B.

that every vapour or fume doth not turn into a storm, so it is nevertheless true that storms, though they blow over divers times, yet may fall at last; and, as the Spanish proverb noteth well, "The cord breaketh at the last by the weakest pull."

The causes and motives of seditions are, innovation in religion, taxes, alteration of laws and customs, breaking of privileges, general oppression, advancement of unworthy persons, strangers, dearths, disbanded soldiers, factions grown desperate; and whatsoever in offending people joineth and knitteth them in a common cause.

For the remedies, there may be some general preservatives, whereof we will speak: as for the just cure, it must answer to the particular disease; and so be left to counsel rather than rule.

The first remedy, or prevention, is to remove, by all means possible, that material cause of sedition whereof we spake, which is, want and poverty in the estate: [6] to which purpose serveth the opening and well-balancing of trade; the cherishing of manufactures; the banishing of idleness; the repressing of waste and excess, by sumptuary laws; [7] the improvement and husbanding of the soil; the regulating of prices of things vendible; the moderating of taxes and tributes, and the like. Generally, it is to be foreseen that the population of a kingdom (especially if it be not mown down by wars) do not exceed the stock of the kingdom which should maintain them: neither is the population to be reckoned only by number; for a smaller number, that spend more and earn less, do wear out an estate sooner than a greater number that live lower and gather more: therefore the multiplying of nobility, and other degrees of quality, in an over proportion to the common people, doth speedily bring a state to necessity; and so doth likewise an overgrown clergy, for they bring nothing to the stock; [8] and, in like manner, when more are bred scholars than preferments can take off.

Also the foresight and prevention, that there be no likely or fit head whereunto discontented persons may resort, and under whom they may join, is a known, but an excellent point of caution. I understand a fit head to be one that hath greatness and reputation, that hath confidence with the discontented party, and upon whom they turn their eyes, and that is thought discontented in his own particular: which kind of persons are either to be won and reconciled to the state, and that in a fast and true manner; or to be fronted with some other of the same party that may oppose them, and so divide the reputation. Generally, the dividing and breaking of all factions and combinations that are adverse to the state, and setting them at distance, or, at least, distrust amongst themselves, is not one of the worst remedies; for it is a desperate case, if those that hold

---

[6] State. — T. G. B.

[7] Sumptuary laws, common throughout Europe in the late sixteenth century, restricted dress and diet according to rank, ostensibly to curb waste but primarily to maintain social distinctions. — T. G. B.

[8] Capital. — T. G. B.

with the proceeding of the state be full of discord and faction, and those that are against it be entire and united.

I have noted, that some witty and sharp speeches, which have fallen from princes, have given fire to seditions. Caesar did himself infinite hurt in that speech — "Sylla did not know his letters, and so he could not dictate [as a dictator]" — for it did utterly cut off that hope which men had entertained, that he would at one time or other give over his dictatorship. Galba undid himself by that speech, "That soldiers were levied by him, not bought," for it put the soldiers out of hope of the donative.[9] Probus, likewise, by that speech, "If I live, there shall no longer be need of soldiers in the Roman Empire," a speech of great despair for the soldiers, and many the like. Surely princes had need in tender matters and ticklish times to beware what they say, especially in these short speeches, which fly abroad like darts, and are thought to be shot out of their secret intentions; for as for large discourses, they are flat things, and not so much noted.

Lastly, let princes, against all events, not be without some great person, one or rather more, of military valour, near unto them, for the repressing of seditions in their beginnings; for without that, there useth to be more trepidation in court upon the first breaking out of troubles than were fit; and the state runneth the danger of that which Tacitus saith, "And such was the state of feeling, that a few dared to perpetrate the worst of crimes; more wished to do so — all submitted to it"; but let such military persons be assured, and well reputed of, rather than factious and popular; holding also good correspondence with the other great men in the state, or else the remedy is worse than the disease.

Copernicus Bids the Sun Stand Still

The following selection is taken from the first book of Concerning the Revolution of the Heavenly Spheres *(1543) — Nicolaus Copernicus' great work climaxing a career of more than a half-century of cosmological theorization. Copernicus (1473–1543) was a Polish clergyman-canon lawyer-physician who in 1500 had attracted large audiences in Rome for lectures on astronomy. His heliocentric (or heliostatic), sun-centered (or sun-static) theory was just about completed and essayed in brief in 1530, but his caution, compounded of scholarly carefulness*

---

[9] Gift to enlist. — T. G. B.

and fear of reaction, delayed its full publication until 1543. Reaction
to it, pro and con, was slight for the half-century following publication.
Luther's was the immediately most condemnatory, and ultimately it
came under strong Catholic censure. Copernicus was a medieval scholastic, imbued with a Renaissance passion for the original Classical
texts, who, in challenging traditional learning, pointed toward the new
science.

The Revolution of the Heavenly Spheres

1. THAT THE UNIVERSE IS SPHERICAL

In the first place we must observe that the Universe is spherical. This
is either because that figure is the most perfect, as not being articulated
but whole and complete in itself; or because it is the most capacious and
therefore best suited for that which is to contain and preserve all things;
or again because all the perfect parts of it, namely, Sun, Moon and Stars,
are so formed; or because all things tend to assume this shape, as is seen
in the case of drops of water and liquid bodies in general if freely formed.
No one doubts that such a shape has been assigned to the heavenly
bodies.

2. THAT THE EARTH ALSO IS SPHERICAL

The Earth also is spherical, since on all sides it inclines toward the
centre. At first sight, the Earth does not appear absolutely spherical, because of the mountains and valleys; yet these make but little variation in
its general roundness, as appears from what follows. As we pass from any
point northward, the North Pole of the daily rotation gradually rises,
while the other pole sinks correspondingly and more stars near the North
Pole cease to set, while certain stars in the South do not rise. Thus,
Canopus, invisible in Italy, is visible in Egypt, while the last star of
Eridanus, seen in Italy, is unknown in our colder zone. On the other
hand, as we go southward, these stars appear higher, while those which
are high for us appear lower. Further, the change in altitude of the pole
is always proportional to the distance traversed on the Earth, which could
not be save on a spherical figure. Hence the Earth must be finite and
spherical. . . .

From Nicolaus Copernicus, *De Revolutionibus, Preface and Book I,* trans. John F. Dob-
son and Selig Brodetsky, Royal Astronomical Society Occasional Notes, No. 10 (London,
May, 1947), pp. 7, 9–11, 16–19. Reprinted by permission of the Royal Astronomical
Society.

4. THAT THE MOTION OF THE HEAVENLY BODIES IS UNIFORM, CIRCULAR, AND PERPETUAL, OR COMPOSED OF CIRCULAR MOTIONS

We now note that the motion of the heavenly bodies is circular. Rotation is natural to a sphere and by that very act is its shape expressed. For here we deal with the simplest kind of body, wherein neither beginning nor end may be discerned nor, if it rotate ever in the same place, may the one be distinguished from the other.

Now in the multitude of the heavenly bodies various motions occur. Most evident to sense is the diurnal rotation, the νυχθήμερον [1] as the Greeks call it, marking day and night. By this motion the whole Universe, save Earth alone, is thought to glide from East to West. This is the common measure of all motions, since Time itself is numbered in days. Next we see other revolutions in contest, as it were, with this daily motion and opposing it from West to East. Such opposing motions are those of Sun and Moon and the five planets. Of these the Sun portions out the year, the Moon the month, the common measures of time. In like manner the five planets define each his own independent period.

But these bodies exhibit differences in their motion. First their axes are not that of the diurnal rotation, but of the Zodiac, which is oblique thereto. Secondly, they do not move uniformly even in their own orbits; for are not Sun and Moon found now slower, now swifter in their courses? Further, at times the five planets become stationary at one point and another and even go backward. While the Sun ever goes forward unswerving on his own course, they wander in divers ways, straying now southward, now northward. For this reason they are named *Planets*. Furthermore, sometimes they approach Earth, being then in *Perigee*, while at other times receding they are in *Apogee*.

Nevertheless, despite these irregularities, we must conclude that the motions of these bodies are ever circular or compounded of circles. For the irregularities themselves are subject to a definite law and recur at stated times, and this could not happen if the motions were not circular, for a circle alone can thus restore the place of a body as it was. So with the Sun which, by a compounding of circular motions, brings ever again the changing days and nights and the four seasons of the year. Now therein it must be that divers motions are conjoined, since a simple celestial body cannot move irregularly in a single orbit. For such irregularity must come of unevenness either in the moving force (whether inherent or acquired) or in the form of the revolving body. Both these alike the mind abhors regarding the most perfectly disposed bodies.

It is then generally agreed that the motions of the Sun, Moon and

---

[1] Literally, "a day and night." — T. G. B.

Planets do but seem irregular either by reason of the divers directions of their axes of revolution, or else by reason that Earth is not the centre of the circles in which they revolve, so that to us on Earth the displacements of these bodies when near seem greater than when they are more remote, as is shewn in the *Optics*.[2] If then we consider equal arcs in the paths of the planets we find that they seem to describe differing distances in equal periods of time. It is therefore above all needful to observe carefully the relation of the Earth toward the Heavens, lest, searching out the things on high, we should pass by those nearer at hand, and mistakenly ascribe earthly qualities to heavenly bodies.

5. WHETHER CIRCULAR MOTION BELONGS TO THE EARTH; AND CONCERNING ITS POSITION

Since it has been shown that Earth is spherical, we now consider whether her motion is conformable to her shape and her position in the Universe. Without these we cannot construct a proper theory of the heavenly phenomena. Now authorities agree that Earth holds firm her place at the centre of the Universe, and they regard the contrary as unthinkable, nay as absurd. Yet if we examine more closely it will be seen that this question is not so settled, and needs wider consideration.

A seeming change of place may come of movement either of object or of observer, or again of unequal movements of the two (for between equal and parallel motions no movement is perceptible). Now it is Earth from which the rotation of the Heavens is seen. If then some motion of Earth be assumed it will be reproduced in external bodies, which will seem to move in the opposite direction.

Consider first the diurnal rotation. By it the whole Universe, save Earth alone and its contents, appears to move very swiftly. Yet grant that Earth revolves from West to East, and you will find, if you ponder it, that my conclusion is right. It is the vault of Heaven that contains all things, and why should not motion be attributed rather to the contained than to the container, to the located than the locater? . . .

There is another difficulty, namely, the position of Earth. Nearly all have hitherto held that Earth is the centre of the Universe. Now, grant that Earth is not at the exact centre but at a distance from it which, while small compared to the starry sphere, is yet considerable compared with the orbits of Sun and other planets. Then calculate the consequent variations in their seeming motions, assuming these to be really uniform and about some centre other than the Earth's. One may then perhaps adduce a reasonable cause for these variable motions. And indeed since the Planets are seen at varying distances from the Earth, the centre of Earth is surely not the centre of their orbits. Nor is it certain whether the

[2] Of Euclid. — T. G. B.

Planets move toward and away from Earth, or Earth toward and away from them. It is therefore justifiable to hold that the Earth has another motion in addition to the diurnal rotation. That the Earth, besides rotating, wanders with several motions and is indeed a Planet, is a view attributed to Philolaus the Pythagorean, no mean mathematician, and one whom Plato is said to have eagerly sought out in Italy. . . .

10. OF THE ORDER OF THE HEAVENLY BODIES

No one doubts that the Sphere of the Fixed Stars is the most distant of visible things. As for the planets, the early Philosophers were inclined to believe that they form a series in order of magnitude of their orbits. They adduce the fact that of objects moving with equal speed, those further distant seem to move more slowly (as is proved in Euclid's *Optics*). They think that the moon describes her path in the shortest time because, being nearest to the Earth, she revolves in the smallest circle. Furthest they place Saturn, who in the longest time describes the greatest orbit. Nearer than his is Jupiter, and then Mars. . . .

Unconvincing too is Ptolemy's proof that the Sun moves between those bodies that do and those that do not recede from him completely. Consideration of the case of the Moon, which does so recede, exposes its falseness. Again, what cause can be alleged, by those who place Venus nearer than the Sun, and Mercury next, or in some other order? Why should not these planets also follow separate paths, distinct from that of the Sun, as do the other planets? and this might be said even if their relative swiftness and slowness does not belie their alleged order. Either then the Earth cannot be the centre to which the order of the planets and their orbits is related, or certainly their relative order is not observed, nor does it appear why a higher position should be assigned to Saturn than to Jupiter, or any other planet.

Therefore I think we must seriously consider the ingenious view held by Martianus Capella the author of the *Encyclopaedia* and certain other Latins, that Venus and Mercury do not go round the Earth like the other planets but run their courses with the Sun as centre, and so do not depart from him further than the size of their orbits allows. What else can they mean than that the centre of these orbits is near the Sun? So certainly the orbit of Mercury must be within that of Venus, which, it is agreed, is more than twice as great.

We may now extend this hypothesis to bring Saturn, Jupiter and Mars also into relation with this centre, making their orbits great enough to contain those of Venus and Mercury and the Earth; and their proportional motions according to the Table demonstrate this. These outer planets are always nearer to the Earth about the time of their evening rising, that is, when they are in opposition to the Sun, and the Earth between them and the Sun. They are more distant from the Earth at the time of their evening setting, when they are in conjunction with the Sun and the Sun between them and the Earth. These indications prove that their centre pertains rather to the Sun than to the Earth, and that this is the same centre as that to which the revolutions of Venus and Mercury are related.

But since all these have one centre it is necessary that the space between the orbit of Venus and the orbit of Mars must also be viewed as a Sphere concentric with the others, capable of receiving the Earth with her satellite the Moon and whatever is contained within the Sphere of the Moon — for we must not separate the Moon from the Earth, the former being beyond all doubt nearest to the latter, especially as in that space we find suitable and ample room for the Moon.

We therefore assert that the centre of the Earth, carrying the Moon's path, passes in a great orbit among the other planets in an annual revolution round the Sun; that near the Sun is the centre of the Universe; and that whereas the Sun is at rest, any apparent motion of the Sun can be better explained by motion of the Earth. Yet so great is the Universe that though the distance of the Earth from the Sun is not insignificant compared with the size of any other planetary path, in accordance with the ratios of their sizes, it is insignificant compared with the distance of the Sphere of the Fixed Stars.

Kepler Applauds Galileo

Galileo built a thirty-power telescope in 1609 upon hearing a report that lens makers in the Netherlands had constructed a practical telescope. Turned heavenward, Galileo's instrument revealed sunspots, Saturn's elliptical shape, the rough surface of the moon, the phases of Venus, and four of Jupiter's twelve moons. Believing that his observations supported Copernicus' heliocentric theory, Galileo published his findings in The Sidereal Messenger *(1610) in Venice. Kepler in Prague was given a copy of the book by Emperor Rudolf II, an avid amateur astronomer. His critique of it,* Conversation with Galileo's Sidereal Messenger, *was written in April, 1610. Kepler's praise was unstinted, though methodologically and temperamentally the two scientists were poles apart. The* Conversation *conveys insight into both men and their contributions to the new science.*

Conversation with Galileo's Sidereal Messenger

NOTICE TO THE READER

When many people asked my opinion about Galileo's "Sidereal Messenger," I decided to satisfy them all by adopting the short cut of circulating in printed form the letter which I sent to Galileo (and which was drafted in great haste, amidst unavoidable obligations, to meet a deadline).

But after it was printed, my friends cautioned me that it seemed a little too unconventional in conception. One of them wanted the introduction done away with; another would have liked to soften certain expressions which, to short-sighted eyes, might appear to impute to my opponent views at variance with scholastic tradition; some also desired less extensive praise of Galileo, in order to make room for the verdict of famous men, whose attitude, they hear, differs from mine.

Therefore I resolved to advise the reader that everybody has his own preference. Whereas most debaters get all heated up, I regard humor as a more pleasant tone in discussions. Other authors strive for impressiveness in the exposition of philosophy by the weightiness of their assertions; yet they often prove amusing, unintentionally. I seem by nature cut out to lighten the hard work and difficulty of a subject by mental relaxation, conveyed by the style.

II

I may perhaps seem rash in accepting your claims so readily with no support from my own experience. But why should I not believe a most learned mathematician, whose very style attests the soundness of his judgment? He has not intention of practicing deception in a bid for vulgar publicity, nor does he pretend to have seen what he has not seen. Because he loves the truth, he does not hesitate to oppose even the most familiar opinions, and to bear the jeers of the crowd with equanimity. Does he not make his writings public, and could he possibly hide any villainy that might be perpetrated? Shall I disparage him, a gentleman of Florence, for the things he has seen? Shall I with my poor vision disparage him with his keen sight? Shall he with his equipment of optical instruments be disparaged by me, who must use my naked eyes because I lack these aids? Shall I not have confidence in him, when he invites everybody to see the same sights, and what is of supreme importance, even

From *Kepler's Conversation with Galileo's Sidereal Messenger* (© 1965 by the Johnson Reprint Corporation), ed. and trans. Edward Rosen (New York, 1965), pp. 5, 12–15, 17–19. Reprinted by permission of Johnson Reprint Corporation, Publishers, New York.

offers his own instrument in order to gain support on the strength of observations?

Or would it be a trifling matter for him to mock the family of the Grand Dukes of Tuscany, and to attach the name of the Medici to figments of his imagination, while he promises real planets?

Why is it that I find part of the book verified by my own experience and also by affirmations of others? Is there any reason why the author should have thought of misleading the world with regard to only four planets?

Three months ago the Most August Emperor [1] raised various questions with me about the spots on the moon. He was convinced that the images of countries and continents are reflected in the moon as though in a mirror. He asserted in particular that Italy with its two adjacent islands seemed to him to be distinctly outlined. He even offered his glass for the examination of these spots on subsequent days, but this was not done. Thus at that very same time, Galileo, when you cherished the abode of Christ our Lord above the mere appellation [of a Galilean], you vied in your favorite occupation with the ruler of Christendom (actuated by the same restless spirit of inquiry into nature).

But this story of the spots in the moon is also quite ancient. It is supported by the authority of Pythagoras and Plutarch, the eminent philosopher who also, if this detail helps the cause, governed Epirus with the power of a proconsul under the Caesars. I say nothing about Mästlin and my treatise on "Optics," published six years ago; these I shall take up later on in their proper place.

Such assertions about the body of the moon are made by others on the basis of mutually self-supporting evidence. Their conclusions agree with the highly illuminating observations which you report on the same subject. Consequently I have no basis for questioning the rest of your book and the four satellites of Jupiter. I should rather wish that I now had a telescope at hand, with which I might anticipate you in discovering two satellites of Mars (as the relationship seems to me to require) and six or eight satellites of Saturn, with one each perhaps for Venus and Mercury.

For this search, so far as Mars is concerned, the most propitious time will be next October, which will show Mars in opposition to the sun and (except for the year 1608) nearest to the earth, with the error in the predicted position exceeding 3°. . . .

IV

The first section of your little book deals with the construction of the telescope. Its magnifying power is so great that the object viewed shows a thousandfold increase in surface. This enlargement is possible if the di-

[1] Rudolf II, an amateur astronomer and astrologer. — T. G. B.

ameter appears 32 times longer. But if the observer's estimate approximates an impression of the normal size, the object must then seem 32 times nearer. For the eye does not see distance, but infers it, as we learn in optics. Suppose, for example, that a man 3200 paces away is subtended by an angle 32 times greater than that which, without a telescope, subtends a second man 100 paces away. Since the eye regards it as certain that the distant man has the usual height, it will judge that he is no more than 100 paces away. A contributing factor is the sharp definition bestowed on the image by the telescope.

So powerful a telescope seems an incredible undertaking to many persons, yet it is neither impossible nor new. Nor was it recently produced by the Dutch, but many years ago it was announced by Giovanni Battista della Porta in his "Natural Magic," Book XVII, Chapter 10, "The Effects of a Crystal Lens." . . .

Nor is it beyond belief that expert sculptors of painstaking workmanship, who use glasses to inspect the details of a figure, may also have accidentally stumbled on this device, while uniting convex lenses with concave in various ways, in order to choose the combination most serviceable to the eyes.

I do not advance these suggestions for the purpose of diminishing the glory of the technical inventor, whoever he was. I am aware how great a difference there is between theoretical speculation and visual experience; between Ptolemy's discussion of the antipodes and Columbus' discovery of the New World, and likewise between the widely distributed tubes with two lenses and the apparatus with which you, Galileo, have pierced the heavens. But here I am trying to induce the skeptical to have faith in your instrument.

After I began to work on my "Optics," the Emperor questioned me quite frequently about Della Porta's aforementioned devices.[2] I must confess that I disparaged them most vigorously, and no wonder, for he obviously mixes up the incredible with the probable. And the title of Chapter 11 ("To Extend Vision to Unimaginable Distances") seemed to involve an optical absurdity; as though vision took place by a process of emanation, and lenses sharpened the ejaculations of the eye so that they would travel farther than if no lenses were employed; or if vision takes place by a process of repetition, as Della Porta acknowledges, as though in that case lenses supplied or increased the light to make things visible. Rather is it true that no lens can ever detect objects which do not of themselves impart to our eyes some degree of light as the medium through which the objects acquire visibility.

[2] In preceding paragraphs, Kepler had discussed Della Porta's very influential book, *Natural Magic*, first published in 1558, especially his speculations on the combination of a concave with a convex lens. — T. G. B.

Furthermore, I believed that the air is dense and blue in color, so that the minute parts of visible things at a distance are obscured and distorted. Since this proposition is intrinsically certain, it was vain, I understood, to hope that a lens would remove this substance of the intervening air from visible things. Also with regard to the celestial essence, I surmised some such property as could prevent us, supposing that we enormously magnified the body of the moon to immense proportions, from being able to differentiate its tiny particles in their purity from the lowest celestial matter.

For these reasons, reinforced by other obstacles besides, I refrained from attempting to construct the device.

But now, most accomplished Galileo, you deserve my praise for your tireless energy. Putting aside all misgivings, you turned directly to visual experimentation. And indeed by your discoveries you caused the sun of truth to rise, you routed all the ghosts of perplexity together with their mother, the night, and by your achievement you showed what could be done.

Under your guidance I recognize that the celestial substance is incredibly tenuous. To be sure, this property is made known on page 127 of my "Optics." If the relative densities of air and water are compared with the relative densities of the aether and air, the latter ratio undoubtedly shows a much greater disparity. As a result, not even the tiniest particle of the sphere of the stars (still less of the body of the moon, which is the lowest of the heavenly bodies) escapes our eyes, when they are aided by your instrument. A single fragment of the lens interposes much more matter (or opacity) between the eye and the object viewed than does the entire vast region of the aether. For a slight indistinctness arises from the lens, but from the aether none at all. Hence we must virtually concede, it seems, that the whole immense space is a vacuum. . . .

That master of all the sciences, Johannes Pistorius, asked me more than once, I recall, whether Brahe's observations were so refined that in my opinion absolutely nothing could be lacking in them. I vigorously maintained that the pinnacle had been reached, and that nothing further was left to human enterprise, because the eyes would not permit greater precision, nor would the effect of refraction, which alters the position of the stars with reference to the horizon. In rebuttal, he steadfastly declared that some day somebody would come along who would devise a more exact procedure with the help of lenses. I objected on the ground that their refractive properties made lenses unsuitable for reliable observations. But now at last I see that Pistorius was in part a true prophet. To be sure, Brahe's observations speak for themselves and need no praise. For what an arc of 60° is in the heavens, or 34′, is known through Brahe's instruments by themselves. But whereas Brahe in this way measured celestial degrees in the heavens (or even I determined the diameter of the moon by optical device), now your telescope, Galileo, surpasses these attainments. Accepting the numerical results recorded by Brahe and me, it subdivides them with the utmost nicety into minutes and fractions of minutes. It couples itself with Brahe's observational method in a most appropriate marriage, so that Brahe has good reason to rejoice at your method of observation, and you must base your method on Brahe's.

Would you like me to express my feelings? I want your instrument for the study of lunar eclipses, in the hope that it may furnish the most extraordinary aid in improving, and where necessary in recasting, the whole of my "Hipparchus" or demonstration of the sizes and distances of the three bodies, sun, moon, and earth. For the variations in the solar and lunar diameters, and the portion of the moon that is eclipsed, will be measured with precision only by the man who is equipped with your telescope and acquires skill in observing.

Therefore let Galileo take his stand by Kepler's side. Let the former observe the moon with his face turned skyward, while the latter studies the sun by looking down at a screen (lest the lens injure his eye). Let each employ his own device, and from this partnership may there some day arise an absolutely perfect theory of the distances. . . .

Descartes Finds Certainty

René Descartes published his intellectual autobiography in his Discourse on Method *(1637). It suffered from no false modesty, and, characteristic of its author, it was less than full in its recognition of those who had contributed to the development of Descartes's extraordinary intellect. His four rules of right reasoning had great vogue and were a major contribution to logic, though not necessarily to scientific investigation. Descartes, in fact, was not always careful in his own diffuse investigations to respect them fully. The major importance of the following selection is its description of the way in which Descartes came to perceive certainty. Cartesianism was founded on this rock, the mind of Descartes, much more than on any necessary derivation from it of the perfect being "which was God." Descartes's disciples, the philosophes of the Enlightenment, were indeed true believers of the master, accepting somewhat uncritically his extreme rationalism, his belief in immutable mechanical laws of nature — for him nature meant everything but the mind — and his aspiration that all knowledge might be combined into one universal science.*

Discourse on Method

But like one walking alone and in the dark, I resolved to proceed so slowly and with such circumspection, that if I did not advance far, I would at least guard against falling. I did not even choose to dismiss summarily any of the opinions that had crept into my belief without having been introduced by Reason, but first of all took sufficient time carefully to satisfy myself of the general nature of the task I was setting myself, and ascertain the true Method by which to arrive at the knowledge of whatever lay within the compass of my powers.

Among the branches of Philosophy, I had, at an earlier period, given some attention to Logic, and among those of the Mathematics to Geometrical Analysis and Algebra — three Arts or Sciences which ought, as I conceived, to contribute something to my design. But, on examination, I found that, as for Logic, its syllogisms and the majority of its other precepts are of avail rather in the communication of what we already know, or even as the Art of Lully, in speaking without judgment of things of which we are ignorant, than in the investigation of the unknown; and although this Science contains indeed a number of correct and very excellent precepts, there are, nevertheless, so many others, and these either injurious or superfluous, mingled with the former, that it is almost quite as difficult to effect a severance of the true from the false as it is to extract a Diana or a Minerva from a rough block of marble. Then as to the Analysis of the ancients and the Algebra of the moderns, besides that they embrace only matters highly abstract, and, to appearance, of no use, the former is so exclusively restricted to the consideration of figures, that it can exercise the Understanding only on condition of greatly fatiguing the Imagination; [1] and, in the latter, there is so complete a subjection to certain rules and formulas, that there results an art full of confusion and obscurity calculated to embarrass, instead of a science fitted to cultivate the mind. By these considerations I was induced to seek some other Method which would comprise the advantages of the three and be exempt from their defects. And as a multitude of laws often only hampers justice, so that a state is best governed when, with few laws, these are rigidly administered; in like manner, instead of the great number of precepts of which Logic is composed, I believed that the four following would prove perfectly sufficient for me, provided I took the firm and unwavering resolution never in a single instance to fail in observing them.

The *first* was never to accept anything for true which I did not clearly know to be such; that is to say, carefully to avoid precipitancy and

From René Descartes, *Discourse on the Method of Rightly Conducting the Reason and Seeking Truth in the Sciences*, trans. John Veitch (Edinburgh, 1873), pp. 59–63, 74–77.
1 The Imagination must here be taken as equivalent simply to the Representative Faculty. — Trans.

prejudice, and to comprise nothing more in my judgment than what was presented to my mind so clearly and distinctly as to exclude all ground of doubt.

The *second,* to divide each of the difficulties under examination into as many parts as possible, and as might be necessary for its adequate solution.

The *third,* to conduct my thoughts in such order that, by commencing with objects the simplest and easiest to know, I might ascend by little and little, and, as it were, step by step, to the knowledge of the more complex; assigning in thought a certain order even to those objects which in their own nature do not stand in a relation of antecedence and sequence.

At the *last,* in every case to make enumerations so complete, and reviews so general, that I might be assured that nothing was omitted.

The long chains of simple and easy reasonings by means of which geometers are accustomed to reach the conclusions of their most difficult demonstrations, had led me to imagine that all things, to the knowledge of which man is competent, are mutually connected in the same way, and that there is nothing so far removed from us as to be beyond our reach, or so hidden that we cannot discover it, provided only we abstain from accepting the false for the true, and always preserve in our thoughts the order necessary for the deduction of one truth from another. And I had little difficulty in determining the objects with which it was necessary to commence, for I was already persuaded that it must be with the simplest and easiest to know, and considering that of all those who have hitherto sought truth in the Sciences, the mathematicians alone have been able to find any demonstrations, that is, any certain and evident reasons, I did not doubt but that such must have been the rule of their investigations. I resolved to commence, therefore, with the examination of the simplest objects, not anticipating, however, from this any other advantage than that to be found in accustoming my mind to the love and nourishment of truth, and to a distaste for all such reasonings as were unsound. But I had no intention on that account of attempting to master all the particular Sciences commonly denominated Mathematics: but observing that, however difficult their objects, they all agree in considering only the various relations or proportions subsisting among those objects, I thought it best for my purpose to consider these proportions in the most general form possible, without referring them to any objects in particular, except such as would most facilitate the knowledge of them, and without by any means restricting them to these, that afterward I might thus be the better able to apply them to every other class of objects to which they are legitimately applicable. Perceiving further, that in order to understand these relations I should sometimes have to consider them one by one, and sometimes only to bear them in mind, or embrace them in the aggregate, I thought that, in order the better to consider them individually,

I should view them as subsisting between straight lines, than which I could find no objects more simple, or capable of being more distinctly represented to my imagination and senses; and on the other hand, that in order to retain them in the memory, or embrace an aggregate of many, I should express them by certain characters the briefest possible. In this way I believed that I could borrow all that was best both in Geometrical Analysis and in Algebra, and correct all the defects of the one by the help of the other. . . .

I am in doubt as to the propriety of making my first meditations, in the place above mentioned, matter of discourse; for these are so metaphysical, and so uncommon, as not, perhaps, to be acceptable to everyone. And yet, that it may be determined whether the foundations that I have laid are sufficiently secure, I find myself in a measure constrained to advert to them. I had long before remarked that, in relation to practice, it is sometimes necessary to adopt, as if above doubt, opinions which we discern to be highly uncertain, as has been already said; but as I then desired to give my attention solely to the search after truth, I thought that a procedure exactly the opposite was called for, and that I ought to reject as absolutely false all opinions in regard to which I could suppose the least ground for doubt, in order to ascertain whether after that there remained aught in my belief that was wholly indubitable. Accordingly, seeing that our senses sometimes deceive us, I was willing to suppose that there existed nothing really such as they presented to us; and because some men err in reasoning, and fall into paralogisms,[2] even on the simplest matters of Geometry, I, convinced that I was as open to error as any other, rejected as false all the reasonings I had hitherto taken for demonstrations; and finally, when I considered that the very same thoughts (presentations) which we experience when awake may also be experienced when we are asleep, while there is at that time not one of them true, I supposed that all the objects (presentations) that had ever entered into my mind when awake, had in them no more truth than the illusions of my dreams. But immediately upon this I observed that, whilst I thus wished to think that all was false, it was absolutely necessary that I, who thus thought, should be somewhat; and as I observed that this truth, *I think, hence I am,* was so certain and of such evidence, that no ground of doubt, however extravagant, could be alleged by the Sceptics capable of shaking it, I concluded that I might, without scruple, accept it as the first principle of the Philosophy of which I was in search.

In the next place, I attentively examined what I was, and as I observed that I could suppose that I had no body, and that there was no world nor any place in which I might be; but that I could not therefore suppose that I was not; and that, on the contrary, from the very circum-

2 A fallacy in reasoning, especially one of which the reasoner is unconcious. — T. G. B.

stance that I thought to doubt of the truth of all things, it most clearly and certainly followed that I was; while, on the other hand, if I had only ceased to think, although all the other objects which I had ever imagined had been in reality existent, I would have had no reason to believe that I existed; I thence concluded that I was a substance whose whole essence or nature consists only in thinking, and which, that it may exist, has no need of place, nor is dependent on any material thing; so that "I," that is to say, the mind by which I am what I am, is wholly distinct from the body, and is even more easily known than the latter, and is such, that although the latter were not, it would still continue to be all that it is.

After this I inquired in general into what is essential to the truth and certainty of a proposition; for since I had discovered one which I knew to be true, I thought that I must likewise be able to discover the ground of this certitude. And as I observed that in the words *I think, hence I am,* there is nothing at all which gives me assurance of their truth beyond this, that I see very clearly that in order to think it is necessary to exist, I concluded that I might take, as a general rule, the principle, that all the things which we very clearly and distinctly conceive are true, only observing, however, that there is some difficulty in rightly determining the objects which we distinctly conceive.

In the next place, from reflecting on the circumstance that I doubted, and that consequently my being was not wholly perfect (for I clearly saw that it was a greater perfection to know than to doubt), I was led to inquire whence I had learned to think of something more prefect than myself; and I clearly recognized that I must hold this notion from some Nature which in reality was more perfect. As for the thoughts of many other objects external to me, as of the sky, the earth, light, heat, and a thousand more, I was less at a loss to know whence these came; for since I remarked in them nothing which seemed to render them superior to myself, I could believe that, if these were true, they were dependencies on my own nature, in so far as it possessed a certain perfection, and, if they were false, that I held them from nothing, that is to say, that they were in me because of a certain imperfection of my nature. But this could not be the case with the idea of a Nature more perfect than myself; for to receive it from nothing was a thing manifestly impossible; and, because it is not less repugnant that the more perfect should be an effect of, and dependence on the less perfect, than that something should proceed from nothing, it was equally impossible that I could hold it from myself: accordingly, it but remained that it had been placed in me by a Nature which was in reality more perfect than mine, and which even possessed within itself all the perfection of which I could form any idea: that is to say, in a single word, which was God. . . .

AGE OF CRISIS, 1600–1660:
ABSOLUTIST SOLUTION

Chapter 9

Absolutism has had a poor reputation since 1789. Tom Paine's ringing condemnation of the *ancien régime* in *The Rights of Man (II)* in 1792 became embedded in the subconsciousness of nineteenth-century historians:

It is impossible that such governments as have hitherto existed in the world, could have commenced by any other means than a total violation of every principle, sacred and moral. The obscurity in which the origin of all the present old governments is buried, implies the iniquity and disgrace with which they began.

The continuing ramifications of the liberalization of man's condition begun by the French Revolution have given to "representative democracy" a universal intellectual and emotional appeal that has loaded "monarchial absolutism" with a pejorative burden so heavy that the most balanced historian finds it difficult to shift it for the purposes of his study. The facts as well as reason argue that absolutism was a realistic response to a real need, a predictable stage in the development of the modern state, and a system of government that had some sort of societal consensus in support of it and a respectable body of theory behind it.

The need was the universally recognized threat posed by internal disorder in an age of ideological confrontation, economic dislocation, and social dynamism. The continuous rivalry of independent sovereign states — ranging from the atomized entities of Germany and Italy to the major European powers (France, Spain, Austria, and England) — unrestrained by any superior legal, political, or moral authority, vying with each other for territory, commercial advantage, and political hegemony by dynastic aggrandizement, created a particularly destructive divisiveness based on differing ideological allegiances and necessitated strong central control.

As a predictable stage in the development of the modern state, the absolutist monarch was the natural beneficiary of the increasing cul-

tural and linguistic particularism of Europe, the embryonic national-
ism that developed rapidly in the later Middle Ages and became recog-
nizable in power relations in the sixteenth century. Identification with
the person of the monarch, with his forbears, and with his heirs — the
dynasty — gave subjects a sense of individual worth, of meaning derived
from the past with the promise of its extension to the subjects' posterity in the future. This identification was a powerful sentiment
among men whose vision remained otherworldly and who, in an age of
short life expectancy and hard existence, had great powers of "delayed
gratification" or else could believe in nothing. An emphasis on heritage
and inheritance as unquestioned social values cemented the subjects'
identification with the hereditary monarchy. The challenge to the
spiritual sovereignty of the Pope in the Reformation everywhere re-
dounded to the benefit of kings, and the results ranged from the assumption of the Supreme Headship over the English Church by Henry
VIII to the special protective role of Catholic kings over the Roman
Church within their kingdoms. The dulled spiritual sword became increasingly dependent upon the keen temporal sword for survival.

The societal consensus in support of absolutism was overwhelming.
Generally the supporters included the clergy of the established church,
whether Protestant or Catholic, though Calvinist clergy were less amenable to absolutism than others were. Absolutism's staunchest supporters were the people in society whose fortunes were immediately linked
with the monarch's: lawyers, bureaucrats, the military, the new nobility
whose honors and wealth were the rewards of service to the absolutist
monarch, and merchants who depended on the good will and assistance
of the state in their ventures. These elements enjoyed tremendous and
increasing power over the lower ranks of society. Significantly, only the
greater nobility and their dependents were not part of the consensus
favoring absolutism. But the feudatories were the principal victims of
absolutism, their power the power to be reduced, their privileges the
privileges to be curtailed, their preeminence and leadership the targets
of absolutist centralism. By 1600 the beneficiaries of absolutism were
more numerous, more wealthy, and more powerful than the victims.

The theoretical justification for absolutist monarchy followed the
substantial establishment of it. The meagerness of the voices raised in
opposition to the concept of absolutism is striking. They consisted of a
few defenders of the republican ideals of Venice, defenders of the
privileges of the representative estates (particularly in England and the
Dutch Republic), ultra-Calvinist resistance on behalf of theocracy, and
Catholic theoreticians such as Bellarmine and Suarez, who assailed
secular absolutism in order to advance the spiritual absolutism of the
papacy. Otherwise, the proponents of the theory of absolutism had a
clear field.

The medieval secular polity, both in practice and in theory, was "mixed monarchy": the king ruled in conjunction with the estates, and his power was shared with the estates, usually composed of the representatives of the three legally privileged orders, the clergy, the nobility and the commoners. The king and the estates were conceived of as separate but cooperating entities in a dualistic government. The absolutist monarch sought to destroy the dualism and to remove the restraining limitation on his authority imposed by the traditional authority of the estates. The Reformation advanced his cause. It gave vogue to Machiavelli's postulate that the preservation of the state was the transcendent morality in politics, for, in the conflict with the Church, the justification of the secular authority depended upon the moral primacy of the state. Justification for the expulsion or reduction of papal authority raised the claim of monarchical sovereignty, that the king was under no power on earth, temporal or spiritual, and was invested with the injunction of God ("divine right") to rule. Two essential ingredients of absolutist theory were already present in the notions of the preservation of the state as the transcendent morality in politics and the divine right of kings.

Machiavelli was the pivotal theorist in the development toward absolutist theory, though he believed "mixed monarchy" was the best system. By making the state central to polity, Machiavelli directed attention to the question of who has ultimate authority in the state, who is sovereign. Jean Bodin, convinced of the indivisibility of majesty, argued a clear preference for a sovereign monarch. Giovanni Botero posited that the state is an ethical entity, and, that since it is difficult to conceive of a conglomeration of persons as one ethical entity, the logical conclusion is to conceive of the single person, the monarch, as the personification of the ethical state.

According to absolutist theory, the king's authority was unbound by a higher earthly authority, but it was bound by God's law and the law of nature. These were poor guarantees for the subject, but they served to remind the monarch that his power was limited, though uncontrolled. The king had to serve God's ends. James VI of Scotland (and later James I of England) gave the classical definition of the divine-right sovereignty of the absolutist monarchy. His definition outlasted absolutism in his kingdoms.

In practice, absolutism in the early-seventeenth-century age of crisis placed a heavy reliance on the loyalty and commitment of the monarch's ministers. This was the age of great ministers: Richelieu and Mazarin in France, Olivares in Spain, Laud and Strafford in England, Oxenstierna in Sweden. The attributes of the absolutist monarch were in their hands. Potentially they were as great a threat to the monarch as the feudal nobility — perhaps greater, because the feudal nobility was already in retreat and disarray. Cardinal Richelieu, who "sacrificed everything in his interest" and "extended his concern for the State no further than his own life" — even if the charges are only partly valid — was too powerful a subject for an absolutist king.

Bodin

Jean Bodin (1530–1596) as theorist was a product of Jean Bodin as politician. He was a councillor to the duc d'Alençon, the leader of the party of the politiques *in the French Wars of Religion, whose position was that the state existed primarily to maintain order, not to establish true religion. The* politiques *looked to an absolutist monarch to establish the order so lacking in France in the 1570's; that monarch would have the full right to demand obedience, and resistance to his authority would be intolerable. This was the burden of Bodin's argument in the* Six Books of the Commonwealth *(1576). Ambitious, diffuse, and pedantic in the extreme, the treatise nonetheless made the essential points for absolutism and reached an enormous audience all over Europe.*

The Well-ordered Commonwealth

BOOK ONE

THE FINAL END OF THE WELL-ORDERED
COMMONWEALTH [CHAPTER I]

A commonwealth may be defined as the rightly ordered government of a number of families, and of those things which are their common concern, by a sovereign power. We must start in this way with a definition because the final end of any subject must first be understood before the means of attaining it can profitably be considered, and the definition indicates what that end is. If then the definition is not exact and true, all that is deduced from it is valueless. One can, of course, have an accurate perception of the end, and yet lack the means to attain it, as has the indifferent archer who sees the bull's-eye but cannot hit it. With care and attention however he may come very near it, and provided he uses his best

From Jean Bodin, *Six Books of the Commonwealth*, ed. and trans. M. J. Tooley (Oxford, n.d.), pp. 1, 6–7, 8–19, 25, 27–29, 34–36, 211–12. Reprinted by permission of Basil Blackwell Ltd.

endeavours, he will not be without honour, even if he cannot find the exact centre of the target. But the man who does not comprehend the end, and cannot rightly define his subject, has no hope of finding the means of attaining it, any more than the man who shoots at random into the air can hope to hit the mark.

CONCERNING THE FAMILY [CHAPTERS II–V]

A family may be defined as the right ordering of a group of persons owing obedience to a head of a household, and of those interests which are his proper concern. The second term of our definition of the commonwealth refers to the family because it is not only the true source and origin of the commonwealth, but also its principal constituent. Xenophon and Aristotle divorced economy or household management from police or disciplinary power, without good reason to my mind. . . . I understand by domestic government the right ordering of family matters, together with the authority which the head of the family has over his dependents, and the obedience due from them to him, things which Aristotle and Xenophon neglect. Thus the well-ordered family is a true image of the commonwealth, and domestic comparable with sovereign authority. It follows that the household is the model of right order in the commonwealth. And just as the whole body enjoys health when every particular member performs its proper function, so all will be well with the commonwealth when families are properly regulated.

CONCERNING THE CITIZEN [CHAPTERS VI AND VII]

. . . When the head of the family leaves the household over which he presides and joins with other heads of families in order to treat of those things which are of common interest, he ceases to be a lord and master, and becomes an equal and associate with the rest. He sets aside his private concerns to attend to public affairs. In so doing he ceases to be a master and becomes a citizen, and a citizen may be defined as a free subject dependent on the authority of another.

Before such things as cities and citizens, or any form of commonwealth whatsoever, were known among men, each head of a family was sovereign in his household, having power of life and death over his wife and children. But force, violence, ambition, avarice, and the passion for vengeance, armed men against one another. The result of the ensuing conflicts was to give victory to some, and to reduce the rest to slavery. Moreover the man who had been chosen captain and leader by the victors, under whose command success had been won, retained authority over his followers, who became his loyal and faithful adherents, and imposed it on the others, who became his slaves. Thus was lost the full and entire liberty of each man to live according to his own free will, without subjection to anyone. It was completely lost to the vanquished and converted into unmitigated servitude; it was qualified in the case of the victors in that they now rendered obedience to a sovereign leader. Anyone who did not wish to abandon part of his liberty, and live under the laws and commands of another, lost it altogether. Thus the words, hitherto unknown, of master and servant, ruler and subject, came into use.

Reason and common sense alike point to the conclusion that the origin and foundation of commonwealths was in force and violence. . . .

Such being the origin of commonwealths, it is clear why a citizen is to be defined as a free subject who is dependent on the sovereignty of another. I use the term *free subject*, because although a slave is as much, or more, subject to the commonwealth as is his lord, it has always been a matter of common agreement that the slave is not a citizen, and in law has no personality. This is not the case with women and children, who are free of any servile dependence, though their rights and liberties, especially their power of disposing of property, is limited by the domestic authority of the head of the household. We can say then that every citizen is a subject since his liberty is limited by the sovereign power to which he owes obedience. We cannot say that every subject is a citizen. This is clear from the case of slaves. The same applies to aliens. Being subject to the authority of another, they have no part in the rights and privileges of the community. . . .

Concerning sovereignty [chapter viii]

Sovereignty is that absolute and perpetual power vested in a commonwealth which in Latin is termed *majestas*. . . . The term needs careful definition, because although it is the distinguishing mark of a commonwealth, and an understanding of its nature fundamental to any treatment of politics, no jurist or political philosopher has in fact attempted to define it. . . .

I have described it as *perpetual* because one can give absolute power to a person or group of persons for a period of time, but that time expired they become subjects once more. Therefore even while they enjoy power, they cannot properly be regarded as sovereign rulers, but only as the lieutenants and agents of the sovereign ruler, till the moment comes when it pleases the prince or the people to revoke the gift. The true sovereign remains always seized of his power. . . . However much he gives there always remains a reserve of right in his own person, whereby he may command, or intervene by way of prevention, confirmation, evocation, or any other way he thinks fit, in all matters delegated to a subject, whether in virtue of an office or a commission. Any authority exercised in virtue of an office or a commission can be revoked, or made tenable for as long or short a period as the sovereign wills. . . .

Let us now turn to the other term of our definition and consider the force of the word *absolute*. The people or the magnates of a common-wealth can bestow simply and unconditionally upon someone of their choice a sovereign and perpetual power to dispose of their property and persons, to govern the state as he thinks fit, and to order the succession, in the same way that any proprietor, out of his liberality, can freely and unconditionally make a gift of his property to another. Such a form of gift, not being qualified in any way, is the only true gift, being at once unconditional and irrevocable. Gifts burdened with obligations and hedged with conditions are not true gifts. Similarly sovereign power given to a prince charged with conditions is neither properly sovereign, nor absolute, unless the conditions of appointment are only such as are inherent in the laws of God and nature. . . .

If we insist however that absolute power means exemption from all law whatsoever, there is no prince in the world who can be regarded as sovereign, since all the princes of the earth are subject to the laws of God and of nature, and even to certain human laws common to all nations. On the other hand, it is possible for a subject who is neither a prince nor a ruler, to be exempted from all the laws, ordinances, and customs of the commonwealth. We have an example in Pompey the Great who was dispensed from the laws for five years, by express enactment of the Roman people, at the instance of the Tribune Gabinius. . . . But notwithstanding such exemptions from the operations of the law, the subject remains under the authority of him who exercises sovereign power, and owes him obedience.

On the other hand it is the distinguishing mark of the sovereign that he cannot in any way be subject to the commands of another, for it is he who makes law for the subject, abrogates law already made, and amends obsolete law. No one who is subject either to the law or to some other person can do this. That is why it is laid down in the civil law that the prince is above the law, for the word *law* in Latin implies the command of him who is invested with sovereign power. . . .

If the prince is not bound by the laws of his predecessors, still less can he be bound by his own laws. One may be subject to laws made by another, but it is impossible to bind oneself in any matter which is the subject of one's own free exercise of will. As the law says "there can be no obligation in any matter which proceeds from the free will of the undertaker." It follows of necessity that the king cannot be subject to his own laws. Just as, according to the canonists, the Pope can never tie his own hands, so the sovereign prince cannot bind himself, even if he wishes. For this reason edicts and ordinances conclude with the formula "for such is our good pleasure," thus intimating that the laws of a sovereign prince, even when founded on truth and right reason, proceed simply from his own free will.

It is far otherwise with divine and natural laws. All the princes of the earth are subject to them, and cannot contravene them without treason and rebellion against God. His yoke is upon them, and they must bow their heads in fear and reverence before His divine majesty. . . .

But if one sovereign prince promises another sovereign prince to keep the agreements entered into by his predecessors, he is bound to do so even if not under oath, if that other prince's interests are involved. If they are not, he is not bound either by a promise, or even by an oath.

The same holds good of promises made by the sovereign to the subject, even if the promises were made prior to his election (for this does not make the difference that many suppose). It is not that the prince is bound either by his own laws or those of his predecessors. But he is bound by the just covenants and promises he has made, whether under oath to do so or not, to exactly the same extent that a private individual is bound in like case. . . .

Edicts and ordinances therefore do not bind the ruler except in so far as they embody the principles of natural justice; that ceasing, the obligation ceases. But subjects are bound till the ruler has expressly abrogated the law, for it is a law both divine and natural that we should obey the edicts and ordinances of him whom God has set in authority over us, providing his edicts are not contrary to God's law. For just as the rearvassal owes an oath of fealty in respect of and against all others, saving his sovereign prince, so the subject owes allegiance to his sovereign prince in respect of and against all others, saving the majesty of God, who is lord of all the princes of this world. From this principle we can deduce that other rule, that the sovereign prince is bound by the covenants he makes either with his subjects, or some other prince. Just because he enforces the covenants and mutual engagements entered into by his subjects among themselves, he must be the mirror of justice in all his own acts. . . . He has a double obligation in this case. He is bound in the first place by the principles of natural equity, which require that conventions and solemn promises should be kept, and in the second place in the interests of his own good faith, which he ought to preserve even to his own disadvantage, because he is the formal guarantor to all his subjects of the mutual faith they owe one another. . . .

A distinction must therefore be made between right and law, for one implies what is equitable and the other what is commanded. Law is nothing else than the command of the sovereign in the exercise of his sovereign power. . . . They err who assert that in virtue of their sovereign power princes can do this.[1] It is rather the law of the jungle, an act of force and violence. For as we have shown above, absolute power only implies freedom in relation to positive laws, and not in relation to

[1] Confiscate property at will. — T. G. B.

the law of God. God has declared explicitly in His Law that it is not just to take, or even to covet, the goods of another. Those who defend such opinions are even more dangerous than those who act on them. They show the lion his claws, and arm princes under a cover of just claims. The evil will of a tyrant, drunk with such flatteries, urges him to an abuse of absolute power and excites his violent passions to the pitch where avarice issues in confiscation, desire in adultery, and anger in murder. . . .

Since then the prince has no power to exceed the laws of nature which God himself, whose image he is, has decreed, he cannot take his subjects' property without just and reasonable cause, that is to say by purchase, exchange, legitimate confiscation, or to secure peace with the enemy when it cannot be otherwise achieved. Natural reason instructs us that the public good must be preferred to the particular, and that subjects should give up not only their mutual antagonisms and animosities, but also their possessions, for the safety of the commonwealth. . . .

If justice is the end of the law, the law the work of the prince, and the prince the image of God, it follows of necessity that the law of the prince should be modelled on the law of God. . . .

BOOK SIX

Concerning distributive, commutative, and harmonic justice . . . [chapter vi]

A wise king ought therefore to govern his kingdom harmoniously, subtly combining nobles and commons, rich and poor with such skill as always to preserve some advantage for the noble over the commoner. For it is right that the gentleman who is as practiced in arms and in law as a commoner should be preferred to him in matters of justice and of war, or that the rich man, equal in all other respects to the poor one should be preferred in those offices which carry with them greater honour than profit. Both will then be content, for the rich man only looks for honour, but the poor man for profit. . . . There is no way of combining great and small, nobleman and commoner, rich and poor, save by giving estates, dignities, and benefices to those who deserve them. But deserts are various. If responsible and honourable charges were only given to the virtuous the commonwealth would always be in a state of confusion, seeing that such men are always few in number, and easily overcome by the rest. But in associating upright men now with nobles, now with rich citizens, even though these last may be quite devoid of virtue, they are flattered to be associated with those who possess it, while they in their turn are gratified to find themselves advanced to some honourable employment. Thus on the one hand the nobility are satisfied that birth is respected in the distribution of honours, on the other the commons are deeply gratified and feel themselves generally honoured. In fact they are so honoured when the son of a poor physician can become the Chancellor of a great kingdom, or the son of a poor soldier High Constable, as happened in the case of Michel de l'Hôpital and Bertrand du Guesclin among many others, whose virtues alone led to their promotion to the very highest offices. But all classes see with impatience the most unworthy promoted to the most responsible positions, though it is occasionally necessary to give some offices to incapable and unworthy persons, provided it is done so sparingly that their ignorance or vice cannot do any great harm in the position they hold. It is not sufficient to entrust finance to the most trustworthy, war to the most valiant, justice to the most upright, censure to the most incorruptible, work to the strongest, government to the wisest, religion to the most devout, as the principle of distributive justice requires, though this in fact cannot be achieved because of the scarcity of good men. To ensure a general harmony one must combine those who can supply one another's shortcomings. Otherwise there will be no harmony than if one sounded separately notes sweet in themselves, but only capable of producing a consonance when struck together. In doing this the prince reconciles his subjects to one another, and all alike to himself. . . .

The prince exalted above all his subjects, whose majesty does not admit of any division, represents the principle of unity, from which all the rest derive their force and cohesion. Below him are the three estates, which have always been disposed in the same way in all well-ordered commonwealths. The estate of the clergy is placed first because of its dignity in ministering to religion. It includes both nobles [bishops] and commoners [priests]. Next comes the military estate, which also includes nobles [officers] and commoners [soldiers]. Last there is the third estate of scholars, merchants, craftsmen, and peasants. Each of these three estates should have a share in public offices, benefices, jurisdictions, and honourable charges, each according to the merits and qualities of persons. Thus an admirable harmony will subsist between the subjects themselves, and the subjects and their prince. . . . Aristocratic and popular states also flourish and maintain a government. But they are not so well united and knit together as if they had a prince. He unites all parts and relates them one to another. . . . One can regard the three estates as characterized by prudence, courage, and temperance respectively. These three virtues complement each other, and that of the king, who supplies the rational and contemplative element. Such a form of commonwealth is harmonious and therefore admirable, for the union of its members depends on unity under a single ruler, on whom the effectiveness of all the rest depends. A sovereign prince is therefore indispensable, for it is his power which informs all the members of the commonwealth.

Botero

Giovanni Botero (1540–1617) was an Italian Jesuit, a man whose experience and ideals were distinct from those of Bodin (whose work influenced him) and poles apart from Machiavelli (whose work Botero intended to counter). Botero accepted Machiavelli's construct of the state, but he denied that the ruler must be unethical. Rather, said Botero, the ruler must be a man of justice and integrity, because the state is an ethical entity. Botero reinstated political morality, but he was never able to resolve the dilemma of the ethical ruler of the ethical state acting unethically. The thrust of his practical advice to the ruler was expediency, as the following selection, especially the part dealing with suppression of rebellion, illustrates. The effect, if not the intention, of the Reason of State *(1589) was to strengthen the moral position of absolutist monarchy.*

The State

BOOK ONE

1. REASON OF STATE DEFINED

State is a stable rule over a people and Reason of State is the knowledge of the means by which such a dominion may be founded, preserved and extended. Yet, although in the widest sense the term includes all these, it is concerned most nearly with preservation, and more nearly with extension than with foundation; for Reason of State assumes a ruler and a State (the one as artificer, the other as his material) whereas they are not assumed — indeed they are preceded — by foundation entirely and in part by extension. But the art of foundation and of extension is the same because the beginnings and continuations are of the same nature. And although all that is done to these purposes is said to be done for Reasons of State, yet this is said rather of such actions as cannot be considered in the light of ordinary reason. . . .

BOOK FOUR

1. HOW TO AVOID RIOTS AND REBELLIONS

It is not enough to possess the art of handling the people, for since this may prove ineffective the ruler must also see to it that the people cannot,

From Giovanni Botero, *The Reason of State*, trans. P. J. Waley and D. P. Waley (London, 1956), pp. 3, 82–83, 86, 111–16. Reprinted by permission of Routledge & Kegan Paul Ltd.

or at least does not, rise in revolt, disturbing the peace of the country and his own majesty. Above all, he must remove whatever may occasion and facilitate rebellion.

2. THE THREE SORTS OF PEOPLE WHO MAKE UP THE POPULATION OF CITIES

. In every state there are three sorts of people, the wealthy, the poor, and the middle class which lies between these extremes. The middle sort is usually the quietest and the easiest to govern, the two extremes are the hardest to govern, because the rich are drawn towards wrong-doing by the power that goes with wealth, while the poor are equally drawn to it by necessity. Solomon prayed to the Lord that he should neither be granted great wealth nor be allowed to fall into extreme poverty. Moreover those who have great riches and are distinguished by their noble birth and influential position are too proud and highly bred to suffer subordination, while the needy are as ready to obey an evil command as an honest one. The former are given to violence and unruliness and will attack their neighbour openly, while the latter turn to underhand forms of villainy. The rich are reluctant to submit to rule because they are fortunate, and Plato was unwilling to provide a legal code for the Cyrenians when they asked him for one on the grounds that it would be difficult to give laws to people who were so fortunately situated. The needy cannot live within the law because necessity, which oppresses them, knows no law. The middle rank are sufficiently wealthy to have no lack of what is required by their station, and yet their affluence is not such as to tempt them into ambitious schemes. They are usually friends of peace, contented with their station and neither exalted by ambition nor prostrated by despair; as Aristotle says, they are most inclined to virtue.[1] We may suppose, then, that these middle folk will be peaceful, and proceed to deal with the extremes and the problem of how they should be prevented from causing riots and rebellions.

3. OF POWERFUL MEN

There are three sorts of people whose power and authority are likely to make them suspect to the ruler. These are his own family and any others whose descent gives them a claim to the throne; the lords of important fiefs and of strategic towns; and any men who have won reputation and prestige by outstanding deeds in war or peace.

4. PRINCES OF THE BLOOD ROYAL

Rule is the greatest source of jealousy and often drives princes to the extremes of rage and fury. Such is the power of jealousy and ambition

---

[1] Aristotle, *Politics*, IV (1295).

over the minds of those dominated by them that they are deprived of their humanity and indeed almost of their human nature. When Alexander the Great set off on his Asiatic enterprise he caused all his relatives to be put to death. The Turkish rulers put their brothers to death on succeeding to the empire, while Amurath III even butchered a concubine of his father's who was pregnant. The kings of Ormuz,[2] before that kingdom came under Portuguese rule, used to deprive their relatives of their sight, and some of the emperors of Constantinople did the same. The kings of China, who were more humane, detested such cruelty and were content instead to confine those of the blood royal in noble and spacious quarters provided with every comfort and delight. . . .

5. OF FEUDAL BARONS

There is both good and bad in the feudal lords of a kingdom. The bad is their authority and power, which are suspect to the supreme ruler as presenting possible sources of aid or refuge to any rebels against his authority (which happened in the kingdom of Naples, where the Princes of Taranto and Salerno and the Dukes of Sessa and Rossano all played this part). The good consists in this, that these lords are, as it were, the bones and strength of the state which without them would be mere flesh and pulp, with no bone or sinew. Such a state would be likely to collapse when faced with an oppressive war or overwhelming defeat in battle or the death of its ruler, for the populace lacks men fitted for high rank by their birth and experience of authority, and may become so confused in the absence of decisive action and policy that they submit to their enemies. This has happened more than once in Egypt, and would happen in Turkey if it should please God that this enemy might once suffer defeat in battle. Kingdoms that have a numerous nobility seem on the other hand to be almost immortal: France and Persia are instances of this, for France had passed almost entirely under the rule of the kings of England, yet she recovered through the infinite strength of her nobles, while Persia was conquered first by the Turks and then by the Saracens, and yet has maintained her position through the valour of her many nobles. And has not Spain been freed from her Moorish servitude by the efforts and courage of her nobles?

Some will say that titled lords are good for the preservation of the country and its government but not for its kings, because just as they can strengthen the country and give heart to the populace so also they can trouble the ruler and make work for him. Of this there can be no doubt, if the ruler is too weak for the position he has to maintain, if he is incapable of greatness and unworthy of his fortune, if he has no sense

2 Ormuz, an island and port on the southern coast of Persia, was once a flourishing trading center: it was under Portuguese domination from 1514 to 1623.

of justice and no light of counsel, if in fact he is otherwise than we have described the ruler. But in this case he will not be troubled by his barons alone, but will be deceived by his counsellors and by his very jesters; he will not be a king but a pawn. . . .

9. How to suppress rebellious movements

However prudent the ruler may be, *necesse est ut eveniant scandala,*[3] and troubles are bound to arise, so we must also consider how rebellious movements may be pacified. Such movements are of two kinds, by the people against the prince and his ministers or by factions or discontented nobles. I must confess first that, just as not all illnesses of the human body are curable . . . so not all disorders of the body politic can be remedied. Kingdoms, and republics too, have their incurable diseases, and their mortal ones. Italy can provide an instance of this, for it was once so divided by the rival parties of Guelfs and Ghibellines that they utterly ravaged and ruined the country without hope of remedy. But, before suggesting what can be done, we must make a distinction between the different circumstances in which troubles may arise: when the ruler sees that he is in the stronger position he should adopt methods quite different from those suited to a ruler who finds himself weaker than the malcontents (and we should include in the latter category a ruler who believes his power to be equal to that of the rebels).

In the first case the ruler should use force and act quickly to eradicate the trouble at once, with as much secrecy as possible, so that the ringleaders will have been removed before the matter becomes generally known. But if the ruler sees that he is in danger, he must achieve victory by different tactics. At first he must yield and give way before the fury of the populace, for mob risings usually lack proper leadership and soon die down when their unity dissolves and with it their strength. The ruler should not move far from the scene of the troubles, as Henry III of France did during the riots at Paris,[4] because his absence diminishes the respect felt for him and gives courage to the crowd and its leaders; the revolutions in Flanders have shown this. . . . Just as a doctor can relieve the disordered humours of the human body by diverting them elsewhere with cauterizing and blood-letting, so a wise prince can placate an enraged people by leading it to war against an external enemy, or by some other means which will turn it from its original evil intention. . . . If the populace cannot all be placated at once, the ruler should find some means of dividing them up.

[3] A quotation from memory from Matthew XVIII : 7, "it must needs be that offences come."
[4] In 1588. — T. G. B.

When none of these remedies is effective it is better to grant the people all or part of what they demand rather than to come to blows. The two foundations on which all authority must be built are reputation and affection, and by yielding you at least retain the affection of your subjects, although your reputation may be diminished: naturally this is to be tried with those who are your subjects by birth rather than with those acquired by conquest. Other devices which may serve to increase your reputation are to appear to desire what you really cannot prevent, and to seem to grant benevolently something which is actually being snatched from you by force (like merchants who sometimes trade wherever the wind blows them when it has not brought them to the country they intended). . . . But such concessions should only involve things, not persons. It is hard to excuse a ruler who consents to hand over one of his ministers to an angry crowd, as Amurath King of the Turks did a few years ago. There is such a loss of dignity in this act that a prince should prefer to have his minister taken from him by force than to give him up. This, of course, supposes that he has been a good and faithful minister, and that it has been impossible to hide him, to help him to escape or to remove him from danger in any other way. It is an excellent thing to pretend to be unaware of some disorder if it can only be remedied by greater disorder. . . .

If the trouble comes from the barons, this may be the result either of a general conspiracy against the ruler, or of the formation of factions. The same remedies can be used against a baronial conspiracy as against the populace, and these have been described. It is easier to foster disunity among the barons than among the multitude, because it is simpler to win over one out of many than many out of an infinite number. . . . But if the nobles throw the kingdom into disorder by quarrels among themselves, owing to the followings they have acquired, then all depends upon whether the dispute concerns private or public matters. If it is a private matter, the parties concerned should be made to submit to judges or to specially appointed arbiters. The prince should be careful not to show favour to one side, lest he lose the support of the other. . . . If, on the other hand, the dispute concerns public affairs (which often conceal personal quarrels) the prince should put himself at the head of the better party, if he cannot quell the trouble or bring it to an end. He who believes that he can secure his power against the threat of such factions by a policy of "balance," backing the weaker against the stronger party, is mistaken. Such a policy was practised in France and it helped the factions to grow and flourish to such an extent that in time the whole kingdom was divided into two powerful parties, the king retaining very little except his title. . . .

I shall conclude this book with the statement that risings and civil wars which are not suppressed at the outset are very rarely put down later unless they end with the complete ruin of one of the parties involved (Roman history, as well as Flanders and France, provides examples of this), or in a change of rule. A tiny stream which can be crossed on foot becomes in time a powerful torrent: suspicion turns into hatred and discontent is transformed into rebellion and crime. If one side is considerably more powerful than the other it will not lay down its arms until it has brought its enemies to utter ruin, while if there is no such disparity the war will end with the exhaustion of both parties, each retaining what it had in the first instance. The height of human wisdom in matters of state is contained in the two words *principiis obsta*,[5] for usually *modicis rebus primi motus consedere. Omne malum nascens facile opprimitur: inveteratum fit robustius.*[6] No one begins to disturb the commonwealth with one great offence: but to overlook small things is to sap the foundation of great ones.

James I of England

James Stuart (James VI of Scotland, 1567–1625, and James I of England, 1603–1625) was the least successful monarch of absolutist inclinations of his day. It was not for want of learning, however, for James was a sound theorist of some articulateness. His problem was practice. The Scotland of his youth was dominated by the feudatories; the England of his later years possessed the most vital representative estates of any monarchy, Parliament. Opportunity avoided him, and his own political and personal shortcomings often frustrated his designs. The Trew Law of Free Monarchies was written in 1598, just as James attained a modicum of success in curbing the Scottish nobility, but only a few years before he succeeded his cousin Elizabeth on the English throne and largely turned his back on Scottish affairs for the rest of his reign. Unlike Bodin's treatise, James' places as much emphasis on the king's obligations as it does on the subject's duties. And in this emphasis it is an improvement on the non–divine-right but uncompromisingly absolutist Leviathan (1651) *of Thomas Hobbes.*

---

[5] Ovid, *Remedia Amoris*, 91: "oppose the beginning."

[6] Cicero, *Philippics*, V, 11: "the first stages in a movement consist of small things. All evils are easily put down at the start but gain strength with time."

The Trew Law of Free Monarchies: Or the Reciprock and Mutuall Duetie Betwixt a Free King, and His Naturall Subjects

AN ADVERTISEMENT

TO THE READER

Accept, I pray you (my deare countreymen) as thankefully this Pamphlet that I offer unto you, as lovingly it is written for your weale. I would be loath both to be faschious, and fectlesse: And therefore, if it be not sententious, at least it is short. It may be yee misse many things that yee looke for in it: But for excuse thereof, consider rightly that I onely lay downe herein the trew grounds, to teach you the right-way, without wasting time upon refuting the adversaries. And yet I trust, if ye will take narrow tent, ye shall finde most of their great gunnes payed home againe, either with contrary conclusions, or tacite objections, suppose in a dairned forme, and indirectly: For my intention is to instruct, and not irritat, if I may eschew it. The profite I would wish you to make of it, is, as well so to frame all your actions according to these grounds, as may confirme you in the course of honest and obedient Subjects to your King in all times coming, as also, when ye shall fall in purpose with any that shall praise or excuse the by-past rebellions that brake foorth either in this countrey, or in any other, ye shall herewith bee armed against their Sirene songs, laying their particular examples to the square of these grounds. Whereby yee shall soundly keepe the course of righteous Judgement, decerning wisely of every action onely according to the qualitie thereof, and not according to your pre-judged conceits of the committers: So shall ye, by reaping profit to your selves, turne my paine into pleasure. But least the whole Pamphlet runne out at the gaping mouth of this Preface, if it were any more enlarged; I end, with committing you to God, and me to your charitable censures.

As there is not a thing so necessarie to be knowne by the people of any land, next the knowledge of their God, as the right knowledge of their alleageance, according to the forme of governement established among them, especially in a Monarchie (which forme of government, as resembling the Divinitie, approacheth nearest to perfection, as all the learned and wise men from the beginning have agreed upon; Unitie being the perfection of all things,) So hath the ignorance, and (which is

From James I, *Workes* (London, 1616), pp. 191–95, 202–03.

worse) the seduced opinion of the multitude blinded by them, who thinke themselves able to teach and instruct the ignorants, procured the wracke and overthrow of sundry flourishing Common-wealths; and heaped heavy calamities, threatening utter destruction upon others. And the smiling successe, that unlawful rebellions have oftentimes had against Princes in aages past (such hath bene the misery, and iniquitie of the time) hath by way of practise strengthned many in their errour: albeit there cannot be a more deceivable argument; then to judge ay the justnesse of the cause by the event thereof; as hereafter shall be proved more at length. And among others, no Commonwealth, that ever hath bene since the beginning, hath had greater need of the trew knowledge of this ground, then this our so long disordered, and distracted Common-wealth hath: the misknowledge hereof being the onely spring, from whence have flowed so many endlesse calamities, miseries, and confusions, as is better felt by many, then the cause thereof well knowne, and deepely considered. The naturall zeale therefore, that I beare to this my native countrie, with the great pittie I have to see the so-long disturbance thereof for lacke of the trew knowledge of this ground (as I have said before) hath compelled me at last to breake silence, to discharge my conscience to you my deare country men herein, that knowing the ground from whence these your many endlesse troubles have proceeded, as well as ye have already too-long tasted the bitter fruites thereof, ye may by knowledge, and eschewing the cause escape, and divert the lamentable effects that ever necessarily follow thereupon. I have chosen then onely to set downe in this short Treatise, the trew grounds of the mutuall duetie, and alleageance betwixt a free and absolute Monarche, and his people; not to trouble your patience with answering the contrary propositions which some have not bene ashamed to set downe in writ, to the poysoning of infinite number of simple soules, and their owne perpetuall, and well deserved infamie: For by answering them, . . . which would rather have bred contentiousnesse among the readers (as they had liked or misliked) then sound instruction of the trewth: Which I protest to him that is the searcher of all hearts, is the onely marke that I shoot at herein.

First then, I will set downe the trew grounds, whereupon I am to build, out of the Scriptures, since Monarchie is the trew paterne of Divinitie, as I have already said: next, from the fundamental Lawes of our owne Kingdome, which nearest must concerne us: thirdly, from the law of Nature, by divers similitudes drawne out of the same: and will conclude syne by answering the most waighty and appearing incommodities that can be objected.

The Princes duetie to his Subjects is so clearly set downe in many places of the Scriptures, and so openly confessed by all the good Princes, according to their oath in their Coronation, as not needing to be long therein, I shall as shortly as I can runne through it.

Kings are called Gods by the propheticall King David, because they sit upon God his Throne in the earth, and have the count of their administration to give unto him. Their office is, *To minister Justice and Judgement to the people,* as the same David saith: *To advance the good, and punish the evill,* as he likewise saith: *To establish good Lawes to his people, and procure obedience to the same,* as divers good Kings of Judah did: *To procure the peace of the people,* as the same David saith: *To decide all controversies that can arise among them* as Salomon did: *To be the Minister of God for the weale of them that doe well, and as the minister of God, to take vengeance upon them that doe evill,* as S. Paul saith. And finally, *As a good Pastour, to goe out and in before his people* as is said in the first of Samuel: *That through the Princes prosperitie, the peoples peace may be procured,* as Jeremie saith.

And therefore in the Coronation of our owne Kings, as well as of every Christian Monarche they give their Oath, first to maintaine the Religion presently professed within their countrie, according to their lawes, whereby it is established, and to punish all those that should presse to alter, or disturbe the profession thereof; And next to maintaine all the lowable and good Lawes made by their predecessours: to see them put in execution, and the breakers and violaters thereof, to be punished, according to the tenour of the same: And lastly, to maintaine the whole countrey, and every state therein, in all their ancient Privileges and Liberties, as well against all forreine enemies, as among themselves: And shortly to procure the weale and flourishing of his people, not onely in maintaining and putting to execution the olde lowable lawes of the countrey, and by establishing of new (as necessitie and evill manners will require) but by all other meanes possible to fore-see and prevent all dangers, that are likely to fall upon them, and to maintaine concord, wealth, and civilitie among them, as a loving Father, and careful watchman, caring for them more then for himselfe, knowing himselfe to be ordained for them, and they not for him; and therefore countable to that great God, who placed him as his lieutenant over them, upon the perill of his soule to procure the weale of both soules and bodies, as farre as in him lieth, all of them that are committed to his charge. And this oath in the Coronation is the clearest, civill, and fundamentall Law, whereby the Kings office is properly defined.

By the Law of Nature the King becomes a naturall Father to all his Lieges at his Coronation: And as the Father of his fatherly duty is bound to care for the nourishing, education, and vertuous government of his children; even so is the king bound to care for all his subjects. As all the toile and paine that the father can take for his children, will be thought

light and well bestowed by him, so that the effect thereof redound to
their profite and weale; so ought the Prince to doe towards his people.
As the kindly father ought to foresee all inconvenients and dangers that
may arise towards his children, and though with the hazard of his owne
person presse to prevent the same; so ought the King towards his
people. . . .

And according to these fundamentall Lawes already alledged, we daily
see that in the Parliament (which is nothing else but the head Court of
the king and his vassals) the lawes are but craved by his subjects, and
onely made by him at their rogation, and with their advice: For albeit
the king make daily statutes and ordinances, enjoyning such paines thereto
as hee thinkes meet, without any advice of Parliament or estates; yet it
lies in the power of no Parliament, to make any kinde of Lawe or
Statute, without his Scepter be to it, for giving it the force of a Law. And
although divers changes have beene in other countries of the blood
Royall, and kingly house, the kingdome being reft by conquest from one
to another, as in our neighbour countrey in England, (which was never
in ours) yet the same ground of the kings right over all the land, and
subjects thereof remaineth alike in all other free Monarchies, as well as
in this: For when the Bastard of Normandie came into England, and
made himselfe king,[1] was it not by force, and with a mighty army? Where
he gave the Law, and tooke none, changed the Lawes, inverted the order
of governement, set downe the strangers his followers in many of the old
possessours roomes, as at this day well appeareth a great part of the
Gentlemen in England, beeing come of the Norman blood, and their old
Lawes, which to this day they are ruled by, are written in his language,
and not in theirs: And yet his successours have with great happinesse enjoyed the Crowne to this day; Whereof the like was also done by all them
that conquested them before.

And for conclusion of this point, that the king is over-lord over the
whole lands, it is likewise daily proved by the Law of our hoordes, of
want of Heires, and of Bastardies: For if a hoord be found under the
earth, because it is no more in the keeping or use of any person, it of the
law pertains to the king. If a person, inheritour of any lands or goods,
dye without any sort of heires, all his landes and goods returne to the
king. And if a bastard die unrehabled without heires of his bodie (which
rehabling onely lyes in the kings hands) all that hee hath likewise re-
turnes to the king. And as ye see it manifest, that the King is over-Lord
of the whole land: so is he Master over every person that inhabiteth the
same, having power over the life and death of every one of them: For
although a just Prince will not take the life of any of his subjects without
a cleare law; yet the same lawes whereby he taketh them, are made by

---

[1] William the Conqueror in 1066. — T. G. B.

himselfe or his predecessours; and so the power flowes alwaies from him selfe; as by daily experience we see, good and just Princes will from time to time make new lawes and statutes, adjoyning the penalties to the breakers thereof, which before the law was made, had beene no crime to the subject to have committed. Not that I deny the old definition of a King, and of a law; which makes the king to bee a speaking law, and the Law a dumbe king: for certainely a king that governes not by his lawe, can neither be countable to God for his administration, nor have a happy and established raigne: For albeit it be trew that I have at length prooved, that the King is above the law, as both the author and giver of strength thereto; yet a good king will not onely delight to rule his subjects by the lawe, but even will conforme himselfe in his owne actions thereunto, alwaies keeping that ground, that the health of the common-wealth be his chiefe lawe: And where he sees the lawe doubtsome or rigorous, hee may interpret or mitigate the same, lest otherwise *Summum jus* bee *summa injuria:* [2] And therefore generall lawes, made publikely in Parliament, may upon knowen respects to the King by his authoritie bee mitigated, and suspended upon causes onely knowen to him. . . .

The Cardinal-Ministers

From 1624 to 1661 French absolutism rested in the hands of two successive clerical-ministers, Cardinal Richelieu (1624–1642) and Cardinal Mazarin (1642–1661). Their red hats would have gladdened the heart of Botero, who urged the new monarchs to use the talents of the clergy, and their policies by and large would also have been satisfactory to him. Richelieu completed the bureaucratization of the French absolutist state, worked ceaselessly for the downfall of Hapsburg power in Spain, the Netherlands, and Germany, further depleted the power of the old nobility and advanced the fortunes of the new, and reduced Huguenot autonomy. Mazarin continued Richelieu's policies, staved off noble reaction in the Fronde, and handed on to his young masterward, Louis XIV, the most considerable absolutist structure in Europe. Louis completed the structure, not least by never again allowing any minister such power as the two cardinals had wielded. Cardinal de Retz (1614–1679), the author of the following passages, was a protégé of Mazarin, then a supporter of the Fronde and bitter enemy of Mazarin. He was not entirely fair to either cardinal, but his commentary illuminates the age of the great ministers of absolutism.

[2] Greatest justice be greatest injury. — T. G. B.

Richelieu and Mazarin

Henry IV,[1] who was not afraid of the laws, because he trusted in himself, showed he had a high esteem for them. The Duc de Rohan [2] used to say that Louis XIII [3] was jealous of his own authority because he was ignorant of its full extent, for the Maréchal d'Ancre [4] and M. de Luynes [5] were mere dunces, incapable of informing him. Cardinal de Richelieu, who succeeded them, collected all the wicked designs and blunders of the two last centuries to serve his grand purpose. He laid them down as proper maxims for establishing the King's authority, and, fortune seconding his designs by the disarming of the Protestants in France, by the victories of the Swedes, by the weakness of the Empire and of Spain, he established the most scandalous and dangerous tyranny that perhaps ever enslaved a State in the best constituted monarchy under the sun.

Custom, which has in some countries inured men even to broil as it were in the heat of the sun, has made things familiar to us which our forefathers dreaded more than fire itself. We no longer feel the slavery which they abhorred more for the interest of their King than for their own. Cardinal de Richelieu counted those things crimes which before him were looked upon as virtues. The Mirons, Harlays, Marillacs, Pibracs, and the Fayes, those martyrs of the State who dispelled more factions by their wholesome maxims than were raised in France by Spanish or British gold, were defenders of the doctrine for which the Cardinal de Richelieu confined Président Barillon in the prison of Amboise. And the Cardinal began to punish magistrates for advancing those truths which they were obliged by their oaths to defend at the hazard of their lives.

Our wise Kings, who understood their true interest, made the Parliament [6] the depositary of their ordinances, to the end that they might exempt themselves from part of the odium that sometimes attends the execution of the most just and necessary decrees. They thought it no disparagement to their royalty to be bound by them, — like unto God, who himself obeys the laws he has preordained. Ministers of State, who are generally so blinded by the splendour of their fortune as never to be content with what the laws allow, make it their business to overturn them; and Cardinal de Richelieu laboured at it more constantly than any other, and with equal application and imprudence. . . .

From *The Memoirs of Cardinal de Retz* (Paris, n.d.), pp. 96–98, 100–06.
  [1] 1589–1610. — T. G. B.
  [2] The Huguenot leader against Richelieu. — T. G. B.
  [3] 1610–1643. — T. G. B.
  [4] Concino Concini, assassinated in the Louvre, 1617.
  [5] Charles d'Albert, Duc de Luynes, Constable of France, died 1621.
  [6] Parlement of Paris — not a legislative body but a high court with power, at this time, to delay royal legislation. — T. G. B.

Cardinal de Richelieu . . . sacrificed everything to his interest. He would govern according to his own fancy, which scorned to be tied to rules, even in cases where it would have cost him nothing to observe them. And he acted his part so well that, if his successor had been a man of his abilities, I doubt not that the title of Prime Minister, which he was the first to assume, would have been as odious in France in a little time as were those of the Maire du Palais and the Comte de Paris. But by the providence of God, Cardinal Mazarin, who succeeded him, was not capable of giving the State any jealousy of his usurpation. As these two ministers contributed chiefly, though in a different way, to the civil war,[7] I judge it highly necessary to give you the particular character of each, and to draw a parallel between them.

Cardinal de Richelieu was well descended; his merit sparkled even in his youth. He was taken notice of at the Sorbonne, and it was very soon observed that he had a strong genius and a lively fancy. He was commonly happy in the choice of his parties. He was a man of his word, unless great interests swayed him to the contrary, and in such a case he was very artful to preserve all the appearances of probity. He was not liberal, yet he gave more than he promised, and knew admirably well how to season all his favours. He was more ambitious than was consistent with the rules of morality, although it must be owned that, whenever he dispensed with them in favour of his extravagant ambition, his great merit made it almost excusable. He neither feared dangers nor yet despised them, and prevented more by his sagacity than he surmounted by his resolution. He was a hearty friend, and even wished to be beloved by the people; but though he had civility, a good aspect, and all the other qualifications to gain that love, yet he still wanted something — I know not what to call it — which is absolutely necessary in this case. By his power and royal state he debased and swallowed up the personal majesty of the King. He distinguished more judiciously than any man in the world between bad and worse, good and better, which is a great qualification in a minister. He was too apt to be impatient at mere trifles when they had relation to things of moment; but those blemishes, owing to his lofty spirit, were always accompanied with the necessary talent of knowledge to make amends for those imperfections. He had religion enough for this world. His own good sense, or else his inclination, always led him to the practice of virtue if his self-interest did not bias him to evil, which, whenever he committed it, he did so knowingly. He extended his concern for the State no further than his own life, though no minister ever did more than he to make the world believe he had the same regard for the future. In a word, all his vices were such that they received a lustre from his great fortune, because they were such as could have no other instru-

---

[7] The Fronde. — T. G. B.

ments to work with but great virtues. You will easily conceive that a man who possessed such excellent qualities, and appeared to have as many more — which he had not — found it no hard task to preserve that respect among mankind which freed him from contempt, though not from hatred.

Cardinal Mazarin's character was the reverse of the former; his birth was mean, and his youth scandalous. He was thrashed by one Moretto, a goldsmith of Rome, as he was going out of the amphitheatre, for having played the sharper. He was a captain in a foot regiment, and Bagni, his general, told me that while he was under his command, which was but three months, he was only looked upon as a cheat. By the interest of Cardinal Antonio Barberini, he was sent as Nuncio Extraordinary to France, which office was not obtained in those days by fair means. He so tickled Chavigni by his loose Italian stories that he was shortly after introduced to Cardinal de Richelieu, who made him Cardinal with the same view which, it is thought, determined the Emperor Augustus to leave the succession of the Empire to Tiberius. He was still Richelieu's obsequious, humble servant, notwithstanding the purple.[8] The Queen making choice of him, for want of another, his pedigree was immediately derived from a princely family. The rays of fortune having dazzled him and everybody about him, he rose, and they glorified him for a second Richelieu, whom he had the impudence to ape, though he had nothing of him; for what his predecessor counted honourable he esteemed scandalous. He made a mere jest of religion. He promised everything without scruple; at the same time he intended to perform nothing. He was neither good-natured nor cruel, for he never remembered good offices or bad ones. He loved himself too well, which is natural to a sordid soul; and feared himself too little, the true characteristic of those that have no regard for their reputation. He foresaw an evil well enough, because he was usually timid, but never applied a suitable remedy, because he had more fear than wisdom. He had wit, indeed, together with a most insinuating address and a gay, courtly behaviour; but a villainous heart appeared constantly through all, to such a degree as betrayed him to be a fool in adversity and a knave in prosperity. In short, he was the first minister that could be called a complete trickster, for which reason his administration, though successful and absolute, never sat well upon him, for contempt — the most dangerous disease of any State — crept insensibly into the Ministry and easily diffused its poison from the head to the members.

You will not wonder, therefore, that there were so many unlucky cross rubs in an administration which so soon followed that of Cardinal de Richelieu and was so different from it. It is certain that the imprisonment

---

8 Purple was the color of a cardinal's dress. — T. G. B.

of M. de Beaufort impressed the people with a respect for Mazarin, which the lustre of his purple would never have procured from private men. Ondedei (since Bishop of Fréjus) told me that the Cardinal jested with him upon the levity of the French nation on this point, and that at the end of four months the Cardinal had set himself up in his own opinion for a Richelieu, and even thought he had greater abilities. It would take up volumes to record all his faults, the least of which were very important in one respect which deserves a particular remark. As he trod in the steps of Cardinal de Richelieu, who had completely abolished all the ancient maxims of government, he went in a path surrounded with precipices, which Richelieu was aware of and took care to avoid. But Cardinal Mazarin made no use of those props by which Richelieu kept his footing. For instance, though Cardinal de Richelieu affected to humble whole bodies and societies, yet he studied to oblige individuals, which is sufficient to give you an idea of all the rest. . . .

Cardinal de Richelieu managed the kingdom as mountebanks do their patients, with violent remedies which put strength into it; but it was only a convulsive strength, which exhausted its vital organs. Cardinal Mazarin, like a very unskilful physician, did not observe that the vital organs were decayed, nor had he the skill to support them by the chemical preparations of his predecessor; his only remedy was to let blood, which he drew so plentifully that the patient fell into a lethargy, and our medicaster was yet so stupid as to mistake this lethargy for a real state of health. The provinces, abandoned to the rapine of the superintendents, were stifled, as it were, under the pressure of their heavy misfortunes, and the efforts they made to shake them off in the time of Richelieu added only to their weight and bitterness. The Parliaments, which had so lately groaned under tyranny, were in a manner insensible to present miseries by a too fresh and lively remembrance of their past troubles. The grandees, who had for the most part been banished from the kingdom, were glad to have returned, and therefore took their fill of ease and pleasure. If our quack had but humoured this universal indolence with soporifics, the general drowsiness might have continued much longer, but thinking it to be nothing but natural sleep, he applied no remedy at all. The disease gained strength, grew worse and worse, the patient awakened, Paris became sensible of her condition; she groaned, but nobody minded it, so that she fell into a frenzy, whereupon the patient became raving mad.[9]

9 The insurrection called the Fronde, 1648–1653. — T. G. B.

ABSOLUTISM VERSUS OLIGARCHY: ENGLAND AND THE DUTCH REPUBLIC

Chapter 10

Alone among the states of Western Europe, England and the Dutch Republic resisted the advance of absolutism in the early seventeenth century. The resistance was stout enough, to the point of revolution in England, to make absolutism forever untenable in both countries. This was an extraordinary feat in the age of absolutist monarchy, full of potential for the evolution of constitutional theory and practice in the next two centuries and beyond. In an age when revolution was unthinkable, condemned by the whole spectrum of opinion, England underwent the first modern revolution of the European world. In an age when republicanism was a dreadful aberration and the sure symptom of fatal weakness, the Dutch maintained their republic, withstood the greatest powers of the age, and built a commercial and colonial empire that rivaled those of Spain and France.

England and the Dutch Republic in some ways were on parallel courses. Both were Protestant, and their Protestantism involved the Calvinist ambivalence toward the "civil magistrate." Both were rising colonial and naval powers, with a seaward rather than a landward bent, with industry as the flesh and commerce as the blood of their beings. In both, the legal and social restrictions on economic endeavor and social mobility comprised in serfdom had long since lost effectiveness. In neither had powerful feudatories survived the sixteenth century, albeit for very different reasons. In both, the representative institutions of the estates remained unimpaired — indeed, had gathered strength over the sixteenth century and had retained the essential powers of sharing with the executive in making laws and raising revenue. In both, the representative institutions represented the interests of a new oligarchy of wealth, talent, education, and involvement in the routine of local governmental administration.

The resistance to the absolutist urge of the Stuart monarchs in

England and the monarchical tendency of the Orange stadtholders in the Dutch Republic centered respectively in Parliament and in the States-General. So long as the executive required new laws and extra revenue, he required the cooperation of the representative institution. At no time in the first half of the seventeenth century, or later, was the executive in either country able to do without that cooperation for very long. The routine revenues of the English king were insufficient to meet his and his government's expenses in peacetime, and, save for the first two decades of James I's reign, war and preparations for war demanded even greater revenue. The stadtholder was in a similar, though more pressing situation because of the necessity to be on a constant war footing against Spain.

In order to obtain cooperation, the executive in both nations had to make substantial concessions in policy to the representatives. In England, these concessions went beyond policy to trench upon the powers of the monarch himself. The Petition of Right in 1628 climaxed a series of such concessions since 1621 that had weakened the position of James I, and afterward Charles I, and had given the political initiative to Parliament. It followed an unpopular and unsuccessful war fought on two fronts by the king's ambitious and hated minister, the duke of Buckingham, in which lack of revenue pressed the king to raise money by forced loans of questionable legality and to billet troops on householders in order to keep the army intact. The oligarchy would not support what it did not want, and it was prepared to make substantial inroads on the executive's powers to prevent a recurrence of what it considered an "unconstitutional" and intolerable exercise of the royal will.

Despite obvious differences, the oligarchical element in both countries was remarkably similar. In England, the numerous, substantial landed gentry, a broad-based aristocracy of new money, educated to a high degree, governed the counties as justices of the peace, deputy lieutenants (in command of the militia), and sheriffs, who controlled elections to the lower house of Parliament and furnished the bulk of its members, even those ostensibly representing the towns. In the Dutch Republic, the numerous merchants, again a broad-based aristocracy of new money, with considerable education, governed the towns of the seven provinces and represented the towns in the provincial States, which in turn furnished the members of the States-General. The description by Sir William Temple, an English oligarch, of the Dutch oligarchs contains a nice touch not lacking a tinge of self-portraiture.

Charles I's attempt to rule without Parliament from 1629 to 1640 proved disastrous. He had to rely on the oligarchy in its local capacity to execute his policy and raise revenue. The resistance of his otherwise neglected northern subjects, the Scots, to the potential curtailment of their Calvinist religious observances raised a rebellion that forced him to summon the English Parliament. With almost total unanimity it forced concessions from him that were really more than he could concede in faith and destroyed his chief minister and forced out his other councillors. With less unanimity, Parliament took up the long-standing demand of the neo-Calvinist Puritans for further reform of the Church of England. When Charles's attempted countercoup against the parliamentary leadership failed, the king withdrew to the north, summoned his loyal subjects to attend him — a great many members of Parliament did — and civil war began in 1642.

The civil war of the 1640's was revolution, political primarily, social secondarily. The only effective force that came from the civil war was the victorious parliamentarian army; the only effective control of that force was in the hands of its general, Oliver Cromwell. The army became the classical revolutionary innovator of change in state and church. It purged Parliament, forced the establishment of a republic, brought the king to trial, and executed him. In his trial, the king's refusal to admit the constitutionality of his judges ended, following his sentence, with the prophetic words, "I am not suffered to speak, expect what justice other people may have."

Charles I's prophecy came true during the eleven years of republican rule. Cromwell was never able to find a satisfactory base for legitimate rule. He was first and foremost an oligarch, sharing with the gentry who had fought with him and the gentry against whom he had fought a deep commitment to the rights and liberties of Englishmen, to the sacredness of property, and to the inviolability of governance with Parliament. He was, secondarily, a revolutionary general required to maintain a tenuous control over a potentially uncontrollable army bent on a course of radical political and religious change. His deep religious faith was of his substance, and it reinforced his conservative nature more than it eased his conscience in radical acts done by necessity. Throughout his rule he sought to rule by Parliament, but his Parliaments represented none but themselves, least of all Cromwell. His forbearance, his essential conservatism, his unwillingness to loose the army for a holocaust of repression determined that the revolution would last no longer than he did, the republic hardly longer.

The restoration of Charles II in 1660 was not the restoration of an absolutist monarch. The machinery of absolutism had been effectively dismantled. Above all the oligarchy was firmly entrenched, and it had extended the invitation to the exiled king.

"Let Right Be Done"

The Petition of Right, hotly debated in Parliament and with great reluctance given the royal assent by Charles I that made it law, has been hailed as a landmark in the growth of English liberty. It was invested with this importance later; at the time, it was a moderate attempt to restrict nonparliamentary taxation, billeting of troops in private houses, and martial law over troops. It was moved by the parliamentary opposition to the war against Spain and France conducted by the king's minister and favorite, the duke of Buckingham. The king assented to the unusual "petition" because it was the only way he could get some of the revenue needed for the war. In the coming years he ignored its provisions.

The citation of older statutes in the Petition indicates the heavy use of precedent, including the Magna Carta, in buttressing the Parliament's erstwhile constitutional position. In fact, the weight of precedent was on the king's side.

The Petition of Right, 1628

The Petition exhibited to his Majesty by the Lords Spiritual and Temporal and Commons in this present Parliament assembled concerning divers rights and liberties of the subject.

To the King's Most Excellent Majesty

Humbly show unto our Sovereign Lord the King the Lords Spiritual and Temporal and Commons in Parliament assembled, that whereas it is declared and enacted by a statute made in the time of the reign of King Edward the First commonly called Statutum de Tallagio non Concedendo [1] that no tallage or aid should be laid or levied by the King or his heirs in this realm without the good will and assent of the archbishops, bishops, earls, barons, knights, burgesses and other the freemen of the commonalty of this realm; and by authority of Parliament holden in the five and twentieth year of the reign of King Edward the Third [2] it is declared and enacted, that from henceforth no person should be compelled to make any loans to the King against his will because such loans were against reason and the franchise of the land, and by other laws of this realm it is provided that none should be charged by any charge or

3 Charles I, c. 1, *Statutes of the Realm*, vol. 5 (London, 1819), pp. 23–24.
1 1297. — T. G. B.
2 1351–1352. — T. G. B.

imposition called a benevolence nor by such like charge, by which the statutes before mentioned and other the good laws and statutes of this realm your subjects have inherited this freedom, that they should not be compelled to contribute to any tax, tallage, aid or other like charge not set by common consent in Parliament.

II. Yet, nevertheless of late divers commissions directed to sundry commissioners in several counties with instructions have issued, by means whereof your people have been in divers places assembled and required to lend certain sums of money unto your Majesty, and many of them upon their refusal so to do have had an oath administered unto them not warrantable by the laws or statutes of this realm, and have been constrained to become bound to make appearance and give attendance before your Privy Council and in other places; and others of them have been therefore imprisoned, confined, and sundry other ways molested and disquieted, and divers other charges have been laid and levied upon your people in several counties by Lord Lieutenants, Deputy Lieutenants, Commissioners for Musters, Justices of Peace and others by command or direction from your Majesty or your Privy Council against the laws and free customs of the realm.

III. And where also by the statute called the Great Charter of the Liberties of England it is declared and enacted, that no freeman may be taken or imprisoned or be disseised of his freehold or liberties or his free customs or be outlawed or exiled or in any manner destroyed, but by the lawful judgement of his peers or by the law of the land.[3]

IV. And in the eight and twentieth year of the reign of King Edward the Third [4] it was declared and enacted by authority of Parliament, that no man, of what estate or condition that he be, should be put out of his land or tenement, nor taken, nor imprisoned, nor disherited, nor put to death without being brought to answer by due process of law.

V. Nevertheless against the tenor of the said statutes and other the good laws and statutes of your realm to that end provided, divers of your subjects have of late been imprisoned without any cause shown; and when for their deliverance they were brought before your justices by your Majesty's writ of habeas corpus there to undergo and receive as the Court should order, and their Keepers commanded to certify the causes of their detainer, no cause was certified, but that they were detained by your Majesty's special command signified by the Lords of your Privy Council, and yet were returned back to several prisons without being charged with any thing to which they might make answer according to the law.

VI. And whereas of late great companies of soldiers and mariners have

[3] Magna Carta, clause 39. — T. G. B.
[4] 1354. — T. G. B.

been dispersed into divers counties of the realm, and the inhabitants against their will have been compelled to receive them into their houses, and there to suffer them to sojourn against the laws and customs of this realm and to the great grievance and vexation of the people.

VII. And whereas also by authority of Parliament in the five and twentieth year of the reign of King Edward the Third [5] it is declared and enacted that no man should be forejudged of life and limb against the form of the Great Charter and the law of the land; and by the said Great Charter, and other the laws and statutes of this your realm, no man ought to be adjudged to death but by the laws established in this your realm, either by the customs of the same realm or by Act of Parliament, and whereas no offender of what kind soever is exempted from the proceedings to be used and punishments to be inflicted by the laws and statutes of this your realm; nevertheless of late time divers commissions under your Majesty's great seal have issued forth, by which certain persons have been assigned and appointed commissioners with power and authority to proceed within the land according to the justice of martial law against such soldiers or mariners or other dissolute persons joining with them as should commit any murder, robbery, felony, mutiny or other outrage or misdemeanour whatsoever, and by such summary course and order as is agreeable to martial law and as is used in armies in time of war to proceed to the trial and condemnation of such offenders, and them to cause to be executed and put to death according to the law martial.

By pretext whereof some of your Majesty's subjects have been by some of the said commissioners put to death, when and where, if by the laws and statutes of the land they had deserved death, by the same laws and statutes also they might and by no other ought to have been judged and executed.

And also sundry grievous offenders by colour thereof claiming an exemption have escaped the punishments due to them by the laws and statutes of this your realm, by reason that divers of your officers and ministers of justice have unjustly refused or forborne to proceed against such offenders according to the same laws and statutes upon pretence that the said offenders were punishable only by martial law and by authority of such commissions as aforesaid. Which commissions and all others of like nature are wholly and directly contrary to the said laws and statutes of this your realm.

VIII. They do therefore humbly pray your most excellent Majesty that no man hereafter be compelled to make or yield any gift, loan, benevolence, tax or such like charge without common consent by Act of Parliament, and that none be called to make answer or take such oath or to give attendance or be confined or otherwise molested or disquieted con-

[5] 1351–1352. — T. G. B.

cerning the same or for refusal thereof. And that no freeman in any such manner as is before mentioned be imprisoned or detained. And that your Majesty would be pleased to remove the said soldiers and mariners, and that your people may not be so burdened in time to come. And that the aforesaid commissions for proceeding by martial law may be revoked and annulled. And that hereafter no commissions of like nature may issue forth to any person or persons whatsoever to be executed as aforesaid, lest by colour of them any of your Majesty's subjects be destroyed or put to death contrary to the laws and franchises of the land.

All which they most humbly pray of your most excellent Majesty as their rights and liberties according to the laws and statutes of this realm, and that your Majesty would also vouchsafe to declare that the awards, doings, and proceedings to the prejudice of your people in any of the premises shall not be drawn hereafter into consequence or example. And that your Majesty would be also graciously pleased for the further comfort and safety of your people to declare your royal will and pleasure, that in the thing aforesaid all your officers and ministers shall serve you according to the laws and statutes of this realm as they tender the honour of your Majesty and the prosperity of this kingdom.

[King Charles I's reply]. Let right be done as it is desired.

The Trial of Charles Stuart, 1649

The trial before a hastily assembled tribunal, the condemnation, and the execution of Charles I shocked Europe. Death in battle, forced abdication and subsequent murder, and assassination were accepted as the hazards of the crowned head. Perversion of the forms of legal procedure to destroy an anointed king, who was himself the fount of law, was novel and terrifying. Probably a majority of his subjects found it so. There was no concealing the revulsion of the crowd of Londoners, heartily sympathetic to the parliamentarian cause and inured to public executions, that watched his head fall on January 30, 1649. He died nobly. More significantly, his death raised an insurmountable obstacle to the legitimacy of the republican regime that was instituted a little more than a month later. Charles' reasons for not recognizing the competency of the tribunal that condemned him were too sound in law and history to be dismissed by even his most virulent opponents. His death and those reasons haunted English statecraft for centuries to come; they haunted Cromwell and his regime as long as both lasted.

Ordinance Establishing a Tribunal to Try the King, January 6, 1649

Whereas it is notorious that Charles Stuart, the now King of England, not content with the many encroachments which his predecessors had made upon the people in their rights and freedom, hath had a wicked design totally to subvert the ancient and fundamental laws and liberties of this nation, and in their place to introduce an arbitrary and tyrannical government, and that besides all other evil ways and means to bring his design to pass, he hath prosecuted it with fire and sword, levied and maintained a civil war in the land, against the Parliament and kingdom; whereby this country hath been miserably wasted, the public treasure exhausted, trade decayed, thousands of people murdered, and infinite other mischiefs committed; for all which high and treasonable offences the said Charles Stuart might long since have justly been brought to exemplary and condign punishment: whereas also the Parliament, well hoping that the restraint and imprisonment of his person, after it had pleased God to deliver him into their hands, would have quieted the distempers of the kingdom, did forbear to proceed judicially against him, but found, by sad experience, that such their remissness served only to encourage him and his accomplices in the continuance of their evil practices, and in raising new commotions, rebellions and invasions: for prevention therefore of the like or greater inconveniences, and to the end no Chief Officer or Magistrate whatsoever may hereafter presume, traitorously and maliciously, to imagine or contrive the enslaving or destroying of the English nation, and to expect impunity for so doing; be it enacted and ordained by the (Lords and) Commons in Parliament assembled, and it is hereby enacted and ordained by the authority thereof, that the Earls of Kent, Nottingham, Pembroke, Denbigh and Mulgrave, the Lord Grey of Wark, Lord Chief Justice Rolle of the King's Bench, Lord Chief Justice St. John of the Common Pleas, and Lord Chief Baron Wylde, the Lord Fairfax, Lieutenant-General Cromwell, and others [in all about 136], shall be and are hereby appointed and required to be Commissioners and Judges for the hearing, trying and judging of the said Charles Stuart; and the said Commissioners, or any twenty or more of them, shall be, and are hereby authorised and constituted an High Court of Justice, to meet and sit at such convenient times and place as by the said Commissioners, or the major part, or twenty or more of them, under their hands and seals, shall be appointed and notified by proclamation in the Great Hall or Palace-Yard of Westminster; and to adjourn from time to time, and from place to place, as the said High Court, or the major part thereof, at meeting shall hold fit; and to take order for the charging

From John Rushworth, *Historical Collections*, vol. 7, 2d ed. (London, 1721), pp. 1379–80.

of him, the said Charles Stuart, with the crimes and treasons above mentioned, and for receiving his personal answer thereunto, and for examination of witnesses upon oath (which the Court hath hereby authority to administer) or otherwise, and taking any other evidence concerning the same; and thereupon, or in default of such answer, to proceed to final sentence according to justice and the merit of the cause; and such final sentence to execute, or cause to be executed, speedily and impartially.

And the said Court is hereby authorised and required to choose and appoint all such officers, attendants and other circumstances as they, or the major part of them, shall in any sort judge necessary or useful for the orderly and good managing of the premises; and Thomas Lord Fairfax the General, and all officers and soldiers under his command, and all officers of justice and other well-affected persons, are hereby authorised and required to be aiding and assisting unto the said Court in the due execution of the trust hereby committed unto them; provided that this Act, and the authority hereby granted, do continue in force for the space of one month from the date of the making thereof, and no longer.

The King Denies the Tribunal's Legality and Jurisdiction, January 23, 1649

Having already made my protestations, not only against the illegality of this pretended Court, but also, that no earthly power can justly call me (who am your King) in question as a delinquent, I would not any more open my mouth upon this occasion, more than to refer myself to what I have spoken, were I in this case alone concerned: but the duty I owe to God in the preservation of the true liberty of my people will not suffer me at this time to be silent: for, how can any free-born subject of England call life or anything he possesseth his own, if power without right daily make new, and abrogate the old fundamental laws of the land which I now take to be the present case? Wherefore when I came hither, I expected that you would have endeavoured to have satisfied me concerning these grounds which hinder me to answer to your pretended impeachment. But since I see that nothing I can say will move you to it (though negatives are not so naturally proved as affirmatives) yet I will show you the reason why I am confident you cannot judge me, nor indeed the meanest man in England: for I will not (like you) without showing a reason, seek to impose a belief upon my subjects.

There is no proceeding just against any man, but what is warranted, either by God's laws or the municipal laws of the country where he lives. Now I am most confident this day's proceeding cannot be warranted by God's laws; for, on the contrary, the authority of obedience unto Kings is clearly warranted, and strictly commanded in both the Old and New Testament, which, if denied, I am ready instantly to prove.

And for the question now in hand, there it is said, that "where the word of a King is, there is power; and who may say unto him, what dost thou?" Eccles., viii. 4. Then for the law of this land, I am no less confident, that no learned lawyer will affirm that an impeachment can lie against the King, they all going in his name: and one of their maxims is, that the King can do no wrong. Besides, the law upon which you ground your proceedings, must either be old or new: if old, show it; if new, tell what authority, warranted by the fundamental laws of the land, hath made it, and when. But how the House of Commons can erect a Court of Judicature, which was never one itself (as is well known to all lawyers) I leave to God and the world to judge. And it were full as strange, that they should pretend to make laws without King or Lords' House, to any that have heard speak of the laws of England.

And admitting, but not granting, that the people of England's commission could grant your pretended power, I see nothing you can show for that; for certainly you never asked the question of the tenth man in the kingdom, and in this way you manifestly wrong even the poorest ploughman, if you demand not his free consent; nor can you pretend any colour for this your pretended commission, without the consent at least of the major part of every man in England of whatsoever quality or condition, which I am sure you never went about to seek, so far are you from having it. Thus you see that I speak not for my own right alone, as I am your King, but also for the true liberty of all my subjects, which consists, not in the power of government, but in living under such laws, such a government, as may give themselves the best assurance of their lives, and property of their goods; nor in this must or do I forget the privileges of both Houses of Parliament, which this day's proceedings do not only violate, but likewise occasion the greatest breach of their public faith that (I believe) ever was heard of, with which I am far from charging the two Houses; for all the pretended crimes laid against me bear date long before this Treaty at Newport, in which I having concluded as much as in me lay, and hopefully expecting the Houses' agreement thereunto, I was suddenly surprised and hurried from thence as a prisoner; upon which account I am against my will brought hither, where since I am come, I cannot but to my power defend the ancient laws and liberties of this kingdom, together with my own just right. Then for anything I can see, the higher House is totally excluded; and for the House of Commons, it is too well known that the major part of them are detained or deterred from sitting; so as if I had no other, this were sufficient for me to protest against the lawfulness of your pretended Court. Besides all this, the peace of the kingdom is not the least in my thoughts; and what hope of settlement is there, so long as power reigns without rule or law, changing the whole frame of that government under which this kingdom hath flourished for many hundred years? (nor will I say what will fall out in case this lawless, unjust proceeding against me do go on) and believe it, the Commons of England will not thank you for this change; for they will remember how happy they have been of late years under the reigns of Queen Elizabeth, the King my father,[1] and myself, until the beginning of these unhappy troubles, and will have cause to doubt, that they shall never be so happy under any new: and by this time it will be too sensibly evident, that the arms I took up were only to defend the fundamental laws of this kingdom against those who have supposed my power hath totally changed the ancient government.

Thus, having showed you briefly the reasons why I cannot submit to your pretended authority, without violating the trust which I have from God for the welfare and liberty of my people, I expect from you either clear reasons to convince my judgment, showing me that I am in an error (and then truly I will answer) or that you will withdraw your proceedings.

This I intended to speak in Westminster Hall on Monday, January 22, but against reason was hindered to show my reasons.

The Tribunal Sentences Charles Stuart, January 27, 1649

Whereas the Commons of England assembled in Parliament, have by their late Act intituled an Act of the Commons of England assembled in Parliament, for erecting an High Court of Justice for the trying and judging of Charles Stuart, King of England, authorised and constituted us an High Court of Justice for the trying and judging of the said Charles Stuart for the crimes and treasons in the said Act mentioned; by virtue whereof the said Charles Stuart hath been three several times convented before this High Court, where the first day, being Saturday, the 20th of January instant, in pursuance of the said Act, a charge of high treason and other high crimes was, in the behalf of the people of England, exhibited against him, and read openly unto him, wherein he was charged, that he, the said Charles Stuart, being admitted King of England, and therein trusted with a limited power to govern by, and according to the law of the land, and not otherwise; and by his trust, oath, and office, being obliged to use the power committed to him for the good and benefit of the people, and for the preservation of their rights and liberties; yet, nevertheless, out of a wicked design to erect and uphold in himself an unlimited and tyrannical power to rule according to his will, and to

[1] James I. — T. G. B.

From John Rushworth, *Historical Collections*, vol. 7, 2d ed. (London, 1721), pp. 1418–19, 1425.

overthrow the rights and liberties of the people, and to take away and make void the foundations thereof, and of all redress and remedy of misgovernment, which by the fundamental constitutions of this kingdom were reserved on the people's behalf in the right and power of frequent and successive Parliaments, or national meetings in Council; he, the said Charles Stuart, for accomplishment of such his designs, and for the protecting of himself and his adherents in his and their wicked practices, to the same end hath traitorously and maliciously levied war against the present Parliament, and people therein represented, as with the circumstances of time and place is in the said charge more particularly set forth; and that he hath thereby caused and procured many thousands of the free people of this nation to be slain. . . .

[He is author of the] unnatural, cruel, and bloody wars, and therein guilty of high treason, and of the murders, rapines, burnings, spoils, desolations, damage, and mischief to this nation acted and committed in the said war, and occasioned thereby. For all which treasons and crimes this Court doth adjudge that he, the said Charles Stuart, as a tyrant, traitor, murderer, and public enemy to the good people of this nation, shall be put to death by the severing of his head from his body.

[After the sentence was read], His Majesty then said, Will you hear me a word, Sir?

PRESIDENT OF THE COURT. Sir, you are not to be heard after the sentence.

HIS MAJESTY. No, Sir?

PRESIDENT. No, Sir, by your favour, Sir. Guards, withdraw your prisoner.

HIS MAJESTY. I may speak after sentence, by your favour, Sir, I may speak after sentence, ever. By your favour, hold — the sentence, Sir — I say, Sir, I do — I am not suffered to speak, expect what justice other people may have . . .

God's "Miserable and Wretched Creature": England's Lord Protector

Oliver Cromwell, Esquire, of Huntingdonshire (1599–1658) remains the most complex figure in English history and the most controversial. His enemies recognized his greatness as they vilified him, his friends denigrated him as they praised him. His career in Parliament, on the battlefield, as republican leader, and later as Lord Protector was astonishing to contemporaries and bewildering to historians. So too was his character, especially his almost mystical religious devotion. The latter was not unique, for it moved many of his fellows, but it makes assessment of Cromwell as general and politician doubly difficult. Cromwell was an incomparable leader of men, and the English revolution became his revolution by force of his personality and astuteness. It died with him by virtue of his will that it should not continue. He could govern the army, he could control the clergy, he could repress the Royalists, but he could not manage even the weakest Parliament. Ruthless and uncompromising, convinced of his rightness and his "election," he lacked the one urge essential in the successful despot: the desire to destroy all existing institutions or to pervert them to his own ends. He would not take the crown (hence the title Lord Protector), he would not govern without Parliament, he would not destroy the law and the courts. He did not destroy the fabric of English government.

Cromwell's Letters

Ely, 10th January, 1643

To the Rev. Mr. Hitch, at Ely: These
Mr. Hitch,

Lest the Soldiers should in any tumultuary or disorderly way attempt the reformation of the Cathedral Church, I require you to forbear altogether your Choir-service, so unedifying and offensive — and this as you shall answer it, if any disorder should arise thereupon.

I advise you to catechise, and read and expound the Scripture to the people; not doubting but the Parliament, with the advice of the Assembly of Divines, will direct you farther. I desire your sermons "too," where usually they have been — but more frequent.

Your loving friend,
Oliver Cromwell

Leaguer before York, 5th July, 1644

To my loving Brother, Colonel Valentine Walton: These
Dear Sir,

It's our duty to sympathise in all mercies; and to praise the Lord together in chastisements or trials, that so we may sorrow together.

Truly England and the Church of God hath had a great favour from the Lord, in this great Victory given unto us, such as the like never was since this War began. It had all the evidences of an absolute Victory obtained by the Lord's blessing upon the Godly Party principally. We never charged but we routed the enemy. The Left Wing, which I commanded, being our own horse, saving a few Scots in our rear, beat all the Prince's horse. God made them as stubble to our swords. We charged

From Thomas Carlyle, *Oliver Cromwell's Letters and Speeches, with Elucidations by Thomas Carlyle*, 2d ed. (London, n.d.), pp. 117, 122–23, 138, 250, 295–96.

their regiments of foot with our horse, and routed all we charged. The particulars I cannot relate now; but I believe, of twenty thousand the Prince hath not four thousand left. Give glory, all the glory, to God.

Sir, God hath taken away your eldest Son by a cannon-shot. It brake his leg. We were necessitated to have it cut off, whereof he died.

Sir, you know my own trials this way: but the Lord supported me with this, That the Lord took him into the happiness we all pant for and live for. There is your precious child full of glory, never to know sin or sorrow any more. He was a gallant young man, exceedingly gracious. God give you His comfort. Before his death he was so full of comfort that to Frank Russel and myself he could not express it, "It was so great above his pain." This he said to us. Indeed it was admirable. A little after, he said, One thing lay upon his spirit. I asked him, What that was? He told me it was, That God had not suffered him to be any more the executioner of His enemies. At his fall, his horse being killed with the bullet, and as I am informed three horses more, I am told he bid them, Open to the right and left, that he might see the rogues run. Truly he was exceedingly beloved in the Army, of all that knew him. But few knew him; for he was a precious young man, fit for God. You have cause to bless the Lord. He is a glorious Saint in Heaven; wherein you ought exceedingly to rejoice. Let this drink up your sorrow; seeing these are not feigned words to comfort you, but the thing is so real and undoubted a truth. You may do all things by the strength of Christ. Seek that, and you shall easily bear your trial. Let this public mercy to the Church of God make you to forget your private sorrow. The Lord be your strength: so prays

Your truly faithful and loving Brother,
Oliver Cromwell

My love to your Daughter, and my Cousin Perceval, Sister Desbrow and all friends with you.

Harborough, 14th June, 1645

For the Honourable William Lenthall,
Speaker of the Commons House of Parliament: These
Sir,

Being commanded by you to this service, I think myself bound to acquaint you with the good hand of God towards you and us.

We marched yesterday after the King, who went before us from Daventry'to Harborough; and quartered about six miles from him. This day we marched towards him. He drew out to meet us; both armies engaged. We, after three hours fight very doubtful, at last routed his army; killed and took about 5000 — very many officers, but of what quality we yet know not. We took also about 200 carriages, all he had; and all his guns, being 12 in number, whereof two were demi-cannon, two demi-culverins, and I think the rest sackers. We pursued the enemy from three miles short of Harborough to nine beyond, even to the sight of Leicester, whither the King fled.

Sir, this is none other but the hand of God; and to Him alone belongs the glory, wherein none are to share with Him. The General served you with all faithfulness and honour; and the best commendation I can give him is, That I daresay he attributes all to God, and would rather perish than assume to himself. Which is an honest and a thriving way — and yet as much for bravery may be given to him, in this action, as to a man. Honest men served you faithfully in this action. Sir, they are trusty; I beseech you, in the name of God, not to discourage them. I wish this action may beget thankfulness and humility in all that are concerned in it. He that ventures his life for the liberty of his country, I wish he trust God for the liberty of his conscience, and you for the liberty he fights for. In this he rests, who is

> Your most humble servant,
> Oliver Cromwell

> Knottingley, 20th November, 1648
For his Excellency the Lord General Fairfax at St. Albans: These
My Lord,

I find in the Officers of the Regiments a very great sense of the sufferings of this poor Kingdom; and in them all a very great zeal to have impartial Justice done upon Offenders. And I must confess I do in all, from my heart, concur with them; and I verily think and am persuaded they are things which God puts into our hearts.

I shall not need to offer anything to your Excellency: I know, God teaches you; and that He hath manifested His presence so to you as that you will give glory to Him in the eyes of all the world. I held it my duty, having received these Petitions and Letters, and being "so" desired by the framers thereof — to present them to you. The good Lord work His will upon your heart, enabling you to *it;* and the presence of Almighty God go along with you. Thus prays, My Lord,

> Your most humble and faithful servant,
> Oliver Cromwell

> Dublin, 16th September, 1649
To the Honourable John Bradshaw, Esquire,
President of the Council of State: These
Sir,

It hath pleased God to bless our endeavours at Tredah.[1] After battery, we stormed it. The Enemy were about 3,000 strong in the Town. They

---

1 Drogheda. — T. G. B.

made a stout resistance; and near 1,000 of our men being entered, the Enemy forced them out again. But God giving a new courage to our men, they attempted again, and entered; beating the Enemy from their defences.

The Enemy had made three retrenchments, both to the right and left "of" where we entered; all which they were forced to quit. Being thus entered, we refused them quarter; having the day before summoned the Town. I believe we put to the sword the whole number of the defendants. I do not think Thirty of the whole number escaped with their lives. Those that did, are in safe custody for the Barbadoes. Since that time, the Enemy quitted to us Trim and Dundalk. In Trim they were in such haste that they left their guns behind them.

This hath been a marvellous great mercy. The Enemy, being not willing to put an issue upon a field-battle, had put into this Garrison almost all their prime soldiers, being about 3,000 horse and foot, under the command of their best officers; Sir Arthur Ashton being made Governor. There were some seven or eight regiments, Ormond's being one, under the command of Sir Edmund Varney. I do not believe, neither do I hear, that any officer escaped with his life, save only one Lieutenant, who, I hear, going to the Enemy said, That he was the only man that escaped of all the Garrison. The Enemy upon this were filled with much terror. And truly I believe this bitterness will save much effusion of blood, through the goodness of God.

I wish that all honest hearts may give the glory of this to God alone, to whom indeed the praise of this mercy belongs. "As" for instruments, they were very inconsiderable the work throughout.

Captain Brandly did with forty or fifty of his men very gallantly storm the Tenalias; for which he deserves the thanks of the State. I rest,

Your most humble servant,
Oliver Cromwell

Cromwell's Speech to the First Parliament of the Protectorate, Dissolving It, January 22, 1655

To say that men bring forth these things when God doth them — judge you if God will bear this? I wish that every sober heart, though he hath had temptations upon him of deserting this Cause of God, yet may take heed how he provokes and falls into the hands of the Living God by such blasphemies as these! According to the Tenth of the *Hebrews:* "If we sin

From Thomas Carlyle, *Oliver Cromwell's Letters and Speeches*, 2d ed. (London, n.d.), pp. 581–83.

wilfully after that we have received the knowledge of the truth, there remains no more sacrifice for sin." "A terrible word." It was spoken to the Jews who, having professed Christ, apostatised from Him. What then? Nothing but a fearful "falling into the hands of the Living God!" They that shall attribute to this or that person the contrivances and production of those mighty things God hath wrought in the midst of us; and "fancy" that they have not been the Revolutions of Christ himself, "upon whose shoulders the government is laid" — they speak against God, and they fall under His hand without a Mediator. That is, if we deny the Spirit of Jesus Christ the glory of all His works in the world; by which He rules kingdoms, and doth administer, and is the rod of His strength — we provoke the Mediator: and He may say: I will leave you to God, I will not intercede for you; let Him tear you to pieces! I will leave thee to fall into God's hands; thou deniest me my sovereignty and power committed to me; I will not intercede nor mediate for thee; thou fallest into the hands of the Living God! — Therefore whatsoever you may judge men for, howsoever you may say, "This is cunning, and politic, and subtle" — take heed again, I say, how you judge of His Revolutions as the product of men's inventions! — I may be thought to press to much upon this theme. But I pray God it may stick upon your hearts and mine. The worldly-minded man knows nothing of this, but is a stranger to it; and thence his atheisms, and murmurings at instruments, yea repining at God Himself. And no wonder; considering the Lord hath done such things amongst us as have not been known in the world these thousand years, and yet notwithstanding is not owned by us!

There is another Necessity, which you have put upon us, and we have not sought. I appeal to God, Angels and Men — if I shall "now" raise money according to the Article in the Government [1] "whether I am not compelled to do it!" Which "Government" had power to call you hither; and did; and instead of seasonably providing for the Army, you have laboured to overthrow the Government, and the Army is now upon Free-quarter! And you would never so much as let me hear a tittle from you concerning it. Where is the fault? Has it not been as if you had a purpose to put this extremity upon us and the Nation? I hope, this was not in your minds. I am not willing to judge so — but such is the state into which we are reduced. By the designs of some in the Army who are now in custody, it was designed to get as many of them as possible — through discontent for want of money, the Army being in a barren country, near thirty weeks behind in pay, and upon other specious pretences — to march for England out of Scotland; and, in discontent to seize their General there [General Monk], a faithful and honest man, that so another [Colonel Overton] might head the Army. And all this opportunity taken from your delays. Whether this will be a thing of feigned Necessity?

[1] The new constitution. — T. G. B.

What could it signify, but "The Army are in discontent already; and we will make them live upon stones; we will make them cast off their governors and discipline?" What can be said to this? I list not to unsaddle myself, and put the fault upon your backs. Whether it hath been for the good of England, whilst men have been talking of this thing or the other [Building Constitutions], and pretending liberty and many good words — whether it has been as it should have been? I am confident you cannot think it has. The Nation will not think so. And if the worst should be made of things, I know not what the Cornish men nor the Lincolnshire men may think, or other Counties; but I believe they will all think *they are not safe.* A temporary suspension of "caring for the greatest liberties and privileges" (if it were so, which is denied) would not have been of such damage as the not providing against Free-quarter hath run the Nation upon. And if it be my "liberty" to walk abroad in the fields, or to take a journey, yet it is not my wisdom to do so when my house is on fire!

I have troubled you with a long Speech; and I believe it may not have the same resentment with all that it hath with some. But because that is unknown to me, I shall leave it to God — and conclude with this: That I think myself bound, as in my duty to God, and to the People of these Nations for their safety and good in every respect — I think it my duty to tell you that it is not for the profit of these Nations, nor for common and public good, for you to continue here any longer. And therefore I do declare unto you, That I do dissolve this Parliament.

Cromwell's Last Prayer
Before His Death in 1658

Lord, though I am a miserable and wretched creature, I am in Covenant with Thee through grace. And I may, I will, come to Thee for Thy People. Thou hast made me, though very unworthy, a mean instrument to do them some good, and Thee service; and many of them have set too high a value upon me, though others wish and would be glad of my death; Lord, however Thou do dispose of me, continue and go on to do good for them. Give them consistency of judgment, one heart, and mutual love; and go on to deliver them, and with the work of reformation; and make the Name of Christ glorious in the world. Teach those who look too much on Thy instruments, to depend more upon Thyself. Pardon such as desire to trample upon the dust of a poor worm, for they are Thy People too. And pardon the folly of this short Prayer: Even for Jesus Christ's sake. And give us a good night if it be Thy pleasure. Amen.

From Thomas Carlyle, *Oliver Cromwell's Letters and Speeches,* 2d ed. (London, n.d.), pp. 775–76.

222

The Dutch Regental Oligarchy
at Its Zenith

Sir William Temple's description of Dutch society in 1672 is particularly valuable because it is of the regental oligarchy in its great golden age. Between 1650 and 1672 the republic was without a prince of Orange at its head, the control of the state resting in the capable hands of the epitome of the regental class, Jan de Witt, from 1653. Despite war with England, Portugal, and Sweden, the republic was strong, prosperous, and confident. The war of resistance, which began in 1672, against Louis XIV's aggression badly shook the latter, resulted in the overthrow of De Witt and a call to Prince William III to undertake the defense of the republic. The republic then entered a long period of increasing dependence on Orange leadership. Temple (1628–1699) had been English ambassador to the republic; he was a friend of De Witt and a man of learning and literary talents. After William III became king of England in 1689, Temple became an influential adviser of the new king.

William Temple: *Observations upon the United Provinces of the Netherlands,* 1672

CHAPTER 4. OF THEIR PEOPLE AND DISPOSITIONS

The people of Holland may be divided into these several classes: the clowns or boors (as they call them) who cultivate the land: the mariners or schippers, who supply their ships and inland-boats: the merchants or traders, who fill their towns: the Renteeners, or men that live in all their chief cities upon the rents or interest of estates formerly acquired in their families: and the Gentlemen, and officers of their armies.

The first are a race of people diligent rather than laborious; dull and slow of understanding, and so not dealt with by hasty words, but managed easily by soft and fair; and yielding to plain reason, if you give them time to understand it. In the country and villages not too near the great towns, they seem plain and honest, and content with their own; so that if, in bounty, you give them a shilling for what is worth but a groat, they will take the current price, and give you the rest again; if you bid them take it, they know not what you mean, and sometimes ask, if you are a fool. They know no other good but the supply of what nature re-

From William Temple, *Works*, vol. 1, new ed. (London, 1814), pp. 133–38, 150–51.

quires, and the common increase of wealth. They feed most upon herbs, roots, and milks; and by that means, I suppose, neither their strength nor vigour seem answerable to the size or bulk of their bodies.

The mariners are a plain, but much rougher people; whether from the element they live in, or from their food, which is generally fish and corn, and heartier than that of the boors. They are surly and ill-mannered, which is mistaken for pride; but, I believe, is learned, as all manners are, by the conversation we use. Now theirs lying only among one another, or with winds and waves, which are not moved or wrought upon by any language or observance, or to be dealt with, but by pains and by patience; these are all the qualities their mariners have learned; their valour is passive rather than active; and their language is little more, than what is of necessary use to their business.

The merchants and tradesmen, both the greater and mechanic, living in towns that are of great resort, both by strangers and passengers of their own, are more mercurial (wit being sharpened by commerce and conversation of cities) though they are not very inventive, which is the gift of warmer heads; yet are they great in imitation, and so far, many times, as goes beyond originals: of mighty industry, and constant application to the ends they propose and pursue. They make use of their skill, and their wit, to take advantage of other men's ignorance and folly they deal with; are great exacters, where the law is in their own hands: in other points, where they deal with men that understand like themselves, and are under the reach of justice and laws, they are the plainest and best dealers in the world; which seems not to grow so much from a principle of conscience, or morality, as from a custom or habit introduced by the necessity of trade among them, which depends as much upon common honesty, as war does upon discipline; and without which all would break up, merchants would turn pedlars, and soldiers thieves.

Those families, which live upon their patrimonial estates in all the great cities, are a people differently bred and mannered from the traders, though like them in the modesty of garb and habit, and the parsimony of living. Their youth are generally bred up at schools, and at the universities of Leyden or Utrecht, in the common studies of human learning, but chiefly of the civil law, which is that of their country, at least as far as it is so in France and Spain. For (as much as I understand of those countries) no decisions or decrees of the civil law, nor constitutions of the Roman Emperors, have the force or current of law among them, as is commonly believed, but only the force of reasons when alledged before their courts of judicature, as far as the authority of men esteemed wise passes for reason: but the ancient customs of those several countries, and the ordonnances of their Kings and Princes, consented to by the Estates, or in France verified by Parliaments, have only the strength and authority of law among them.

Where these families are rich, their youths, after the course of their studies at home, travel for some years, as the sons of our gentry use to do; but their journies are chiefly into England and France, not much into Italy, seldomer into Spain, nor often into the more northern countries, unless in company or train of their public Ministers. The chief end of their breeding is, to make them fit for the service of their country in the magistracy of their towns, their Provinces, and their State. And of these kind of men are the civil officers of this government generally composed, being descended of families who have many times been constantly in the magistracy of their native towns for many years, and some for several ages.

Such were most or all of the chief Ministers, and the persons that composed their chief councils, in the time of my residence among them; and not men of mean or mechanic trades, as it is commonly received among foreigners, and makes the subject of comical jests upon their government. This does not exclude many merchants, or traders in gross, from being often seen in the offices of their cities, and sometimes deputed to their States; nor several of their States from turning their stocks in the management of some very beneficial trade by servants, and houses maintained to that purpose. But the generality of the States and Magistrates are of the other sort; their estates consisting in the pensions of their public charges, in the rents of lands, or interest of money upon the Cantores, or in actions of the East-India company, or in shares upon the adventures of great trading merchants.

Nor do these families, habituated as it were to the magistracy of their towns and provinces, usually arrive at great or excessive riches; the salaries of public employments and interest being low, but the revenue of lands being yet very much lower, and seldom exceeding the profit of two in the hundred. They content themselves with the honour of being useful to the public, with the esteem of their cities or their country, and with the ease of their fortunes; which seldom fails, by the frugality of their living, grown universal by being (I suppose) at first necessary, but since honourable, among them.

The mighty growth and excess of riches is seen among the merchants and traders, whose application lies wholly that way, and who are the better content to have so little share in the government, desiring only security in what they possess; troubled with no cares but those of ·their fortunes, and the management of their trades, and turning the rest of their time and thought to the divertisement of their lives. Yet these, when they attain great wealth, chuse to breed up their sons in the way, and marry their daughters into the families, of those others most generally credited in their towns, and versed in their magistracies; and thereby introduce their families into the way of government and honour, which consists not here in titles, but in public employments.

The next rank among them is that of their Gentlemen or Nobles, who, in the Province of Holland (to which I chiefly confine these observations) are very few, most of the families having been extinguished in the long wars with Spain. But those that remain, are in a manner all employed in the military or civil charges of the Province or State. These are, in their customs, and manners, and way of living, a good deal different from the rest of the people; and, having been bred much abroad, rather affect the garb of their neighbour-courts, than the popular air of their own country. They value themselves more upon their Nobility, than men do in other countries, where it is more common; and would think themselves utterly dishonoured by the marriage of one that was not of their rank, though it were to make up the broken fortune of a Noble family by the wealth of a Plebeian. They strive to imitate the French in their mien, their cloaths, their way of talk, of eating, of gallantry or debauchery; and are, in my mind, something worse than they would be, by affecting to be better than they need; making sometimes but ill copies, whereas they might be good originals, by refining or improving the customs or virtues proper to their own country and climate. They are otherwise an honest, well-natured, friendly, and gentlemanly sort of men, and acquit themselves generally with honour and merit, where their country employs them.

The officers of their armies live after the customs and fashions of the gentlemen; and so do many sons of the rich merchants, who, returning from travel abroad, have more designs upon their own pleasure, and the vanity of appearing, than upon the service of their country: or, if they pretend to enter into that, it is rather by the army than the State. And all these are generally desirous to see a court in their country, that they may value themselves at home, by the qualities they have learned abroad; and make a figure which agrees better with their own humour, and the manner of courts, than with the customs and orders that prevail in more popular governments.

There are some customs, or dispositions, that seem to run generally through all these degrees of men among them; as great frugality, and order, in their expences. Their common riches lie in every man's having more than he spends; or, to say it more properly, in every man's spending less than he has coming in, be that what it will: nor does it enter into men's heads among them, that the common port or course of expence should equal the revenue; and, when this happens, they think at least they have lived that year to no purpose; and the train of it discredits a man among them, as much as any vicious or prodigal extravagance does in other countries. This enables every man to bear their extreme taxes, and makes them less sensible than they would be in other places. . . .

To conclude . . . , Holland is a country, where the earth is better than the air, and profit more in request than honour; where there is more sense than wit; more good nature than good humour; and more wealth than pleasure: where a man would chuse rather to travel than to live; shall find more things to observe than desire; and more persons to esteem than to love. But the same qualities and dispositions do not value a private man and a state, nor make a conversation agreeable, and a government great: nor is it unlikely, that some very great King might make but a very ordinary private gentleman, and some very extraordinary gentleman might be capable of making but a very mean Prince.